Amber
A Very Personal Cat

For Kim Schneider
A rock and refuge—

Holly
Amber
Gladys Taber

Conversations
with AMBER

For OLIVE
and her two cats and one small Trinka

HELEN and VICKY
who so loved one Irish Setter that
they named their home Holly Hill

Amber
A Very Personal Cat

———

Conversations
with AMBER

———

This edition, encompassing both books,
published by arrangement with
Harper & Row, Publishers, Inc.
All Rights Reserved
ISBN 0-940160-41-2

PARNASSUS IMPRINTS
Orleans, Massachusetts

Amber

A VERY PERSONAL CAT

by Gladys Taber

PARNASSUS IMPRINTS
Orleans, Massachusetts

Her amber eyes
Regard me steadfastly
With the grave wisdom of long ages past.
I am bewildered by their mystery
Too infinite to realize.

But suddenly I find I hold a kitten here,
Purring a love song in my ear.

Chapter 1

It was a cold November day and the sugar maples along the winding road to Stillmeadow stood bare against a pale sky. The air smelled of snow. I was coming home from Cape Cod to Connecticut with three friends, Helen, Vicky, and Margaret, but the little white farmhouse built in 1690 for once had no welcome. It was empty and so was the car. For the first time in fifteen years no Irish setter took up the whole back seat. My beloved champion Holly was not coming home again.

There seemed to be a loud stillness in the house as we stacked the luggage in the back kitchen beside the dog leashes, feeding pans, extra collars, combs and brushes. Nobody had a word to say.

Then I heard another car drive up, and I opened the back door (nobody ever uses the front door at Stillmeadow). I saw my daughter Connie climb out of the car and lift up an oblong black-handled case. When she came in, she put it down beside me and carefully unhooked the clasps and raised the cover.

A small triangular-shaped face set with a pair of topaz

eyes poked out, and after it came about eight ounces of kitten.

I almost never cry, but I burst into tears and simply sobbed while the morsel hopped in my lap and began to purr.

"It's an Abyssinian," I managed to say finally as the kitten kneaded my arms.

Now when my Siamese, Esmé, used to make the trip from New York to Stillmeadow and we opened the carrying case, she always uttered an ear-splitting screech, sped upstairs and hid behind the bathroom pipes. She usually stayed there three or four days, with room service up the steep ancient stairs. Tigger, our Manx, was raised in the country, and only once underwent the trip in the car to the veterinarian. His screams stopped a good many cars on the road as drivers craned their necks.

And when Aladdin, my first Abyssinian, came from Hollywood, he traveled in the Super Chief in a compartment with Smiley Burnette's wife. No carrying case for him to worry about. He slept in a basket lined with pink satin and had special meals cooked for him by an anxious chef.

Normally a cat takes some time to adjust to change, and I understand this very well since I hate change myself. But this new kitten was taking over socially from the first moment, and as soon as I stopped crying, she indicated that she was hungry and skipped ahead to the kitchen.

Connie unloaded her equipment. This included an aquamarine bathroom with plastic liners, a scoop for cleaning, two bags of sterilized kitty litter, a scratching

Aladdin, my first Abyssinian, came from Hollywood.

post covered with green wool carpet and topped with a catnip mouse on a coil, cans of special catfood, a bottle of vitamins, an envelope of instructions about diet, a bag of toys, and a folder of papers so that I could register her properly as the offspring of champions.

"We knew the house would be empty," Connie said as she put up the scratching post in the middle of my bedroom, "but Curtis and I felt you shouldn't be alone."

Abyssinians are rather rare and Connie and Curt had quite a time locating one. They finally found mine in, of all places, Staten Island.

This kitten had kept quiet all the way from Staten Island to Southbury, Connecticut.

I am not disparaging the Siamese or Manx, for any cat lover should have at least one of each. The Siamese is charming, passionate, uninhibited, beautiful. The Manx is steady, sensible as a banker, and the best mouser possible. Tigger reserved his deepest emotions for Esmé and kept bringing her mice and moles and laying them worshipfully at her paws. She never gave them a look.

Esmé was a one-person cat and I was the person. When I went away on a business trip, she would not speak to me when I got back. This might last two or three days. At the end of the time, she would stand on my desk and deliver a scorching indictment of people who left their cat. Then she forgave me in a dramatic scene worthy of Duse.

"I've brought everything," said Connie now, "so you won't need to let her out." She laid a small harness, collar and leash in my lap. "You wouldn't let her out in the snowdrifts anyway," she observed.

She was tactfully referring to Aladdin, that first Abyssinian, who went out one summer day when he was eight months old and was never seen again. Half the county turned out to hunt for him, and the loss was advertised on radio and in newspapers. We finally felt that someone had opened a car door to look at this unusual cat and sociable Aladdin hopped in and they went off. Aladdin never had a sense of direction; earlier he had got himself to the top of a 150-foot maple and did not know the way down. Our farmer neighbor, Frank, went up the tree and saved him while I stood dizzily below expecting them both to crash to death.

"Don't worry," said Frank, handing Aladdin over, "someone up there is looking after me." He pointed to the sky and smiled.

Naming the new kitten was quite a project. It was, in a way, just a matter of registering her, for I began calling her Sweetheart at once. Connie pointed out this would not look well on the papers although some of her champion ancestors had odd names, one called Eric and one Penny.

Of course she came to me when she felt like it, called or uncalled, and she felt like it so constantly that she might have been named Adhesive. Even now I often have to forego the can of French fried potatoes on the cellarway shelves because I cannot get the door ajar without having a golden shadow disappear into the catacombs of the cellar.

The first time I sat down to type, a small wedge-shaped head kept popping over the machine just in case an unwary key came up for her to catch. When I opened the drawer for manuscript paper, she vanished into the back of the drawer and settled into a four-inch space while I wondered whether getting her out would ever be possible.

Still, she did need some sort of official name. When you decide to name an Abyssinian, the unusual apricot color seems important, and so does the history. Faith Baldwin suggested some Egyptian and Oriental names which were fascinating but which we finally decided were too imposing for such a small morsel. I liked Topaz, and Connie thought Buttercup would be good. But neither of these made good call names. My son-in-law settled it with Amber, which is euphonious and easy to say and fits the color.

Now the Abyssinian is supposed to be The Cat the Egyptians worshiped in the days of the pyramids. She was the cat goddess. From 3500 B.C. to 1970 is quite a span to retain a likeness, but Amber looks like some bas-reliefs I have seen of the Egyptian cat. The Abby has what experts call an oriental bone structure similar to the Siamese and is a small graceful slender cat with a coat difficult to describe. The undercoat and the delicate ears are apricot. The face is apricot with some darker overlay at the top, the eyes are golden or topaz and the nose itself is a small triangle of pinky brick. The whiskers are silvery with charcoal roots. The top coat has three different colors on each hair, and my own Amber has no intention of having me pull out a couple to put under a microscope in order to check whether the tip color is black or seal brown. The whole effect is luminous.

The tail is long and tapering, dark on the upper side and apricot on the under. The ears are sharply pointed triangles so delicate you can see light through them. The

Amber and I.

(Worcester Telegram Photo)

face below is another triangle, as is the jawline. The paw pads are charcoal.

It is no wonder the Egyptians felt this cat was a goddess!

Sometimes the Abyssinian is called the water cat, for according to one legend it was used as a fishing cat. What this means today is that I never turn on the hot water without being sure Amber is not in the sink. She spends a good deal of time in the shower too, just hoping a few drops will come down. There often is a trickle as well as some water on the stall itself, since the drain is not too reliable. She also likes to sit under the bathtub faucets to catch a drop or two.

I do not know whether other breeds ever love water so much. But Amber empties her own water dish daily and often takes a sip from my glass at breakfast time.

I always keep a glass of water on my bedside table, and the other night around midnight I heard a faint sound and turned the light on. Amber lifted her head from the glass and then dipped in and sipped earnestly. She drank a third of that water and then leaped to the bed and scrubbed her face before curling up to go to sleep again. I told her sleepily that we always provided room service at Stillmeadow.

Perhaps related to this love of water is her fanaticism for cleanliness. Like most cats, she washes herself constantly, polishing and repolishing, folding her ears flat with the impact of her paws and angling her hind legs out to scrub them thoroughly. But she also likes to be brushed four or five times a day, purring and kneading her paws as the brush goes over. And soon afterward she is washing her paws again. Being a short-hair she does not lose much hair, but she likes the feeling of being groomed.

One special characteristic of the Abyssinian, which may go back to the mysterious age of the pyramids, is the tone of voice. The miaow is so faint and deprecatory that it is hard to hear. I never had this trouble with the Siamese or the Manx. I began to wonder at first whether Amber could miaow. But when I took her to Dr. George Whitney in New Haven for a check up, she got bored in Ansonia and uttered a single lutelike cry and thrust both forelegs out of the breathing holes in the carrying case.

But the moment the case was open in the treatment room she began to purr. Then, instead of hiding behind the waste container, she leaped lightly to the cabinet and started taking caps from the medicine bottles. From there a swift leap took her to the high window ledge, where she could watch the dogs in the yard outside. When Dr. George came in, she greeted him happily and only uttered a delicate miaow as he gave her an enteritis injection. Afterward she sat on the table and scrubbed the disinfected area and purred again.

Buying a pedigreed cat is not always easy. Occasionally ads appear in a local newspaper when someone has a litter of Blue Point Siamese or of Persians, and some telephone books have listings. The directory of my nearest large city, however, only lists kennels. If you write The Cat Fanciers' Association, Inc., 20615 Patton Court, Detroit, Michigan, you will be able to get the names of breeders. Also *Cats' Magazine*, 2900 Jefferson Avenue, Washington, Pennsylvania, in every issue advertises cats and kittens of various breeds.

If there is a cat show in your area, this is an excellent

way to study the cats. Then you can choose the particular type of personality that fits yours best.

The Abyssinian, a rare breed, is expensive. Also the litters are small; two or three kittens is the usual number. Still, considering the Abby's charm, stability and loving disposition, I am sure the number available will increase markedly.

Once you have your pedigreed kitten, you register him or her as you register a pedigreed puppy. Even if you do not plan to have litters or go to cat shows, it is a good idea to have the registration, just as it is to have a school diploma!

There are various other ways to acquire a cat. In the country where I live, kittens bloom like the flowers in spring. One of the few free things in this expensive world is a kitten. Neighbors call one another up and suggest that they have the darlingest new batch of kittens. People run ads in the country newspaper. Notices on brown paper are posted regularly on trees or in store windows.

Or you can adopt a cat who is already in your yard. As I write, three cats are sitting by the well house, a smoky gray, a light orange, and a striped cat with white paws. They are thrifty, plump and able to fend for themselves. They are what we call barn cats and earn their shelter by keeping the rats from nearby barns. They are shy, but any of them would come in before long if I left the door ajar and in a week or two would be running the house.

Chapter 2

Cat nature has been speculated about for probably 4000 years, since the Egyptians first began to deify them. One thing is certain, the Egyptians used a cat head on the body of a woman for the goddess Bastet, who was the divinity of femininity and motherhood. Cats were mummified when they died, and anyone who killed a cat was likely to be put to death. Possibly this had a basis in economic necessity, for some authorities believe that only because the Phoenicians brought cats into Egypt was Egypt's grain saved.

When an Egyptian cat died, the man of the family is said to have shaved his eyebrows.

The Egyptians had a corner on cats until the Greeks began to steal them when most of the Greek granaries were being depleted by rats. I like to imagine Greek spies stealing in and trying to snag a few cats: they are not so easy to catch.

In the Middle Ages cats became associated with witches and were burned, buried alive and otherwise cruelly mistreated. This in turn helped the rat-carrying plagues of that period to decimate populations.

Today cat shows are held all over the land and cat breeding has become big business. Country cats are respected and cherished, and animal shelters pick up the unwanted kittens some summer people toss from their cars as they head back to what they feel is civilization.

But there are still some misunderstandings about cat nature. Many people think all cats are alike. The same people will discuss the difference between a hunting dog and a toy poodle, both of which are dogs. When they buy a dog, they will not get an Irish setter if they live on the top floor of a big city apartment house; they will get what I call an inside dog, one that needs a minimum of exercise.

But when it comes to cats, these same people feel all cats are alike. A cat is a cat. Cats are indifferent and solitary, they say. Cats do not care for anybody. They cannot be taught anything. They cannot be trusted. You must never leave them alone with a baby.

I do not know where the superstition arose that cats will suck a baby's breath and should never be left alone with a baby. This is absolute nonsense. Amber, for instance, tiptoes up to a baby and goes so far as to sniff the nearest minute foot waving in the air (she is a great sniffer). Then she folds herself up and contemplates this fascinating phenomenon.

Most cats seem to realize that a baby is somehow human although in a diminished version. Some feel protective and some retire to the nearest ample lap to watch from a secure distance. Even cats who are afraid of

Esmé and Tigger. The Siamese is beautiful and uninhibited; the Manx is sensible as a banker.

jumping-jack older children apparently understand that the baby-carriage set is not going to grab them suddenly.

As for "indifferent" and "solitary" Amber only smiled when I told her this (both cats and dogs smile). "Indifferent" and "solitary" do not exactly fit her. Whatever I am doing, she is doing with me and wherever I go I have to watch out not to step on that small form. She just happens to be right there and usually wants to be reassured that I still love her as much as I did ten minutes ago. Sometimes I have to stop whatever chore I am doing and sit down and hold her for twenty minutes while she purrs and spreads her toes.

When I have to leave her and put her in the bedroom, she does not speak a word but stands looking at me with desperate wide eyes. How can you desert me? The anguish of a forever-good-by is in that small face.

As for learning, the fourth time I got out the harness —which meant going for a walk—she jumped on the table and began to purr while I struggled with the buckle. And the first time she traveled to Cape Cod from Connecticut in her carrying case, the five-hour trip did not faze her. She began to investigate the new home with great interest the minute the case was opened.

A few days later, I got out the case to take her to the veterinarian. She tiptoed over, inspected it and then got in, folding her tail around her. I decided, as I lugged the case to the car, that I had an intellectual genius inside.

After two trips to the veterinarian she accepted the whole routine with no struggle. I had seen a cat in the same office who needed three people to hold her down, all of whom bore scars of the conflict. But Amber has an acceptance of inevitability that I wish I could always have.

One cat book I read says the Abyssinian is timid, but I know one who is not. When a friend brought in an elderly cat, Amber stiffened her small self. Her fur rose, doubling her size, and she drew back her lips and hissed until her whiskers vibrated. The hiss was loud as a steam engine. Smutsie, the guest, sat quietly looking at her without twitching an eyelid. Amber added a low menacing sound between hisses and started toward him. She was as deadly as four pounds could ever be against twenty or more.

When I hastily gathered her up, I could feel a heartbeat too fast to count. And Smutsie was removed, still ignoring her.

When a group of strangers comes in, she vanishes briefly, but soon that small triangular face pokes around the corner and she looks the gathering over. She makes her choice, which is usually a man, and shortly is perched on his shoulder from which it is easy to reach down when he holds up a sliver of sharp Cheddar cheese. I notice that even if he happens to be indifferent to cats, he begins to talk to her and then, of course, to rub her behind the ears. Her purr joins the conversation.

However, when the voices climb to that unfortunate level so typical of parties, she finds the noise too much for her sensitive ears and retires to the quiet of my bedroom. When the group thins out, she is ready to come back and be admired again.

I have one very dear friend who has a cat phobia. The first time she came over after Amber arrived, I did not know this, so Amber was on the sofa industriously washing herself. This time she did *not* go over to the guest, she minded her own laundry. Later, the friend said if she could ever like a cat, it would be Amber.

The customary picture of a cat is one of serenity. There is usually a fireplace and the cat is folded up in front of it. Or the cat dozes on a wide window sill. Amber's idea is to get as close to the fire as is safe and then to jump up and down as the flames leap. On the window sill she swivels her small head so as to see everything outside, always hoping a bird may fly past so she can start quivering and chittering. There is nothing somnolent about her, whether she is smelling the roses on the table or bounding after a moth.

There are still people who worry about having a black cat cross their path. This must be a special hangover from the witchcraft days. My Tigger was blacker than Waterman's black ink, but he brought nothing but good luck to Stillmeadow for he was a born mouser and cleaned up the ancient cellar in no time. He also diminished the moles that ate the bulbs and tunneled the lawn. One day he made history in the garden as he inspected a mole hole. He sat with his bullet head cocked for a few minutes and then he moved back and pulled up a length of weed (we always had weeds available). Tiptoeing over, he stuck the weed stem in the edge of the hole and then removed himself a short distance and sat. I had seen this from the kitchen window and called the rest of the family. We could not decide what Tigger was up to, but we found out. When the weed moved, he bolted like black lightning and grabbed the mole.

It was fortunate I had witnesses or everyone would

Esmé, like Amber, was a dainty person.

have said my imagination was working as usual. But the most practical member of the family, Jill, admitted Tigger had planted that weed so that when it moved he would know the mole was coming out. Jill said he was miscast in life and should have been in Wall Street.

Occasionally I meet people who say they could never have a cat because a cat kills birds. None of my cats has been able to fly, and the birds that cloud the sky over Stillmeadow simply soar away when the cats come around.

One of the most unfortunate superstitions about cats is that if you feed them well, they will not catch mice or rats. Some owners actually withhold food so that kitty will get the mice. This is not only cruel but senseless. A well-fed cat has more energy for hunting and does not lose his strong instinct to chase small scurrying creatures.

Rats and mice carry more deadly disease than I can name, including bubonic plague. Recently the government has been embroiled in the problem of rats in city ghettos. Rats spread lice, fleas and mange. They bite babies in their cribs and destroy food, which is not too plentiful in ghettos at best.

Rat control could be possible at minimum expense in all cities, I think. Cats could be obtained from any A.S.P.C.A., which has to destroy so many who have been deserted. If every ghetto family had one cat and an allowance of those catfood pellets that are inexpensive and will keep indefinitely, I feel confident that the rat problem would be solved. This is probably too simple a solution for the government—and would be too inexpensive.

Someone once told me about a Southern town that had

a plague of rats some seventy-five years ago. Then a smart man in a neighboring state advertised rattraps to solve the problem. The rattraps were simply cats. The cats cleaned up the town and only cost a dollar each.

Amber enjoys hunting ants in the yard and moths against the windowpane and an occasional spider. The final pounce is like a meteor on a summer night. She has an unfortunate tendency to swallow the victim before I can fish it out of that delicate pink mouth. But all of these unscheduled snacks seem to agree with her, so I tell myself to stop worrying and concentrate instead on her marvelous hunting skill.

Chapter 3

To Amber, daily life is always exciting. On Cape Cod it is especially so. The house on Mill Pond is not so isolated as Stillmeadow, and people drop in at all hours of the day and night. There is a sign at the front door which says PLEASE DO NOT LET THE CAT OUT OF THE DOOR. So visitors peer through the glass timidly and then venture to open a small crack in the door and call nervously, "Is it all right to come in?"

I swoop Amber up until the door is closed again. Only the grocery boy and the milkman are agile enough to get through by themselves without having Amber go with them. Most cats, fortunately, can be let out to run free. Very often my friend Petie decides to go out at midnight on a good moon-bright night. But he can take care of himself. The cat next door, who was not so intelligent, was run over as he was crossing the road in the middle of the afternoon.

Certainly Amber is not equipped to fend for herself in the big outside. A small cat cannot get out of the way of danger and is hard to find if she gets lost. I was especially thankful that Amber was inside last night when I saw a stately enormous skunk walking sedately down the steps. A skunk is no menace if you leave him alone, but Amber's curiosity is boundless. She never leaves anything or anybody alone. And one real encounter with a skunk might even blind her.

There are also stray dogs who would love to chase her to a treetop. The Rescue Squad might not like to bring extension ladders too often to retrieve one small cat. Country cats, like Tigger, can climb high into a tree and sit on a branch for a long time and then descend easily. But house cats like Aladdin and Amber can get up very well but never seem able to figure out how to get down again.

Theoretically, you could train any cat to climb down a tree by backing him down paw by paw, holding on to him firmly. But I have never attempted this, partly because the cat is always too high to reach and partly because he is usually so scared he tightens his hold on that top branch, while he screams.

Walking on a leash is a different matter altogether.

Amber's training began with a collar which a neighbor gave her. I put it on her and went to answer the telephone. By the time I hung up, Amber was also hung up on the collar. She had her lower jaw hooked under the leather and was rapidly strangling. Before I got it off we were both near death's door. I decided immediately that collars are for dogs but not for cats. At least my cats.

Subsequently I heard of other cats whose collars caught on branches or hooks or whose paws had been damaged by being caught in the collar as the cats tried to claw it off.

The idea of belling a cat does not appeal to me because this would make any cat nervous. as well as warning mice or stray dogs as to just where the cat is.

I never had a dog who was bothered by a collar. The argument against harnesses has always been that they tend to spread the shoulders, and show dogs never wear them. When I thought it over, I doubted whether Amber would really have her shoulders spread by a small light harness if I didn't haul her around by it.

I began by leaving the harness on the floor so she could investigate the buckles and clasp. Then I put it on her and left it for five minutes, letting her run around the floor and pull the leash. I followed this procedure for several days and then I carried her out of doors with the harness on and set her on the grass. I kept the leash loose. The first time she just stood on tiptoe with quivering whiskers. The second time she took a few steps. The third time she caught an ant. The fourth time I said, "Want to go outdoors?" and she jumped to the corner of the table by the door and waited, purring loudly, for the harness to be put on.

Now all I have to do is ask the question and she flies onto the table and pokes her nose at the harness. So she has learned one whole sentence—"Want to go outdoors?" In fact, if I am telling someone that I plan to take Amber for a walk soon, I have to spell the words. And even when I spell them she somehow happens to be on the harvest table, just in case.

In general, I do not think words as words will ever mean as much to her as to the dogs, but she knows enough for her purposes. "I am going to fix you something to eat" is an easy one. "I have to go down to the

Tigger was a great mouser.
Amber met only one rat and demolished him.

village for the mail but I'll be back soon," is understandable.

The tone of voice is more important to her than words, however. She reacts with pleasure to compliments no matter what the words are because of the heartwarming tone. I experimented by telling her she was just impossible but in an admiring tone, and she purred and kneaded her paws and was delighted.

Harsh sounds bother her. The rotary mower going at a neighbor's makes her nervous, as it does me. The sound of a jet plane flattens her ears. But thunder is only mildly bothersome to Amber, whereas it terrified several of my dogs.

Any sudden crash sends her high in the air. I dropped a broiler pan the other day in the kitchen and Amber really levitated. But she came out immediately afterward to see what was going on. The sound of a small child screeching drives her under the nearest bed, but she pokes a wary nose out before long to see what it is all about.

Cats hear sounds even beyond the range of a dog's ears, and a dog is said to have a range of twenty-five thousand cycles a second. The human has fifteen thousand. With this extrasensitivity, any harsh sound must be painful.

Amber has no difficulty in distinguishing the sounds of various automobile motors. She knows our friend Margaret Stanger's car very well, and when it draws up, she flies to the door ready for the treat that always comes with Margaret. The grocery truck sends her to the kitchen, in case there may be a steak in the carton. When a strange car drives up, she tenses and stands ready to seek refuge in the bedroom until she knows who has come. But the retreat is brief and she emerges on tentative paws to inspect the intruders.

Purses are fun to explore and she tries to push the clasps with her nose. There might be morsels of chicken or beef inside for a cat who is starved by a cruel owner. If a jacket has any kind of fringe, like Scotch plaid, she chews the fringe and usually gets a strand or two of wool before she is discovered.

I understand that some biologists are experimenting with communication between animals and man by spoken words. I may say I doubt the value of most of the experiments conducted on domestic animals because no laboratory can reproduce the natural conditions of living as a part of the family. When I say "careful" to Amber as she is biting my hand in an excess of affection, she does chew more gently, but I candidly cannot say I think the word "careful" is the reason. I think it is the warning, admonitory tone of my voice she responds to.

It was on Mill Pond when I first discovered how far Amber can see. I am farsighted myself, but long after I cannot glimpse the flight of a gull, Amber follows it with nose lifted, eyes shining, tail lashing. She swivels her head to catch the last wing-beat out to the sea. Often she will inform me a bird is coming inland, and eventually I see it myself.

In bright daylight, her eyes are topaz with a dark slit of pupil (which cuts down the intensity of the light). As afternoon draws on, the pupil grows larger and more oval-shaped and by dusk her eyes are onyx. If all the clocks stopped I could almost tell the time of day by her eyes. At night, her eyes shine, and I am told this is because there is an iridescent layer of cells there which we do not have and which reflect light we cannot see.

This again suggests inheritance, for cats in the beginning were probably nocturnal, and I know quite a few who still are, really wanting to begin to live just as the tired owner is ready to drop from fatigue. Fortunately for me, Amber does not prowl all night. Perhaps if I retired at a reasonable hour it would be different, but I usually stay up quite late. She stays up too and we both watch television.

Her favorite hour is the weather report. As the weatherman assumes his academic pose before a generally troubled-looking map, she folds herself into a compact ball on the back of the armchair. And then he raises the pointer—oh lovely moment—and she springs into the air and soars across the room. On tiptoe, she tries to catch the tip of the pointer. As the weatherman, smiling, predicts hurricanes or floods, Amber is all over the map with him. She works so hard that when the report is over, she has to wash herself.

She also enjoys some musical hours, especially those with horns such as the Tijuana Brass. With a Bernstein concert, she may doze through part of a symphony, but when the camera pans to the violin section she is wide awake.

My television habits have changed slightly since Amber came to stay. I never used to watch wild-animal shows or circus acts with little dogs dressed in petticoats and walking on their hind legs. Now I have to turn on jungle-adventure programs for her, as well as the variety shows that have performing animals.

34

Perhaps the most exciting show she has seen was one which showed a lioness with her cubs. Amber knocked an ash tray from the table while leaning over the edge to watch one cub leap around.

The reason I find this surprising is that the cockers and Irish never bothered much with television, and I assumed they felt the world would be as well off without that silly screen. But Amber even finds radio interesting and often pokes around behind the small set trying to discover where the sound is born.

When the TV set is finally turned off at night, Amber has a wild race, tearing through the house, leaping from chair top to window sills and back again. Then she is ready to go to sleep and curls up until she is no larger than a baby's mitten. Her seal-dark tail folds around her and her apricot nose rests under tucked paws. I wish human beings could fall instantly to sleep the way cats can. The moment she is folded up comfortably she is sound asleep.

If I get up in the night to check a banging window or tighten a faucet, she opens one eye and yawns. She implies that I am silly to wake up after we are all settled down for the night.

If Amber gets up before I do in the morning, she is so quiet I do not know it. I doubt whether any animal can be as noiseless as a kitten. I have to see Amber to believe in her. About nine thirty she decides it is time to start the day, and she jumps on my pillow with helicopter purrs and spreading paws. She even sometimes gives me an encouraging lick, and if that fails, a soft bite.

Her tongue feels like warm fine sandpaper and is

surprisingly strong. The top is textured, with tiny hooks, which is why Amber can keep her fur so clean, for the hooks literally comb out the fur.

When I look at her with her face so close, I can see her golden eyelashes. They are invisible to a casual glance, partly because her silvery whiskers are so noticeable. These have very sharp nerves at the roots and are better than man-made antennas for receiving messages. Anyone who trims a cat's whiskers should spend some time in a jail cell.

If I stroke Amber's whiskers, moving my hand gently back from her muzzle, they feel as delicate as cobweb lace. But when she investigates something strange, they quiver vibrantly. I always think I should like to count them, but I get distracted trying to time her purrs!

Amber's purrs are a mystery. They vary in intensity from a drowsy thread of sound to a deep full throb when I get out her harness. Sometimes they are rapid and sometimes light as dew. The experts seem to agree on only one thing, which is that the cat is the only animal which purrs. But they do not know why.

Purring begins at the age of a week. Does the mother teach the kittens? Or does something just develop in the vocal cords or elsewhere in the throat? And what relation does this have to prehistoric times when the first cats roamed the jungles?

The earliest purr is a monotone, but later on two purr tones may be heard, even three. The sound is happiness distilled. A purring kitten can comfort the sad heart like music.

On the other hand, a miaow is one of the saddest sounds I have ever heard. But the miaow itself is varied.

Country kittens can take care of themselves.

The hunger miaow is thin and sharp. The miaow when danger seems imminent is louder and wilder. Then Amber also has a questioning miaow which means she is bored and wants me to do something about it. Fortunately I have rarely heard the miaow of pain which has a desperate screeching tone.

There is one time Amber never uses her voice. When a stranger comes to the door she is absolutely silent. If she decides this is not a friend, she stiffens her slight self and raises every hair until her tail balloons and there is a ridge down her back. Her whiskers quiver and she stands on tiptoe. Most dogs utter at least a tentative bark when someone comes to the door, and mine always wagged their tails at the same time. But Amber lets me know someone is coming simply by standing and swelling!

The language of Amber's tail is eloquent. When she is happy, her tail stands straight up like a slim flagpole. When she waves it back and forth slowly, it means she will have more brushing, please. If she is asked to take a pill, the tail whips violently. And when a bird or rabbit comes too near the window, it lashes even more forcibly.

Communication is never static. People who love one another communicate by an expression, a lift of the eyebrow, a touch of the hand. Words are scarcely necessary. This is also true when you live with an animal you love. Every day Amber and I understand each other better and communicate with more ease. But developing this understanding rests with the owner. If you consider your cat just a convenient mousetrap, you will never have any other relationship.

Chapter 4

Living with a kitten or cat is a rewarding experience. Like dogs, they ask so little and give so much. And they still carry within themselves so many traits that have come down from the ancient past.

Man has had for thousands of years what the biologists call a symbiotic relationship with certain other species, which means that both live together for their mutual benefit. It is not exactly fair because we are always at the top and the animal has to adjust to us. We have seldom, if ever, tried to maintain this symbiosis on a fair basis.

We began the association for our own uses. Dogs could chase the primitive hunter's prey and bring it in and receive a bone for reward. Cats could keep down the rat and mouse population, not to mention moles and other small predators, and in return get a few inches by the fire to curl up in.

We had the best of both worlds, using the skill of our symbiotic associates but feeling no responsibility in return. Now we are supposed to be highly civilized creatures, although we alone deliberately kill our own kind, the lower animals do not—except perhaps in the heat of sexual competition.

In the long history of mankind, dogs have been easiest to subjugate. A dog will put up with almost anything. Dogs have infinite patience with this peculiar breed that controls their destinies and will even wear skirts and headdresses and run around on their hind legs to amuse people.

Cats, on the other hand, have managed to keep a kind of independence. They are determined to preserve a little of their original personality. This is the reason so many people say they would never have a cat because a cat is unmanageable. As one who loves and admires both dogs and cats, I may say this is exceedingly silly. We do not expect everyone to be exactly alike, and if we feel a cat should be like a dog, we are missing something important.

For instance, I never had a dog who felt it was vital to leap to the mantelpiece or swing on the Venetian-blind cords. But I am always picking Amber out of the milk-glass cupboard or disentangling her claws from the fringe of the bedspread.

I also fish her out of my desk drawer before I forget and close it. I watch the refrigerator to be sure she hasn't slipped in when the door swung open. I expect her to spend more time in the air than on the floor because she is, by inheritance, a climbing and leaping creature. As far as she is concerned, the floor is a take-off place for the upper regions.

I notice she has a definite route for anywhere in the house, and I marvel that her small head holds so many exact maps. And she seldom has to set a paw on the floor. In the beginning, she fell once, trying to leap from one kitchen counter to another across the room. She was ashamed and showed it. She thought it over and the next time made an interim landing on a chair back. I now have to be sure that this one high-backed chair is never out of place. People who expect their pets to stay right on the floor should never live with a cat.

In prehistoric days the cat family must have lived a great deal in trees, which were both a refuge and a vantage point for attack. Dogs never climbed trees so far as we know. So if you find you are nervous when four delicate paws land in the middle of the worktable, you do not need a cat.

I find Amber's aerial quality a delight! Perhaps I wouldn't feel as I do if I were an Olympic pole vaulter or skier, but as I make my pedestrian way about the house I love to watch Amber leaping from window sill to sofa back, from chair back to the top of the cupboard that reaches almost to the ceiling. The incredible grace of movement and the freedom satisfy a deep need in me. It gives me a sense of weightlessness which perhaps the astronauts enjoy.

I also love the extra companionship which results. I like to start typing and have a beautiful apricot kitten make a perfect landing in the middle of my desk or to be scrubbing the sink and suddenly find an interested wedge-shaped face beside me as Amber balances on the narrow edge of the sink. If I sit by the fire to read, a small person lands soundlessly on the chairback and someone is purring in my ear.

Then we come to the controversial problem of birds.

In the days of the cave dwellers cats ate birds, it is said, and I see no reason to deny this. It may not fit in with my devotion to birds to realize that the three wild, country cats in my yard are there mainly because the bird feeder is there. They wait for their natural heritage.

Amber certainly never has to worry about where her next meal is coming from. It is coming from the refrigerator and will be warmed on the stove. However, as she sits on the kitchen window sill and watches the sparrows on the well house, a curious thing happens. She begins to make an odd chittering sound. The pulse in her throat beats rapidly. Her lips draw back and quiver and her whiskers tremble. Her tail switches. Her body is tense. Her sharp teeth are visible, which they almost never are.

She is merely repeating the pattern set thousands of years ago, and she feels deep within her that those twittering birds are prey. I doubt whether she could ever catch a bird, for she has had no training in the art. But the feeling is there. And I respect it.

We all have basic instincts which we have inherited from the beginning of our breed. Since we have no fur covering as the rest of the mammals have, we must have warmth. When we sit around the applewood fire at Stillmeadow, we are happy because it gives us a feeling of protection, and if the furnace heat is too much we open a few doors to cool the house so we can still toast ourselves by the leaping flames. I have seen tense and troubled people sink down on the couch and look at the hearth and sigh with relief.

We must have food, and although now we buy it at supermarkets, the hunting instinct is still with us. If we

PLEASE
•DO NOT LET THE CAT OUT•
OF THE DOOR.

Amber never goes out alone.

gather the sweet, dark wild strawberries or high bush blueberries or hunt for Morel mushrooms, we revert to the prehistoric times when men fed on wild fruits and berries. The hunter who boasts of getting his deer has satisfied the same instinct. As for the fisherman who sits all day in a boat, broiling in the sun or soaked with rain, just to bring in a few fish, he too is a happy throwback. He may spend countless sums on fishing tackle and the boat, but in his bones he feels he is providing fish for the family.

We also have an instinct to provide shelter for the young. It may be a small cabin or a mansion, but as soon as people have children, they wish to give up any nomadic existence they once enjoyed and maintain a homeplace. I have noticed that though the Hollywood stars, the theatre people, the musicians depend mainly on hotel living and jet travel, they always speak with pride of their homes. Sometimes they have several in different places, obviously so they will have a home wherever they go.

Most of us have basic fears too. Snakes and spiders seem high on the list. It is not really rational to be afraid of either except in tropical places. But the smallest green snake in the yard at Stillmeadow can throw a guest into fits. I myself do not like spiders and feel sure some ancestor was bitten by a large hairy poisonous spider.

When you consider how much we react as our early forebears did, we should not blame our house pets if they respond to their own heritage. It is not a sin for a cat to chase a bird. And it is wrong to punish a cat who manages to get a bird. The reason my cats never have is because the birds are so healthy around here and have plenty of sense. My cats have settled for moles and mice. Actually a bird has a marvelous awareness of danger and can be airborne too fast for a cat to catch it.

However, I do not plan to let Amber try her skill with the birds I feed. And I doubt whether she would be very energetic in pursuit since she dines so well right on the kitchen counter. A homeless hungry cat may be able to snare a bird who cannot take off fast enough, and thus survive for another day or two.

Flies are Amber's chief prey. She will try to climb the wall when a fly buzzes around. So I assume that in the early days, cats also ate small flying insects as well as birds.

But in case she ever does catch a bird, I shall not greet her with cries that she is a bad, bad girl and shame on her. I shall realize that she is a product of evolution as I am but that we haven't evolved in quite the same direction. (Wouldn't most of our mammals look on a human battle line with absolute disbelief!)

When I began to write about Amber, I made the statement that she would probably never see a mouse and would have no idea what it was. But one evening when I had been working late I went to the kitchen for a snack, and there in the middle of the doorway was a half-grown rat, composed in death. He was nearly as big as Amber. She was prancing around with her tail like a wind-blown flag and was obviously stuffed with pride.

Somehow the rat had found a way to get in the cellar and had come up a drain pipe and into the ancient corner cupboard which houses the milk glass.

Amber flew over to show me where she had found him. The remarkable thing was that there was not a scar of battle on her small fragile person and there had been no sound. If I had known about it, I might have had a heart attack and would certainly have made a mess of things trying to rescue my darling and prevent her from protecting our house.

As it was, I praised her extravagantly, wrapped the rat in a paper towel and laid him in the woodshed to show Connie and Curt when they came for the weekend. I did not want them to think Mamma was imagining things!

The amazing thing was that Amber knew exactly how to attack and kill this monster although she had never had any experience except with a catnip toy mouse. Somehow she reached instantly into her heritage and instinctively found the skill, not to mention the strength, to dispatch her hereditary foe.

However, she had no idea of dragging her victim to a secret lair. She wanted me to admire her victory and present her with a special dish of diced chicken.

Amber might have been named Topaz....

Chapter 5

Recently I read that there are ten million cats in the United States, which means five million more cats than dogs. I always wonder how experts arrive at these round figures. Even as they estimate, more puppies are turning blind noses to the daylight and thimble-sized kittens are reaching for the first mouthful of warm life-giving milk. So who knows?

But the preponderance of cats does suggest that the cat can take care of himself better than a dog. A cat can pry open a garbage can and fish out something or sneak in an alleyway and find a mouse or rat. A homeless dog either starves or gets run over or shot by some ambitious hunter. In the city, a cat can jump from one apartment-house roof to another. A dog cannot even get up there. Also, a chased cat can vanish as no dog can. In my part of the country, an unlicensed dog is picked up and, if no home is found, is destroyed. But nobody pays any attention to the cats that live off the land and do not wear licenses.

The country cats that visit my yard would never

submit to a collar and license. Sometimes I wonder what would happen if cats had to have licenses—spayed female so much, altered male so much, unspayed females more, etc. I would very much like to have Amber registered at the Town Hall and listed with a number and my address, but I realize wearing a small metal tag would drive her crazy.

It would also, again, involve a collar to hang the license on. A harness would be useless because when the harness is used, the owner is there. Recently I met a charming Golden Retriever puppy shipped from Canada and he had a serial number for identification tattooed on one ear.

But a Golden has firm thick ears, whereas no cat has ears thick enough to tattoo. And the Golden could not tell me whether this hurt a good deal at the time or not. It is, however, a permanent insurance against anyone stealing a valuable dog, whereas dog stealers toss collars away as they go about their business of marketing stolen dogs.

So far, I cannot think of any way to attach a label and phone number to a cat!

Advertisements for lost dogs usually give the license number, but advertisements for lost cats are pathetic. "Lost in the vicinity of———one spayed female with white paws and a white forefront. Answers to the name of Baby." Since Baby is not apt to rush up to a stranger, this is not very helpful.

Also cats do not identify so readily with a name. Amber comes when I call her either Amber or Sweetheart. But since she is nearly always underfoot, calling her is seldom necessary except when she gets shut in a closet. Then I wish that when I call "*Amber*" she would call back instead of just sitting in the dark and waiting.

Esmé knew her name very well but paid no attention unless she was on her way already. And Tigger, the Manx, would turn his green-glass eyes to me and imply I was very silly because I could see him, couldn't I?

This curious indifference to a label may be peculiar to Amber. She understands very well when I say "Let's go for a walk." Or, "I have something for you to eat —come in the kitchen." Or, "I am going for the mail but I shall be right back." And, as I have said, she knows what the word No means. After one nibble of the best African violet, she waits for that No.

I talk to her about everything and would advise any cat owner to do the same with his cat. Too many cat owners accept a cat's apparent indifference to special commands. Since I have lived with Amber, I know the variations in her voice and can understand almost everything she tries to tell me. I think this is reciprocal. Otherwise when I explain I am going to the typewriter to work, why does she fly ahead of me and jump on the machine and begin pushing the buttons to see the keys hop up?

And even when I don't talk to her, Amber understands what I am thinking. When I have to shut her in the bedroom preparatory to my going out, I have to sneak in and turn the rug back so the door will close. I try not to have her observe this tactic. If she sees me shove the rug over, she vanishes and I am late for the party because I can't find her.

"Well, this is a surprise," one friend said as I turned up ten minutes late for dinner, "you are always so early

(Jacques Chepard)

Stairs are for climbing.

we just rush to get ready and even so we are always late. But here *you* are! Late."

"Amber didn't want to be left alone," I explained.

When I get back I call from the front door, "I'm back, Sweetheart!"

She is at the door of the bedroom, yawning. She has been asleep on the pillow and probably hasn't missed me at all, but she is like an actor in the third act of a play. She rises to the drama of my coming home and not abandoning her forever. Jumping around, purring, kneading her paws, rubbing her head against my hand, twitching her tail and putting an occasional melancholy miaow in the middle of a purr. She has, she implies, suffered excruciatingly.

Which brings me to the point of sleeping. A puppy who is left alone may yell his head off until his lips are foam-flecked. He may claw the door, tear up the furniture and make a career of suffering. When he is older, he gets over this. A kitten goes to sleep. This is partly because cats sleep more than dogs. Recently I read another one of those doubtful statements to the effect that a cat may sleep seventeen hours a day.

If so, it is because a cat exercises violently and completely. The acrobatics of a kitten remind me of Ringling's circus. After Amber goes at a dizzying speed, up in the air, the whole length of the house, for half an hour, she takes a nap with paws folded under her chin, tail quiescent.

A hunting dog may run all day and after a brief rest be ready for an automobile ride. But he does not use every muscle in his body the way a cat does. He seldom leaps, climbs, swings in the air; he just runs through brush. This observation is purely my own without benefit of experts.

The agility of a kitten is amazing until you get used to it. I watch Amber and decide this is the nearest thing to flying without wings. Also, she uses a lot of energy washing, which involves one hind leg at an acute angle while she scrubs, the head swiveled completely while she works at her ears. Her muscles seem to be fluent. The one place she cannot reach is behind her head between the ears, so I give special attention to that and she thanks me with a large enthusiastic purr.

When Amber is asleep, she is motionless as a figurine. This interests me because the dogs always dreamed. Holly, the Irish, would twitch her paws as if she were running a race and often wag her plumed tail wildly. She was a happy dreamer. Amber is quiet as still water. I have been told that all mammals dream (and perhaps birds too) and that the mind is eased by working things out while we sleep. If this is so, I conclude that Amber keeps her dreams inside her mind without reacting physically. The absolute repose of a sleeping cat somehow eases the tensions of a watcher. Often I reach out and touch Amber to be sure she is still warmly alive.

Amber wakes instantly. She may yawn once widely and then she is leaping-active. My cockers and Irish yawned and stretched and yawned again with sleepy-lidded eyes. I belong to this type myself, for the first hour I am up is like being on a slow boat to China, as it were.

But one interesting thing about Amber's sleep is that the slightest sound alerts her. Occasionally I can tiptoe past a dog-tired dog, but if I get up noiselessly in the night for a drink of water, Amber is already on the bathroom bowl, leaning over the faucet to catch the first drip when I turn it on. And when I move silently to the wing at the Cape to work at the typewriter, I often think she is sound asleep on the bed. But when I get to the wing, she is already perched on the carriage of my machine.

Finally, as to sleep, cats like secret places some of the time. Dogs usually choose their own bed and never sleep anywhere else. But Amber may emerge from the linen closet or the kitchen cupboard. She has two kitten houses, one especially made by the grandchildren and one bought at a fancy pet store and equipped with a rug and an upper porch, but she almost never uses them. I have learned when I open a drawer never to close it entirely in case she has slipped in for a nap. Or I may find her tucked in the bookshelves, warmed by Keats and Shakespeare.

Once I closed the closet door in the wing and went peacefully to bed, assuming she was in the chair by the open fire. In the morning I called her and had no answer and began a frantic search. After combing the whole house, I opened that one closet door and out came Amber, a little cross at being confined in there all night but otherwise quite self-possessed. Now I leave that door ajar too, for her melancholy confinement did *not* give her a horror of the closet. It is full of fine things to play with, she says.

The one place where she never lies down is the right half of the best sofa. Even if I am sitting on that sofa at the other end, she leaps from the table to my side without invading the right end, which was Holly's. Since she never saw Holly, there can be no memory pattern, and certainly none of that sweet-hay scent of an Irish is left, so I am happy to assume that Amber has an understanding with Holly herself.

In our Connecticut house a lot has happened. The previous owner murdered his wife one night and then committed suicide, which must have been hard on their houseguest, who had come to the country to visit them after a nervous breakdown. My own feeling about the household ghosts is that they are companionable. They all, in their time, loved Stillmeadow. No matter what tragedies they endured, the fact that this house was cherished is evident in every hand-hewn stone and hand-cut beam. But I wondered about Amber who is so very sensitive.

At first when she heard footsteps and nobody was there, her ears went out like wind-blown sails. A ridge of fur rose along her backbone. Occasionally she uttered a faint hiss. But before long she was only curious and interested. Sometimes around two in the morning she stands on tiptoe at the foot of the old pineapple-post bed. She rests her triangle of chin on the footboard and stares wide-eyed through the bedroom door into the family room beyond. When the footsteps cease, she yawns and tucks up again on my pillow.

The only time she objected was one night when suddenly two books flung themselves from the top shelf in the bedroom. They were books dating back to 1800, bound in ancient leather. One was *Poems of Old Age* and one *Poems for a Young Man*. I have no idea whose they were in the beginning, but they landed on the maple daybed with muffled bangs, and Amber leaped six inches in the air.

Most of the animals that have owned me have had perceptions I could not have. When they prowl around nervously, I stop whatever I am doing and look to see what has gone wrong in the house. When they jump on the window sill and look earnestly down the road, I take off my apron and powder my face hastily. Long before the sound of a motor is heard, they *know*. But if the car coming down the road is not going to stop at Stillmeadow or Still Cove, as the case may be, they pay no attention.

Amber, naturally, does not bark but she is a good watcher. She jumps up and down, tail flashing back and forth. She unfurls her ears and points in the direction of the menace. If she hears the car of her favorite friend Margaret Stanger, she flies to the door, purring up a storm. Margaret always brings a snack. One time, though, she came directly from a party where she couldn't sneak even a morsel in her purse. Amber tried to open the purse, then went through the pockets of Margaret's sweater, and then sat down and miaowed pitifully. A week or so later, Margaret telephoned to say that she had started over to my house and got as far as the nearest neighbor's, but then realized she had forgotten Amber's snack so she turned around and went home.

This probably proves that a small kitten has no difficulty managing her subjects!

But I must add that the subjects are more flattered when she flies into their laps and spreads her paws and

Amber always prefers Christmas-tree decorations to toys.

rubs her head against them and purrs and purrs than they would be if Queen Elizabeth awarded them something to hang around their necks.

Amber's self-appointed role as watchcat always surprises me. With Esmé, the Siamese, her reaction to strangers at the door was to spin upstairs and hide in the bathroom. Tigger, the Manx, sat by the fire and scrubbed his blunt square face no matter who came in. But Amber hears a car coming far down the road. She always recognizes the sound of friends' cars, as I have said, although she had some trouble when Margaret bought a new one. The first time Margaret came in from that car Amber jumped on the harvest table and stared with disbelief. It took several minutes before she hurried over to say hello. The second or third time the car pulled in the drive, Amber was at the kitchen window waiting.

When a strange car turns down our road, Amber rushes to the front door and lashes her tail. If she thinks I have not noticed it—and I often haven't—she dashes in and jumps on my desk and then runs back to her watch-point.

Naturally she could never fall on an intruder and mangle him as a dog could. She cannot bark a warning. Even when she hisses you have to listen hard to hear her. But I feel perfectly secure with Amber to notify me someone is coming and which door he or she is coming toward and whether he or she is familiar or not. Furnace men, painters, electricians she greets with joy. But one night a strange man came to the door. He was trying to deliver a package from the next town and was hopelessly lost. Amber greeted his arrival like a miniature leopard (all five pounds of her).

No German Shepherd could be a more dedicated guardian of the home than this small Abyssinian kitten.

Chapter 6

Amber was three and a half months old when she came to Stillmeadow. When I picked her up, it was like holding a handful of milkweed fluff. I felt she must have been the size of a golden thimble when she was born. A kitten, according to the books, should be at least seven weeks old before leaving the mother. By then the kitten has been trained by the mother in sanitary habits and can go on a basic diet served in a crystal bowl.

The proper diet for a cat seems to be a controversial subject. I had a list from the breeder which I approved of and I also read my whole shelf of cat books. Hardly one agreed with another, which shows that cat people have much in common with dog people! I agreed with Dr. Leon Whitney who believes cats should have vegetables in the diet. While some people feel cats must be meat—or fish—eaters exclusively, Leon points out that cats who live on rats or mice get predigested vegetables in the innards of the prey. He also points out that cats have been domesticated for thousands of years more than many mammals and are adapted to life in man's world.

I started Amber on baby food—lamb and vegetables, beef and vegetables, liver and vegetables, chicken and broth. I omitted those gay jars of bacon and vegetables since ham and bacon, and probably any variety of pork, do not seem to me advisable for a kitten. I also gave her warm milk on the side. Since liver and milk are presumably laxative, I kept them at a minimum since she arrived troubled with diarrhea, possibly because she had roundworms.

I must digress and say that any puppy or kitten should be checked for worms. Even in the days when we raised litters of cocker puppies in the most sanitary conditions, now and then roundworms would turn up. When they are four weeks old, it is time to check. Worming nowadays is very simple with modern drugs, and Amber never lost a meal.

I think a varied diet is better for cats, just as I believe in it for dogs. Man himself in the prehistoric days presumably ate raw meat when he was lucky, but man became omnivorous as the centuries rolled on, and the two who have lived closest to him, dogs and cats, have adapted to changing circumstances in their physical requirements. I have never known a cocker or an Irish who would have survived if he had to kill game and subsist on what he caught. Even country cats that are on their own find supplements in milk in the cowbarns, leftovers around garbage cans, scraps tossed from cars. They nibble sweet fresh grass. If they wander to the town dump, they add a good many odd things to their diet. We keep a pan of kibbled food by the well house for visitors.

There are two digestive differences, however, between cats and humans. I found out at once that Amber's front teeth are sabre-sharp and designed for tearing. Cats normally tear their food and gulp it. Human beings, if they are not starving, chew their food with those flat back teeth. This means starchy food or nuts are pulverized and digest easily. Amber gulps, dipping her head down, throwing her head back and swallowing with a rippling movement in her throat. She even gulped the first baby food, which is already puréed.

The second difference in the cat's digestive system is that the cat does not have the efficient starch-digesting enzyme which human beings have. So starchy meals are not advisable unless the starch is precooked and easily digested.

But I soon discovered that Amber has her own ideas about the need for some starch. I left part of a stuffed baked potato on the table when I went to answer the phone one night, and when I came back, Amber was innocently scrubbing her face and only the potato skin was left. Now when I have baked potato, I put a teaspoonful of it in her dish.

We live in a vitamin-loving age, but a good basic and varied diet provides, in my opinion, enough vitamins. However, a small amount of something like viosterol or a similar type of vitamin mixture may be advisable, and the veterinarian will suggest his preference. When you adopt a starving kitten, vitamin therapy is needed, but it is better to have the veterinarian prescribe than to go to the drugstore and pick out something yourself.

At one time when Amber was still recovering from worms, I made an extra trip to Kim Schneider, the Cape Cod veterinarian adored by patients and owners. He pulled a small tube from his magic cabinet and suggested that Amber should have some extra vitamins until she was fully on her paws again.

When I took the cap from the tube, Amber advanced with interest; and as I squeezed some of the dark substance out to dab on her paws, she put out her minute pink tongue and licked the tube. This, she said, was delicious! So after that I simply called her, took the cap off and squeezed one-sixth of an inch out, and she polished both tube-end and cap.

Now all I do is pick up the tube and call, "Amber, time for vitamins!"

Even when she is busiest she comes flying, and I have to be careful not to squeeze out too much. She would eat a quarter of the tube if she had the chance.

Nobody as far as I know has ever done a study of the modern advances in pet medication, but I am an ardent admirer of the men who have worked in this area. Having spent a good deal of time trying to persuade cockers and Irish that milk of magnesia and such remedies really were fit to swallow, then mopping myself and the floor, I am grateful for a tube of laxative from which a suspicious kitten will take a nice swallow.

When we had thirty-five cockers and two Irish and two cats, I had a whole medicine cabinet stocked for them, and not one single type of medicine was really appealing! Fortunately dogs are easier to persuade than cats, and it is not hard to pull out that lower lip and tuck the medicine in. Amber's lower lip would never pull out. And her throat is so small that only Doctor Kim could ever treat her without a strangle.

The diet chart that came with Amber is a sensible one. For a kitten, it suggests ground chuck, chicken, very little fish, and not more than once a week. Liver and kidney not more than twice a week plus .03 ounce liquid vitamin daily.

This brings me to the question of fish. My dear friends Millie and Ed have a beautiful domestic short-hair (whose coat looks like that of a Persian), one of the healthiest and loveliest cats I have known. Peter decided at an early age that he only wanted to eat tuna fish. He went further. He only wanted one particular brand of tuna fish. He would condescend, tail waving, to nibble one brand of catfood based on the type of tuna he liked. He would not drink milk, or eat chicken, turkey, steak tidbits. When I am at the Cape, I have dinner every Monday night with Millie and Ed, and for several years we spent hours discussing ways of persuading Petie to eat a more balanced diet. Nothing worked. My experience has been that you can persuade a dog into almost anything if only to please you and keep you from bursting into tears.

But a cat will only eat what he or she feels is desirable. No smacking of lips and cooing will make any difference. With a sick puppy, I have gone so far as to get down on the floor and pretend to eat a spoonful of the food he needed. With a cat, it would be useless. Amber, for instance, would watch me with interest and bat at the spoon but never open her mouth. I know this, and it saved me a lot of energy when I discovered she didn't care for eggs. She does not like them raw with milk or soft-boiled or poached or scrambled. So I hard-cooked one and mixed a quarter teaspoon of it with chicken. This she would tolerate, but without undue enthusiasm.

As far as Petie's diet is concerned, I must point out that he is a wonderful mouser, going far afield for mice since the house does not provide them. All the time we worried about him, he was dining on the vital parts of some mice, including the partly digested material in the intestines, which includes some vegetable material.

Then came the worst winter on record. Suddenly Millie imparted the wonderful news that Petie was eating a can of kidney or beef at one sitting plus half a dozen snacks a day. It seems to me reasonable to suppose that with a sudden shortage of the food he got for himself, he sensibly decided that he would eat some of the junk his devoted mistress and master kept urging on him.

However, in view of Petie's addiction to one brand of tuna, I felt I would not start Amber on fish. When she was used to a variety of other things would be time enough. She would never be a mouser, I thought, or an outdoor-country cat. But I discovered how she felt about fish when I dished up a plate of creamed Alaskan King Crab and she tried to get in the plate. I settled for a teaspoon and a promise that life would hold more fish later on. Especially, I said, after she ate her lamb and spinach.

Cats do need some fat. Farm cats manage to get about 25 per cent of fat in their diet. House cats get some in the natural course of events. A balanced diet, says Dr. Whitney, allows around 20 per cent fat. Cow's milk has a considerable amount if it is whole milk. Amber enjoys milk, but is not above licking a stick of butter left on the counter if her meals haven't enough fat in them.

Water is essential. Tigger seldom drank any, but he probably dipped his blunt nose in the pond when he was thirsty. House cats should have *fresh* water available, and Amber drinks frequently. Aladdin used to sit under a leaky faucet and catch the drops as they fell and swallow them. Esmé, the Siamese, drank sparingly, but enjoyed beaten egg yolk which provided some liquid.

For a kitten, I was advised to serve the food slightly warm, never directly from the icebox. At first I had a problem with this for one jar of baby food added up to almost three meals for Amber. I did not want to keep heating up the same food. The right amount set in a pan over a low heat instantly dried into a leathery blob, and most of it had to be scraped from the pan. Adding half a spoonful of liquid turned it into soup. After great thought, I solved this by putting the food on a piece of plastic kitchen wrap, folding the edges tight and dropping it into hot water for a couple of minutes.

With regard to the use of regular catfood, I consulted Dr. Whitney. There are dozens of canned catfoods, catfoods in boxes, all sorts of combinations. Some are made of what they call by-products. Some have a good deal of filler. Some are meals-in-one, some are not.

Considering Amber's tendency to diarrhea, Dr. Whitney suggested adding one of two brands of the tiny

Amber's wedge-shaped face is never far away.

pellets. I'll call them Brand A and Brand B. He said if I put them in her dish, she would play with them (B is made in fancy stars and other shapes). Then she would crunch one and finally eat a few.

Amber admitted she enjoyed tossing them around, dropping them on the floor, chasing them all over the kitchen. But crunch she would not. I added the brand of canned catfood Dr. Whitney recommended, and she sat down and stared at me. I put some of the baby strained beef in with it. She licked up the beef, leaving no pellet so much as cracked.

There may be hardy souls who can defeat a small kitten, but I am not one of them. This was what is called an unequal contest, like having the Green Bay Packers play a high-school football team. I opened a can of lobster bisque and put it on to heat for my own lunch after the morning's struggle, and when I dished it up, Amber advanced, purring loudly. I dribbled a spoonful of the bisque over those controversial pellets and then heard the sweetest music in the world, the sound of a definite *crunch*.

So we reached a compromise. The pellets will be mixed with something added that Amber thinks is fit to eat. Chicken, beef, lamb—and of course, lobster bisque —are her favorites. And there is no problem with diarrhea.

In short, every animal is an individual, and feeding cannot be regimented. Just why Holly, the Irish, wanted her food soupy, while Honey, the cocker, insisted on its being chewy and rather dry, I do not know.

When Amber yawns, I realize how tiny her mouth is and what a small aperture provides a throat. She likes her food to be fairly mushy but varied with bits of meat or chicken that she can tear to pieces, holding one end in her paw. This terrified me at first, for I felt sure she would strangle on anything larger than a pinhead.

I do not give Amber bones. I know the veterinarians say that there is a digestive juice in a cat's stomach which is more powerful than that in a human's and that a bone will be softened in around an hour. But a sharp shard of bone might not get that far, I feel. I also remember that when kind neighbors gave my Irish some steak bones she had to go to the veterinarian because her intestines were packed tight with bone meal. Chewing on a veal knuckle is satisfying for a cat, and that is the limit to which I go.

Cats like to eat up on a table or counter rather than on the floor. Very little of Amber's life is spent on floor level. Leaping is the favored mode of locomotion. I feed Amber on one end of the long counter under the kitchen window and I eat at the other end. This means we both look out on the old well house and the wisteria and can watch the birds.

It has also led to some interesting discoveries as to taste in food. Amber is so fond of Petite Marmite that she must have a teaspoonful in a separate dish. If I have the lobster bisque, I either give her some or a wedge-shaped nose is in my soup spoon. If I have beef stew, she enjoys a portion, even to the onions and carrots. A little potato does no harm, she says.

She likes cheese so much that when I have a cheese sandwich she will go so far as to miaow unless her own sliver is ready.

And recently Amber decided, after all my worries

about vegetables in her diet, that she did like asparagus. I had by then given up the struggle with string beans, spinach soufflé and so on. But one time I fixed a dish of frozen asparagus for supper and the phone rang (it always does at mealtime). When I came back to the kitchen Amber was braced against the dish, eating asparagus tips as fast as possible. I praised her extravagantly and gave her all she could eat.

I couldn't remember that the experts recommended this particular vegetable, but it agreed with her very well. I went to the market and laid in a supply the next day. I found that having asparagus night after night got rather boring for me, especially since I had to eat the stalks while Amber consumed the tips. After two weeks, she decided she had had enough of that particular edible and went back to an occasional binge on mushrooms.

I haven't given up hope that she will change her mind about egg yolks, but so far her answer to egg is to draw back her velvet lips and walk away proud-legged. But I shall keep at it, remembering that even a kitten can change her mind.

Last week end my dear friend Olive brought me a jar of homemade cream of leek soup which I planned to have for lunch. Amber decided that was what she wanted for lunch also, and in the end, after assuring her she could not possibly like it, especially since it was well-seasoned, I gave in and put a spoonful in her dish. She actually seemed to breathe it in and came purring back for another round. At that point I decided that her diet was well-balanced in an odd way even if it did not exactly follow the lists provided by the experts.

Amber's silhouette became superb in adolescence.

I have heard the theory that cats never overeat, but judging by some cats I have known, this cannot be true. Country cats seldom do get too fat because they have so much exercise. Barn cats work for their living and generally live long and stay in good shape. But house cats sometimes are so fat they seem hardly able to move. Overfeeding shortens their lives, as it does with dogs.

As long as I can feel Amber's ribs, I shall not worry, but I do check on them every day or so to be sure she doesn't need to join a weight-watchers' club. Some days she wants more to eat, some days less, and her own system seems to balance it out very well so far. An Abyssinian seldom miaows at all, but occasionally she will leap to my desk, stare fixedly at me and utter that minute sound. It means she is absolutely starving and where is her dinner?

Usually it also means I have been working and forgot to notice the time, while her personal clock has been working. But now and then she decides in the middle of a late television show that she needs something. She gets it.

And one endearing thing about her is that every time she is fed, she jumps in my lap and thanks me with loud, persistent purring. Then she settles down on the desk and scrubs, even flattening her ears which never do get in her food.

One difference between dogs and cats is in the manner of eating. A cat uses her paws like hands, scooping up bits of food and putting them in her mouth. A dog uses his muzzle to push and arrange tidbits or shoves the whole dish around with his nose.

Once when Amber had a dreamy moment I examined

her paws. The four small parts tipped with pale raspberry-colored cushions are prehensile, very like fingers.

"You've got an extra bend in them," I told her.

She purred and spread her toes apart with pleasure.

Her wrist is very flexible, more so than mine, I must say. There is no thumb but I felt a small semipad tipped with a flat claw. I think it is what we call a dewclaw in dogs.

I read somewhere, probably in *The Territorial Imperative*, that it is the thumb which is largely responsible for the difference between man and the other mammals. This seems reasonable to me, since I once hit my thumb with a hammer and decided a thumb was basic.

When Amber sees me put down her food dish, she advances on tiptoe, sniffing. If it is something she really likes, she gulps and when she has finished goes over the dish with a scouring pink tongue, sometimes putting one paw inside to hold it still. If the food is chopped up, she picks out the best morsels and carries them to the corner of the counter, turning her back for privacy while she holds them and pulverizes them. The less attractive bits she pushes to the side with one paw.

She is fastidiously neat. If she spills a drop of anything, she cleans it up. When she is finished, she laps a small amount of milk and then begins the eternal washing up, which she takes very seriously. It's important to tidy up when the mealtime chores are done.

Chapter 7

My first experience in housebreaking a kitten was with Amber. Esmé and Tigger went outdoors when they needed to. Tigger would go to the back door, lie down, and roll over and over, which always worked. Esmé screamed. Occasionally in the coldest weather, Esmé used the toilet seat in one bathroom.

But Amber was to use her own pan since she could not go out in ten-below-zero weather. I was not worried since all of the books I read advised me housebreaking a cat was no problem at all. Generally the mother cat housetrains her kittens—and cats are naturally neat.

I had housebroken dozens of cockers, paper-training them. Most of ours were raised on *The New York Times* and the *Newtown Bee*. Now I had an elegant pale-green plastic rectangular pan with waterproof liners and a bag of kitty litter with a cleaning scoop.

I decided on my dressing room for the location since it was out of the way but near my room. The dressing room is nothing but the front entry on the east side.

There are five doors to the ancient house, and this one has never been used except for letting dogs and cats in and out. There is no path to it. It has room for a chest of drawers and one straight chair.

I knew a kitten couldn't be expected to run all over the house looking for a pan when the house must have seemed as large as a museum. It was quiet and dark in the dressing room; indeed it resembles a closet. I knew cats like privacy for the toilet.

The local Food Center carried the litter, so I could always get more. It smelled a little like cedar and was more absorbent than sand, and in any case I know how sand tracks around since I spend part of my time on Cape Cod. Most Cape floors look as if sandpaper had been rubbed into them.

As soon as Amber had her first meal, I took her to the pan and put her in it. A little later, I put her in again. Later I added some shredded newspaper since she had been used to that at the cattery. When a damp spot appeared, I scooped up the litter and put in fresh.

This worked perfectly as far as wetting was concerned.

However, Amber had never read a cat book and she had her own ideas about the rest of the bathroom business. Her first choice was at the foot of the stairs leading to the upper story. I felt it could scarcely have been a more unfortunate choice since people were always pounding up and down those stairs. I used some ammonia on the area, which took off all seven coats of Butcher's Wax.

Her next chosen location was at one end of the trestle table where nobody who sat down to eat could miss it. I took off some more wax and hoped for the best. Meanwhile I kept her in my room most of the time, feeling sure she would remember her pan because it was so nearby.

A few days passed and the pan got damp spots and that was all. Finally I discovered she had a fine secluded spot under the radiator behind the maple daybed. This old hot-water radiator has bookshelves built around it that go to the ceiling, and my business-office metal desk is at one end. To get under that radiator involves moving the daybed and the desk (both weigh tons). It then means lying flat on the floor and reaching in with soap and water. It took my agile teen-age friend Tommy to accomplish this feat.

While Tommy crawled under, he discovered she also liked the lower shelf of the bookcase—empty because inaccessible. The desk is in front of it. So the desk came out again. The cleaning job took, in all, two hours, and the kitten watched with interest, her head cocked.

"I don't want to do that again," said Tommy, shaking his red head.

So we tried to figure out how to close up the space. An old window screen was jammed in behind the desk, sealing off the bookshelves. Pieces of cardboard cartons went in and some old books were stuffed in the open end of the radiator.

Certainly a mature person should be able to outthink a small apricot kitten, I thought. I felt happy about everything until I decided to get back to work on the current book and discovered Amber had used the floor under the well of my desk as her newest bathroom.

At that point, I cleaned the floor again and spread

(Cape Cod Photos, Orleans, Mass.)

Amber enjoys TV (weather reports most) and Herb Alpert.

newspapers all over the surface and moved her pan from the dressing room to the fine cave under the desk well. And there it has stayed. This means that at regular intervals I stop typing and withdraw. Then Amber slips under the desk and turns her back and lifts her head high, staring at the top of the well. When she has finished her chores she leaps out and goes through the air like a jet plane, wild with triumph.

On the whole, I am satisfied. The pan and extra newspapers do not show, and they occupy what has never had anything but a wastebasket before. True, the wastebasket now sits in front of the daybed and is no object of art. It is a huge metal container I once painted smoky blue. It has rusted right through the paint. So I face the prospect of hunting in antique shops in the valley for an old sugar bucket to use for trash.

But I remember a woman I once met who had a cat that would only use the strings inside the grand piano for her toilet. So nobody could ever play the piano with the top up, and some musical works seem to demand an open top. And one cat I knew insisted on using the fireplace. This should have been cured by filling the pan with ashes, but the fireplace had more charm.

Most cats are more reasonable. Their own pan and some privacy is all they ask. If you do not have a special cat pan, a shallow pan from the hardware store will do very well. Plastic is easy to handle and to clean, but be sure to buy a shallow one. Cats like to see where they are. In case you cannot find the pan liners, plastic kitchen wrap will do.

The advantage of a liner is that you can lift the contents of the pan out all at once and dump it into the trash can. The pan stays clean, but if you want to wash it out, use only a mild soap. The smell of ammonia or carbolic acid will keep your cat away from the pan forever. The smell may make a cat actually ill, and this does not surprise me at all for I feel dizzy if I get near either one.

Once you have the pan located where you and the kitten agree is a satisfactory place, never change the location. You wouldn't like to hunt for a bathroom all over the house either!

Tay Hohoff disagrees with this as her own cat, Shadrach, will put up with having his pan moved when there are guests coming. She says he accepts it like a gentleman. I think she has a most unusual cat. Mine would never put up with it!

In general I feel any established pattern is easier for a cat. Amber does not even like a chair put in a different place. If I change the arrangement of milk glass on the harvest table, she approaches gingerly, then goes over each piece, inspecting it thoroughly and disapprovingly. A pile of laundry on the bed is stalked, examined, and finally accepted as good to nest in.

Although Esmé, Tigger, and Aladdin did not have pans, I think this was a serious mistake on our part. You cannot be sure you won't have a flat tire and be late getting home. In New England in winter there are a good many blizzards when even opening the door can be a problem. Or you may have an appointment with the doctor and expect to be in his office twenty minutes (hope does spring eternal) and sit two hours or more while the doctor is on an emergency call. Cats have a great deal of endurance and patience, but nature has a definite schedule. It is better to have a bathroom available at all times.

A small kitten may need to use the pan a dozen times a day, but the main bathroom business comes after the biggest meal. Amber flies to her pan at almost exactly four in the afternoon. She scratches up the paper with great vigor, following the basic tradition of cats. Afterward she races around the house leaping up and down and then works hard at her scratching post. And then naturally she washes herself from ear tip to tail.

Amber does have one rather odd reaction to her bathroom. She uses her pretty pastel pan with the fine kitty litter in it. But she uses it only for wetting. For the more serious business she steps carefully outside of the pan and nothing will persuade her this is not as good as using the pan for the whole affair!

We had to compromise after a prolonged struggle. I spread *The New York Times* all around the pan in thick layers topped with the smaller folds of *The Cape Codder* or *Newtown Bee*. She uses the newspaper and then scratches frantically, trying to bury everything neatly. After she has panted and heaved and clawed with discouraging results, I rescue her. And I may say she enjoys being rescued. She watches with interest as I pull out the necessary folds of paper, roll them up and slip a rubber band around the roll. Then she flies triumphantly about the house, waving her tail like a banner.

Actually this is easier than emptying the pan so often.

The whole problem of a cat's sanitation is relatively simple. It is not true, as some people think, that a house begins to smell of cat. If it does, the owner is failing to keep the cat clean and to empty the pan daily. If a kitten does make a mistake before she has settled down, a couple of tissues will clean it up. A damp sponge dipped in a mild detergent (no carbolic acid) will prevent a stain on the rug. I have been told that sprinkling salt on the spot will also fix it, but I have never tried this.

It turned out that Amber's original problems were due to the diarrhea from the intestinal infection she arrived with. It was always too far to the regular bathroom. But once the diarrhea was checked, that difficulty was over.

Chapter 8

There may be some stolid cats, but I have never known one. A cat has a naturally lively mind, and my life with Amber has kept me lively too. As for discipline and training—we have learned from each other.

Amber does not care too much for toys that are meant for cats, but sometimes in the night I hear her pouncing in the living room. If I am still up watching a late show, I investigate. I find she has been taking the cigarettes from the small pewter mug and tossing them all over the floor. Every cigarette is full of pin-sized holes.

I learned very soon to keep a cigarette on her counter so she could attack it.

She has also taught me to appreciate pencils. I like soft drawing pencils and so does she. She takes a newly sharpened one and knocks it to the floor, scoops it up, and tosses it and shoves it under the radiator where I cannot reach it. When I retrieve it with the dust mop, the point is gone and the whole pencil mangled.

She does have a few habits which some people might

consider need disciplining, but I am learning to accept them.

She enjoys doing over bouquets, especially roses. I keep a half-dozen sweetheart roses in my grandmother's silver teapot and spend some time arranging them just so. Amber watches, with her head cocked, and as soon as possible she takes the best rose and plays games with it. Next to chicken and roast beef and White Lilac perfume, rose is her favorite scent. She prefers it to catnip.

In a short time, petals are all over the floor and she is pouncing on the rose leaves. When I come in the room, she looks up with innocent eyes and with a rose petal under one paw. She indicates she likes roses and I explain that I do not know whether or not they would be a good thing in her small insides. Many house plants, I am told, are poisonous to cats. So I distract her with a small bit of chicken while I hastily sweep up the rose leaves.

The next thing I know she is inside the television set and I am terrified that she may be electrocuted. The television repairman told me terrible tales of this happening. I fish her out, complaining. Then I glue the television cord up on the bookcase with Scotch tape. (I wonder why they call it Scotch?)

As I have said earlier, one of her favorite sports is playing with water. I have learned to be careful about turning on the hot water. Lately she has become a flower-water addict too, so it is hard to keep flower vases filled. It is her theory that water tastes better if roses or daffodils are standing in it. In April she lowered the level in the forsythia pitcher until the pale gold flowers turned paler and paler. She can elongate her neck and somehow make her head slide around stems.

The vacuum cleaner is a delight for her, which is one of the few things we do not have in common. My hostility to the vacuum cleaner is no secret, but I think more kindly of mine since it means so much to Amber. That long snaky hose which trips me and winds around chair legs is a special treat to her. In the beginning, I wondered whether she might be sucked in by that hose, but she never was.

We have disagreed about one other thing. I cannot type when that golden head is in the key well and two deft paws are picking up the keys. It bothers my concentration and makes the keys knot up and stick. Also I have had to discourage her from unrolling the ribbon— I have trouble enough changing it even when that becomes absolutely necessary.

Then there is the matter of kitchen safety. The kitchen at Stillmeadow is U-shaped and the refrigerator, which goes almost to the ceiling, bisects one set of counters. I was happy about this when Amber came because it meant I had plenty of counter space inaccessible to her. The range was protected. And the counter under the window was free so that she could eat, play and doze in the sun there while I did kitchen chores.

But one night I got up to have a snack and turned on the kitchen lights. From the top of the refrigerator a small wedge-shaped face peered at me. The next minute she flew through the air and landed in the sink. From there it was easy to leap to the range.

No problem at all, she assured me.

(Cape Cod Photos, Orleans, Mass.)
Amber can look startled, but not much.

Her feat was comparable to my leaping to the top of the two-hundred-year-old sugar maples. It was equally dangerous. I uttered my most anguished *No* and she vanished. But the next morning when I went out to plug in the coffee pot, a little golden face hung over the refrigerator top.

By standing on tiptoe, I reached her, and for the first time I spanked her. Now when I go into the kitchen, she flies from the refrigerator top and vanishes. But when I am safely in my room typing, I can hear the thud which means she has pushed the roll of aluminum foil from the top of the refrigerator. And by the time I run out, I find a beautiful Abyssinian tail waving in the sink.

This is probably good for my housekeeping because I cannot leave a single morsel of food on any counter in the kitchen and dishing-up goes at sixty miles an hour. Stacking the soiled plates is not feasible either, so they get washed immediately. I decided this when I found her eating broiled mushrooms that were on a breakfast plate. No cat expert ever said anything about mushrooms on a cat diet. How did I know they wouldn't poison her?

In fact, they agreed with her so well I wondered whether in the wild state cats ever nibble a mushroom on the way to a hunt.

Her games seldom cause me any bother.

When it comes to regular kitten toys, as I have said, Amber finds them dull. She cast a tentative paw over those she got for her first Christmas and settled for munching the ribbon and the tissue paper they came in. A paper grocery bag is better, according to her. She did enjoy taking ornaments from the Christmas tree, and I spent some sleepless hours wondering whether she had really eaten any of those bangles and baubles or just hidden them in cracks in the old floor.

String, erasers, rubber bands, pens, bits of kindling from the wood basket and my best stockings are on the honor list. Crumpled balls of aluminum foil she often drags around, and a ripe olive lifted from the cocktail tray is delightful.

If all else fails, she scoops up a corner of the irreplaceable wool rug and builds a cave in it and chews off nubbins of wool. She also likes bed linen and I often hear Millie, the friend who comes to help me with the weekly household chores, advising her that this time she cannot punch holes in the sheets because these are the *good* ones! Next week, Millie promises, she will use the patched one and it will be all right. A few pillowcases have acquired frayed edges but are still usable, so I do not go into the No-No routine on those.

I have strong opinions on discipline. It should, I think, be sparing. If life is one long negative, nobody is benefited whether it be a child, a pet, or a husband or wife. Most of the problems of living might be solved if we emphasized only the essential.

Cats traditionally do not respond to commands as dogs easily do. I think perhaps the reason Amber obeys me when I say No is that I use it so seldom. If she is pulling the stuffing out of a shabby worn chair I keep quiet. If it is a chair covered with a documentary print, I firmly speak the word "No" as loudly as my rather light voice permits. She gives me an incredulous stare and rakes one last streak down the upholstery and then stops. In three minutes she forgives me and jumps in my lap.

Also, I am sure the reason she always comes when I

call her is that I only call her when it is necessary. Ninety per cent of the time when I worry about whether she has gotten stuck in a drawer or under the sink, I silently hunt. But if a strange dog is coming or unknown children (who invariably leave the door open), I call her. She has never failed to materialize from somewhere when I do call. She seems to know that this is not an idle exercise of authority but that it is important.

I admit it has been my theory as a dog raiser for years that much of the trouble owners have is their own doing. As my favorite reader once said, enough is too much of everything. Incessant repetition of commands, which is really nagging, works no better with animals than with humans.

My list of essential negatives for Amber has resulted in her paying attention to them. She knows she cannot slip into the refrigerator just because the door is open and I am getting out the lamb chops. She knows she cannot leap on the stove (although I always put a pan of water over a recently used burner, just in case). She knows she cannot rush out of the door when the groceryman comes in with a carton of groceries. And she knows she should not claw the newly upholstered sofa; when she hears this particular negative command, she flies over to her scratching post and claws at that, watching me with limpid innocent eyes.

One special characteristic of Amber's would melt the stones at Stonehenge. When I combine the No-No-No with a cuff (as when she chews the television wire), she might be expected to run away and hide. Instead she flies to me. Then we comfort each other! This certainly does not add to ease in discipline. I think a psychologist might say she feels I am her protector in time of trouble, and that I still am even when I myself cause the trouble.

This morning we had a new adventure. Over the fireplace on the Cape, two carved pale-gold-and-brown whales are silhouetted against a sea-gray background. They were copied by a gifted artist from a very old engraving. They each have two holes in the backs which fit supports about as big as broom handles in diameter and about two or three inches long.

It is a big fireplace and the whales are placed well above where a mantel would be if there were one. They are probably the most valuable pieces of art in the entire house, and seem to symbolize the whole mystery of the ocean as they swim forever on the imitation deep.

Early this morning for some reason Amber woke up and discovered the whales. They were not just decorations, they were creatures. Now the only fish she has ever seen is her own flounder fillet, which is headless, tailless, just a flat bit of pinky sweetness. But some deep instinct invaded her—the Abyssinian is said to have been the fishing cat of the Egyptians 4,000 years ago and who can know. . . .

I heard the sound and jumped out of bed, reaching the living room just as Amber landed on the right-hand whale, knocking it loose from one peg. Fortunately I just caught it before it crashed and cracked. Amber's leap was halfway to the ceiling from a flat take-off with no window sill or shelf as a help. The back of the whale she landed on is about ¼ inch thick and would not quite accommodate all of her.

She was preparing for another launch when I used a seldom-word very sharply. *No-No-No.* Then I started out to fix coffee and looked back to see her tensed on the chair top nearest the fireplace, gazing up with passion at the two somnolent whales. In the end, I added a small slap to the *No-No-No.*

I am grateful I do not have to say "No" often. It is upsetting to discipline a kitten and have her rush to you to be comforted immediately afterward.

Chapter 9

Grooming Amber was difficult at first because she wanted to play with the brush and comb. Her idea was to put both arms around the handle and wrestle with this odd gadget. It was a fine game, but her fur was only brushed in spots. She purred like a small motorboat.

Some experts advise a soft brush, and some a fine steel comb. I worried about this briefly and solved it by using both. So I had to be right half of the time. I can see that for a long-hair like an Angora or Persian, a comb would be advisable because the soft long hair mats so easily and a comb would make it possible to separate clumps, providing pussy went along with the idea. But Amber's coat is short and since she washes incessantly is pretty well polished. I sometimes get as many as three loose hairs with the comb. The brush gives an extra satiny gloss and that is about it.

And, of course, since I spend a good deal of time rubbing her, she is also hand-polished. A good many times in the day and night, she feels like being rubbed and leaps to my neck and begins nudging me and kneading her paws back and forth.

Dr. Whitney suggests that if your cat gets soiled, you can wet your hand and rub the body well, and the dirt and dead hair will cling to your hand. As of now, Amber has not fallen in the ashes or gotten in the trash basket, so I have never tried this.

Eventually she will get a bath. I know all the arguments against bathing both dogs and cats. Soap dries out the natural oils. It may cause irritated skin. The animal may catch cold. I am sure this is also true of human beings, but we manage to survive washing, and so have my own dogs and cats.

Even when we had thirty-five cockers, they had baths. Their coats were like silk velvet, their skins glowed. We washed them in the set tub in the back kitchen, which has a spray attachment fine for rinsing. The Irish setters were too heavy to lift into the tub, so they were washed with buckets of water in the yard, using a shampoo put out by a famous house and intended to preserve the natural oils in glamour girls' hair.

The dogs liked being bathed, but I cannot say the cats enjoyed it. Especially Esmé, the Siamese. We popped the cats in orange sacks and lowered them into the warm water gently. Then we rinsed them, still in the sacks, with the spray and wrapped warm bath towels around them. Esmé, although she objected strenuously, felt wonderful afterward. And if anyone who thinks bathing is wrong saw the color of the bath water, I could stop arguing.

As I reflect on this subject, it occurs to me that wild

(Cape Cod Photos, Orleans, Mass.)

Amber loves to be fed from a teaspoon.

animals get rained on and snowed on and run in the foggy foggy dew. Some of them go into brooks and ponds after prey. They run in wet fields or through damp high grass. They do not live in overheated houses where an endless battle with the vacuum cleaner goes on. Nature herself provides a soapless washing fairly often.

Probably primitive man got cleaned up too when caught in a driving rain far from the cave. And the women must have been soaked now and then when they went out for roots or berries or had to ford streams.

A cat's coat is naturally water-resistant, so if you don't want to use an expensive shampoo, one with a coconut-oil base is best as it penetrates the fur. There are many of these available. I have a lovely friend, a bank president's wife, who makes her own soap of bacon grease and lye, but I have never tried it! And she doesn't use it for the cat.

It is important never to let a cat get a chill, so warm bath towels are best for the drying process, followed by a good brushing. A cat's skin renews itself by sloughing off or scaling plus the hair shedding, and a good bath helps to remove the excess. It also helps if you have anyone with asthma in the house. Two members of my family lived comfortably with three cats even though the afflicted ones hung over a steam kettle in haying season.

Hair balls are often a problem with cats but not if the cats are kept clean. Long-hairs must be groomed with extra care because of the fine thick fur. A cat that has no help with this problem sometimes gets hair balls as big as a golf ball in the stomach or intestines, which may require surgery. Amber's close short hair sheds comparatively little.

The time-honored remedy for hair balls is vegetable oil added to the food. A teaspoonful of oil is enough for a kitten and a tablespoon for a grown cat. For a long-haired cat a teaspoonful once a week is a good precaution. Amber will not need it unless she begins to shed in midsummer. I do put a dab of butter on her dish, but if she did not happen to enjoy butter I would spread a dab of it on her paws, for anything on the paws gets licked off. A cat friend of mine prefers the oil from a tin of sardines, which tastes good and lubricates painlessly.

Ears are the most vulnerable part of a cat. Amber's ears stand up like wind-filled sails. When I noticed a waxy deposit in them and saw her scratch first one and then the other, I suspected ear canker or ear mites. Cleaning the ears with cotton swabs is better done by an expert since the ear is extremely sensitive and delicate. It does not take long. For a short time I dropped in some of the doctor's magic medicine and gently wiped out Amber's ears with a soft tissue. She enjoyed this immensely because ear mites cause an almost unbearable itch.

Once the condition was corrected, her ears acquired the delicate pinky glow which is characteristic. Occasionally I now wipe out her ears since they are natural dust catchers, particularly with Abyssinians who have especially large ears.

The care of teeth is simple. An adult cat has thirty teeth (we have thirty-two if we go regularly to the dentist). The enamel is thicker in a cat's teeth and the way they are set in the mouth discourages food particles from lodging between them. When Amber yawns, I can see the shearing teeth at the front, looking like minute ivory daggers. The inside of her mouth is seashell pink. This is the only time I can study it because she has an aversion to having her mouth opened except when she snips up her food or washes herself.

We used to take the cockers and Irish to the veterinarian once a year to have the tartar scraped off, but dogs' teeth resemble human teeth. As a cat grows older, it is advisable to check occasionally with the doctor, but if a cat gets some chewy food, such as pellets, bits of toast, or diced roast beef, there will be no problem. Bones are dangerous as they can splinter and rupture delicate tissues inside the cat.

When you pick up a cat for any purpose, whether for grooming, giving medication or just plain loving, there is only one way to do it. The mother cat picks her baby up by the scruff of the neck for just one reason, it is the only way she can. But a mother cat stops this as soon as the baby can get around by itself.

Small kittens, like puppies, should be picked up gently with one hand under the body to give a sense of firm support. I pick up Amber this way, and am always sure one hand is holding her hind feet. What is more important, I never dangle her in the air but hold her close to my chest. I can carry her all around the house in this manner, hold her to the window to wave good-by at departing guests, or show her the snowflakes falling outside. She purrs the entire time. But if a guest swoops her up so all four legs are hanging, Amber is plainly frightened and struggles to escape.

"Well, I can see Amber doesn't like me," says the guest.

I cannot say sharply, "Well, look at how you grabbed her, you idiot." On the other hand, I cannot say that Amber adores her since the evidence won't support this. But to assure the doubter that Amber really loves everyone but is shy does not solve the dilemma.

I am purely an amateur, knowing nothing about biology or any other ology, but as I watch Amber practically fly through the air, I try to think as she thinks. I decided that when she takes off from a dizzy height and levitates, she knows exactly where she will land and how firm the base is. The base is always solid. But if she is suddenly snatched up, she feels insecure.

Then too moving slowly and speaking softly is a basic rule for being popular with all animals. And with birds too, for the famous quail Robert, who was such a close friend of mine, was originally taken by the fact that I did not try to grab her, ruffle her feathers and make clucking noises. I kept as quiet as possible until she hopped on my shoulder and leaned against my neck.

Strange chirping noises or rattling keys or shrill whistling noises leave most animals and birds cold. They also immediately sense whether you really like them or not. This may have something to do with an acute sense of smell, for there is obviously an odor of fear which humans have in common with all mammals.

It may also be that people who are afraid of or reject animals make involuntary movements of withdrawal which we do not see but which animals perceive at once. It all boils down to the fact that you cannot fool a dog, a cat, or a bird!

When several people sit in front of the fire at Still-meadow, Amber may ignore those who are trying hard-est to please and suddenly land with an enormous purr on the shoulder of one guest. She rubs her cheek against his or her neck, waves her tail, kneads her paws and tries to be as seductive as a movie starlet. But this is always a quiet guest.

It is generally better to keep a kitten away from small children if they have not had experience with animals. The one time Amber screamed was when a lively three-year-old grabbed her around the middle and squeezed as hard as she could, shrieking with excitement. Amber hid under the bed. My own granddaughters, Alice and Anne, happen to be exceptions to the rule since they have (I assume) inherited an empathy with animals as well as birds, butterflies, frogs, and so on.

Even very young children can be taught how to handle kittens or dogs. They should first watch how adults approach animals and rub the fur from head to tail—not backward—and how to pick up small animals gently and support the hind legs with one hand. Both cats and puppies feel nervous if there is no firm support for the back legs. Just dangling in air would not suit most people either!

My Irish setter, Holly, was a big dog and naturally loved children of any age. But she did not like to have her tail suddenly pulled with all the energy a small child could muster. Her reaction was a quick withdrawal from the scene.

Once children learn how to treat animals, a real affinity is established. And practically all children need to love a kitten or dog.

Chapter 10

I do not know who first said a cat has nine lives, but there are times when one fervently hopes it is true.

Another adage, "Experience is the best teacher," would, in my case, mean that I am now qualified to diagnose and treat a number of ailments. Most of the cats I have known have never had a sick day in their lives. Amber, however, is an exception. Together she and I have learned about a whole list of health problems (all of them quickly solved, I am happy to say). I know about gingivitis, for instance, because Amber had it. This is what happened. My beloved Cape veterinarian, Kim Schneider, was already examining her for some other minor ailment and opened her mouth.

"Well, well," he said in his light, comforting voice, "Amber has gingivitis, I see." And sure enough, all along the gums was a burning red line.

"Now you stop at the drugstore on your way home," said Kim, "and pick up a can of sodium perborate powder. Just make a paste of it and dip a bit of cotton in and hold it on the gums two seconds, then wipe it off with a clean damp bit of cotton. That's all you have to do."

I went to the drugstore and asked for the medication, and the clerk brought out a can holding about two quarts of powder.

"I only want it for a small kitten," I said weakly.

After thinking it over on the way home, I began to wonder if when people have gingivitis it takes two quarts to cure them. If so, I thought, I would never live long enough to cure Amber even with the small can the clerk finally found.

When we got home, I sat down and studied the directions on the label, and then waited for Margaret Stanger to come over and read them. The contents were to be kept away from children, it said in big print. Do not swallow. Dissolve one teaspoonful in a quart of warm water (this would make enough to drown a kitten). If inflammation sets in, discontinue treatment.

Margaret read the label three times.

"I thought you'd better come and help me," I said.

"Oh no!" exclaimed Margaret, "Suppose she swallows a drop or two?"

We discussed it, pro and con, for an hour and a half. How thick should the paste be? What if Amber choked?

Finally Margaret said, "I think we'd better take her back to Kim."

"You are a trained nurse," I pointed out, "and I have had years of experience with animals. We should be able to cope with a little adolescent kitten."

"I'll come over around ten tomorrow," Margaret announced, "and we will take her to Kim. We will just tell him we are chickenhearted."

Amber preparing to leap to my typewriter.

We turned up at the clinic at three minutes past ten, when the office opened. Kim did not seem surprised to see us, but in view of the times I have been there, I can understand why!

He took a Q-tip, rolled it in the powder and slid it along the gums so deftly that Amber did not even miaow. Then he used a small wad of cotton and rinsed the gums. The whole thing took only a moment.

"Now I think you two might manage this," he commented.

So I am now in a position to advise anyone who has a cat with gingivitis exactly how to proceed, for subsequently Margaret and I did manage very well. After all, a trained nurse and a kennel owner can certainly give medication to a kitten, as we told each other rather too frequently.

Be sure your kitten has the inoculations for enteritis, a deadly form of distemper which is no longer necessary in this day of modern medicine.

The most common ailment of cats and dogs is, of course, worms. Born and raised under the proper conditions, your newly acquired pet is not likely to have infestations of any of the various types of worm. But it is always well to check even so, whether you pick up a stray kitten or buy one from a mink-lined cage.

Roundworms are probably the most common, and a puppy or kitten can get them from the uterus of the mother. In short, Mamma passes them along to her offspring unless she is free from worms herself. Most reliable breeders check the brood matron before the babies are due—but don't count on it. The legend that milk causes worms is just that—a legend.

The symptoms are easy to spot. The kitten's belly seems bloated and there is a watery diarrhea. Sometimes the worms are coughed up, sometimes they appear in the stool. The breath has a strange sweet smell. The worms, when you see them, are like whitish rubber bands. If they persist, the coat becomes dry and thin and the kitten has no energy. (How could it when it is supporting a stomach full of enemy aliens?)

A veterinarian is the best help here as most of the patent medicines are not adequate. Garlic is thought to be a specific, if you use plenty of it, which is fine provided your kitten likes garlic. But a trip to the doctor is better.

Amber's first cleanup of roundworms was highly successful, but she had a recurrence later on and needed more medication. This time she threw up the green capsule, framing her mouth with foam. I called Kim, who assured me she would not die and had undoubtedly absorbed some of the medication before she threw it up. This must have been true for the worm problem was solved.

For comments on tapeworms, I have to go back to the dogs. Fish, raw, is a comfortable host for these parasites. Since Amber never has raw fish, this is no problem for her, but I have had dogs who brought home fine dead fish from the beach. Tapeworms, as I know, are easily identifiable for segments appear in the stool, looking rather like grains of rice. These worms are more difficult to eliminate than roundworms and cause vomiting, lack of energy, dull fur and, once again, a ballooning belly. The veterinarian can prescribe the necessary capsules and outline the treatment.

Fleas, which may also spread tapeworm, are a common

hazard. As you know if you have ever tried to catch them, fleas can hop very quickly. The eggs develop in the ground, but once you get fleas in the house they will flourish in cracks in the floor or in your kitten's blanket.

Most of the commercial flea powders are not safe for cats, who lick it all off. Derris powder is safe and may be mixed with 3 per cent rotenone and unmedicated talcum powder. DDT is fatal, and any product containing it may kill your cat in a hurry.

When using powder, be sure not to get it too close to the eyes or in the ears, but begin back of the neck and work it in carefully, including between the toes. My cats have never had fleas, but fleas are rare in my location, perhaps because they do not like twelve-below-zero nights in winter. Or perhaps because my pets have baths.

Ticks I have had plenty of experience with, although not with Amber. So far I have picked exactly one tick off her when we were walking in the yard on Cape Cod. It was wandering around hesitantly on her dense fur, as if it couldn't quite decide where to embed itself.

Actually ticks prefer dogs but will camp on anything from woodwork to kitchen towels if they have a chance. Most of them are bothersome but harmless, but there are those that carry spotted fever. When I am removing them, I never study them closely; an expert can identify the poison bringers but I can't. My definition of a tick is that it is the one thing that prevents Cape Cod from being Paradise itself.

The tick was originally imported to the Cape along with some Belgian hares or some kind of rabbit. However, it has now spread. There are ticks in the Rocky

Mountain areas which could not have come from Cape Cod; also there is the Lone Star tick which moves northward from Texas, and the brown tick which prefers to live in houses.

But I had lived in the Middle West, in Virginia and in New York City without ever realizing there was such a hideous creature as a tick. I found out when we came to Cape Cod with two cocker spaniels and an Irish setter. I was, then, in a state of euphoria because the Japanese beetles which were so thick in Connecticut were not evident on the shores of Mill Pond.

Then I learned about ticks. When we went back to Connecticut I spent the whole five-hour trip deticking the dogs so as to be sure we didn't import one to Connecticut. Others who crossed the bridge did not work so hard at it, however, so there are now ticks also in my part of Connecticut, although they are still rare.

Ticks bite through the skin and burrow into the body of the host. Then the tick body swells until it is like a small balloon. What fills it is the blood of your pet.

The best treatment for ticks is to get them off before they engorge. The procedure is a matter for endless argument as all experts have their own methods, many of which do not go along with mine. Mine has worked for some years. First I believe in catching the tick as soon as it gets on the animal. With cats or dogs who run free on Cape Cod, I check every time they come in the house. To be sure, it may seem difficult in the middle of a cocktail party to ask to be excused while you check your dog or cat for ticks. If you are with understanding friends, you sit on the floor and so do they and you all work at it. If not, excuse yourself and disappear with

Buff into a back room. In any case, you get those ticks off *before* they are embedded.

To remove them many people use tweezers and alcohol. You put a drop of alcohol on the tick, and when it feels the effect, use the tweezers. There are also various sprays, but I advise getting prescriptions from the veterinarian.

My own method has never failed. I seize as much of the tick as possible between my forefinger and thumb and twist it clockwise with a quick lifting motion. Then I drop it in a can of kerosene (I keep one ready during the tick season) and wash my hands thoroughly. I have a friend who also uses this method but holds the captured tick, flicks on a cigarette lighter and burns it up. Most people would get their hands burned up too, but she has a special gift.

If you do not twist the tick properly, you may leave half of it still imbedded in the animal. So for most owners, the alcohol method is safer. My method also involves getting them before they have set up house and home but are still on a rental basis.

A cat or dog who has not been deticked regularly may have a host of ticks. In that case a bath of Derris and soapsuds is indicated, using a proportion of one tablespoon of Derris to a gallon of warm water. Do not rinse off at once but pat the cat or dog with dry towels. Rinse the next morning and check again.

Ticks do not fly or run. They tend to hang on beach grass or in a wild stretch of meadow. When a cat or dog goes past, they drop on board. If your pet stays on mowed lawns, the danger is slight. But when I find a tick on a lamp shade, I wonder just what kind of immigration laws he followed!

Ticks are seasonal, but in recent years they seem to arrive earlier and stay later. I suspect they live all year long on rabbits. And I am not sure what part they play in nature's pattern, because few birds eat them and ticks do not eat other pests.

The cat's excessive cleanliness involves licking earnestly a good many times a day. This is the reason that cats develop hair balls, especially when they are shedding. Usually the cat will throw up a hair ball, but if it should move on to the intestines, only the veterinarian can save her.

Prevention is the best remedy. It takes only a few minutes to brush the fur daily. It is easy to put a dab of butter or a bit of oil on the paws. Many cats favor the taste of oil from a tin of sardines. Amber helps herself to the butter from the dish on the counter.

Ear mites affect both dogs and cats, as I have already said, but it bears repetition. Puppies and kittens from a commercial kennel or cattery are often well supplied with them. You can see a dark-chocolate waxy substance inside the ears and there is a sweetish odor, rather like stale cheese. The kitten shakes its head, rubs against furniture and is restless. The first treatment should be from the veterinarian because he can clean out the infection without damaging the delicate ear. He will give you an ointment to take home, which you can squeeze in gently yourself. Once you are rid of ear mites they are not likely to recur.

Skin infections sometimes occur too. If a kitten has

dermatitis—also called eczema—it may begin with a moist scab, generally under the front legs (at least in my experience, which is limited). At first you diagnose it cheerfully as the result of an insect bite. Then you notice that the kitten licks it constantly and the area is spreading. There appear a few raw places where a meticulous tongue has worked too hard.

A tube of salve from the veterinarian works magic. You just rub it in thoroughly so the kitten cannot lick it all off, and repeat as often as prescribed. Most kittens will run to you when they see that tube because this is one medication that feels so good they enjoy it. You need not worry about contracting the infection yourself.

When I first began treating Amber, I hid the tube and then nipped it out when she was on my lap. But I learned from her, as one should learn from one's cat. The surprise treatment upset her. When I started taking out the tube and telling her it was time and that the paste would really help the itching, she would sit quietly in my lap for the whole procedure. And then one day she poked at the tube cap with a tentative paw and waited for the paste to come out. And began to purr. I would like to have exhibited her to one of those people who believe cats are impossible to medicate.

The eyes of a cat are a special miracle. Cats do not actually see in the dark but they manage very well when there is not enough light for us to see by. Their pupils adjust according to the light rays. Cats also have a third eyelid in the lower part of the eye, which is a protection we do not have.

Usually all you need to do about your kitten's eyes is

wipe them occasionally with a soft tissue as sometimes a drop or two of fluid comes to the eyelid.

But when Amber began to look at me with only one eye, while the other was tightly shut, I got out the familiar carrying case and off we went to the veterinarian. Conjunctivitis is an eye infection easy to diagnose and simple to treat. A tiny squeeze of ointment once or twice a day clears it up. And the world looks better when you see it with both eyes wide open!

Sometimes a cat may get a weed seed or bit of sand in the eyes because of going through life hull down as it were. A bit of damp cotton may swab it out, but do not try human eyedrops unless the doctor says it is all right.

Mouth ulcers are often called rodent ulcers in the belief that cats get them from rats or mice. Kim Schneider has done a good deal of research on this, however, and says there is no truth in it. Cats raised in apartments where there is never a sign of a rodent have mouth ulcers as often as barn cats do. Amber had one, although she did not know a mouse from a handsaw at that time. The cause is unknown, says Kim firmly.

The cure is a treatment with pills. And a smooth easy-to-swallow diet. I used baby-food meats and the strained green beans with tidbits of minced chicken and beef and fish.

The diet was no problem. The pills were something else again.

When I myself have to take pills, they always stick crosswise in my throat, so I am not surprised it is hard for a dog or kitten to swallow them. The construction of a cat's throat makes it easy to choke on a foreign object.

I discovered that the best way to give pills is to mash them to a powder and mix them with something delicious.

Amber is very deft at sorting out small grains of something she doesn't like, but if pills are mashed very fine, she will eventually ingest them.

A capsule is a different matter, as I have indicated, and I would always go to my patient veterinarian to have it slipped in. He pinches the mouth open and holds the capsule with a pair of slender forceps. One lightning move and Amber is ready to wash her face. Fortunately most medication for cats comes in the form of pills or salves or smooth tasty liquids in tubes.

For example, the modern medication for constipation comes in a tube. You squeeze half an inch on the kitten's paws and it is rapidly licked off. When Amber developed this ailment, all I had to do was open the cap of the tube and she was beside me on the counter, waiting to have some of this marvelous stuff. She would gladly eat the whole contents of the tube and felt that a mere half inch was a very stingy portion!

It reminded me of the days when milk of magnesia went all over my Siamese, the floor and my dress. I can't stand the taste of milk of magnesia either. It is also about as easy to clean up as liquid cement.

The classic remedy for diarrhea used to be Kaopectate, but now mashed pills will do the trick.

Both constipation and diarrhea may come from many causes, but a change in diet often helps. For constipation strained baby food, green beans, a little olive oil, chicken broth and so on are advisable. For diarrhea omit vegetables and concentrate on protein.

(Cape Cod Photos, Orleans, Mass.)

Amber on my desk, more or less at rest.

If you have an outdoor cat with a private bathroom under the lilac bush you can still diagnose bowel ailments. Constipation makes the stomach hard and round as a golf ball. Diarrhea makes a cat thin from flanks to shoulders, and excessive eating does not bring any gain in weight.

Kidney disease may result from a number of causes, such as infections, injuries, or for no apparent reason. It is important to consult a veterinarian at once so curative treatment may be started early.

A loss of appetite and a constant thirst are warning signals. In chronic kidney disease the cat will be dehydrated and there will be a smell of urine on the breath.

Ice cubes, if the cat will lap them, help with the thirst and provide some water absorption. A low-protein diet is usually indicated, with cereals and fats and vegetables as a mainstay. (It is not easy to persuade your cat to do without meat and fish!) There is a special diet now available for cats with kidney ailments, which the veterinarian may advise. Half a can a day is sufficient for an adult cat.

A urinalysis is necessary and will have to be repeated until the veterinarian decides a return to normal diet is feasible. Modern antibiotics and penicillin are generally useful.

Kidney stones sometimes develop, which the veterinarian can detect by X ray. If a cat is in pain under his loins and runs a temperature and shows traces of blood in the urine or has diarrhea, a trip to the veterinarian is a must, and as soon as possible.

A not unusual ailment in some cats is bladder trouble, which is indicated by a male cat being unable to urinate or a female crying in pain. This is caused by an irritation from a kind of fine gravel. The veterinarian will take measures to reduce the inflammation and restore normal functioning in the bladder.

One ailment I have had no experience with is irritation of the anal glands. These are two small sacs at each side of the anus under the tail region. When a dog or cat grows older, these glands sometimes produce an excess of fluid which must be squeezed out. Some experts believe the glands are related to the musk glands of a skunk, but in any case, if a cat drags along the floor and bites the base of her tail it may indicate anal-gland secretion.

The cure for this is to press on both sides of the anal opening firmly with a piece of cotton, holding the tail up with your third hand. But I know one owner who has a regular appointment with the veterinarian instead, and I favor this myself.

Aside from eczema, ear mites, hair balls, and such, illnesses are rare in cats. With a minimum amount of care your kitten will be as rugged as the Pillars of Hercules. Occasionally, however, medical treatment may be needed. If you are near a veterinarian, this is not your problem; it is his. But if you live in the country, you may not want to drive miles to get to the doctor unless it is a case of life or death.

If you love your cat, you will sense at once when he or she is really sick. A cat's behavior is as readable as a book. But you should have a rectal thermometer on hand to check the temperature, before phoning the doctor.

An adult cat's temperature is 101.5 degrees Fahrenheit but can vary up or down a degree or so without being serious. If it is much above or below that, there is something wrong. Kittens may safely run a higher degree than an adult cat. To take the temperature, lift the tail and gently insert the thermometer, which you have greased with Vaseline, plain uncarbolated Vaseline.

Most cats do not mind this. In fact one time when Kim was taking Amber's temperature, the phone rang and he had a long conversation with a distracted owner while Amber stood patiently with the thermometer in her rear and I rubbed her ears.

A first-aid kit is a good idea, beginning with the thermometer and Vaseline. Then you should have gauze bandage rolls for compresses or whatever. Sterile cotton pads are always useful and rubbing alcohol for cleaning the thermometer or for dropping on ticks. A bottle of baby aspirin is helpful for easing pain or bringing temperatures down.

For my own kit I also have the miracle tubes of eye ointment, constipation medication and ear mite salve, just in case. If you are taking to the woods for a vacation, be sure to include a can of tomato juice in case your darling does decide to establish a beachhead by a skunk. Wash the cat in tomato juice after a skunk rendezvous. Cats, however, are much less likely to get in trouble with skunks and porcupines than are dogs. As for snakes, cats do occasionally kill them. This is not a problem in New England, but it may be in areas that abound with poisonous snakes. If you live in snake country, you should keep snake serum on hand and ask your veterinarian how much to give your cat.

A swelling with two small punctures indicates the location of the snake bite. You inject the serum, and while you wait for the veterinarian, cut the swelling with a razor blade and squeeze out the poison. Keep warm water running over the area—someone in the family can hold a teakettle over it and keep pouring.

I am told cats take care of a great many poisonous snakes, so they must have been natural enemies in the dawn of history. My cats have never killed so much as a grass snake. We did have one blonde cocker who brought them in, but the cats never did. Amber has never even seen one and wouldn't know what to do except swell up and hiss.

After all this about cat health, I am reminded of a nervous friend of mine who has raised a block-busting family of boys and whose husband could qualify for a quarterback. But she keeps a medical dictionary on hand and if anyone coughs, immediately looks up lung cancer. It is not necessary to suspect your cat of lethal ailments or Excedrin headaches. Most kittens and cats are as healthy as anything on this planet. They have a natural stamina which I envy and a will to survive that front-line soldiers possess.

Chapter 11

That ancient Egyptian cat goddess was, among other things, the fertility deity. Since the country is overrun with homeless cats and Animal Rescue Shelters are full of abandoned kittens, it is obvious that female cats still produce litters with impressive regularity. The number of kittens varies from cat to cat and breed to breed. The Abyssinian usually has only two, but country cats have more. I have heard of one cat who had three hundred kittens during her lifetime.

Of course there was the case of Josephine, who belonged to some friends. When they decided it was time to have kittens, they invited a male cat to the house. A major battle ensued. Josephine was a beautiful cat, so they did not give up. They entertained another male. Josephine nearly lost an ear. On the third try, the visitor retired bloody and bowed.

They decided to consult the veterinarian: why did Josephine refuse to have kittens?

"I can tell you one reason," he said. "This is a male cat."

So they went sadly home with Joseph.

If Joseph had been a female, she might have come in season as early as six months. The average male is ready to mate at about eleven months. But it is not possible to mark a calendar for cats, as you usually can for dogs, because their times of season vary. Some males are mature at around six months, some not until a year and a half. Amber, at ten months, still showed no interest in sex.

The question of whether to spay a female or neuter a male is a difficult one to answer. If you own a female who comes in season regularly you can let her run loose the rest of the time. One litter a year is enough if you care about the cat herself, and when she comes in heat and is not bred, the caterwauling begins.

The male in heat sprays the furniture and also caterwauls. If he can go out at will, he will find a mate somehow, but if he cannot, the house will smell like a subway toilet.

Amber first came in season when she was exactly a year old. I had planned to board her when necessary but decided to put it off as long as possible, and she agreed with me that we were happier together no matter what. Fortunately we were on Cape Cod where all our visitors, from the milkman to the gentle neighbors down the road, are very careful about standing in the open door to talk. Also we do not have five male country cats regularly patrolling the yard, as we always have at Stillmeadow.

There are dozens and dozens of rabbits who are only interested in eating my best Peace roses. And plenty of hoppety-hopping quail that expect you will not run over them. But cats are scarce.

So we decided to stick it out at home.

117

Amber began by rolling on the beige rug and digging her claws in, then adopting the stance of a lioness about to pounce, switching her tail as rapidly as a flag in a nor'easter. The second day she discovered new vocal cords, and my whisper-soft miaower uttered a sound that made me drop Kennan's *Memoirs* and run to rescue her. But I could not rescue her from nature!

The sound began deep in her small throat and progressed to high C, reminding me of an opera diva in Act III. Her eyes were deep and big as jungle pools. When I picked her up to offer futile comfort, she trembled, but was much too involved to give me the usual sandpaper kisses. I put her down, and she ran the length of the house, leaping halfway up the living-room drapes.

Now all this is *not* easy, but I discovered one thing that none of the experts I knew of had mentioned: the hyperactivity is not incessant. After the first seizure, Amber retired to my bed and dozed. When she woke up, she slipped into my workroom and took part of my typewriter ribbon off as usual.

The spells of course recurred, but we felt we could manage.

The first two days she did not care much about food, but she did consent to eat from a teaspoon. A good many cats I have known would benefit from a brief period of dieting, but since Amber barely managed to make five pounds on her birthday, I fed her with the teaspoon.

The season lasted five days, and during the entire time she never kept me up at night. The only problem was that she was in a moaning spell when someone came to interview me for a feature article, and they decided, I knew, that I had a dying kitten on my hands. I shut Amber in the bedroom, and the sound was diminished enough so we could talk above it.

My conclusion was that Amber was better off being able to race through her own house than to be shut in a small cage, with the added misery of being away from home. The inconvenience of the sobbing fits was not too much to bear.

At the risk of being called sentimental, I must say I was better off too for being able to offer some small comfort and enabling her to go through this experience without adding rejection to it.

Any relationship between living beings has times of trial, but the soundest involve sharing the difficult times as well as the easy. And when her season ended and Amber jumped on the typewriter keys and started the usual purring and put out a raspberry-pink tongue to kiss my hand, I felt that she subconsciously was grateful that I had not put her away when she was miserable!

In this day of new medications there are pills which will help during the main season, but since cats are so sensitive to medicine, I have not tried this. I have heard of cats who died when the owners gave them sedative pills at this time, and I feel the risk is too great just to save oneself a short period of inconvenience.

The exception to this is when a cat comes in season every month or so. I have a friend with such a cat, and in this instance heartily advised spaying.

No cat should be altered before eight months of age, and no female bred before the second season. As far as neutering a male is concerned, it is not a serious operation and the cat can come home the same day.

Spaying the female cat costs from twenty to forty dollars. The cat must be perfectly healthy and have a thorough medical check-up first. For a male, since the operation is simpler, it is less costly. The price runs from ten to twenty-five dollars. One advantage in sterilizing a male is that he no longer engages in battles and comes home with torn and bleeding ears. He also is less likely to wander so far as to be lost. He should be at least eight months old before being altered.

But with a female the operation is not so simple.

Spaying the female requires cutting the abdomen open and taking out the ovaries and means a stay in the hospital to allow healing. This is nothing to be undertaken casually. Sometimes there is an emotional change in the cat, and a lovely, affectionate, lively companion may become cranky or eccentric or lethargic.

My own feeling is that if it isn't possible to keep a female confined while in season, a few days at the veterinarian's is far better than having that operation. The time is from four to seven days, and it seems to me preferable to cope with those days than run the risk of a major operation.

Our male cat, Tigger, spent a lot of time outdoors with lady friends at certain times, and since he was a most beautiful satin-black Manx, the kittens he sired were always welcome. Even now I sometimes see a handsome bullet-headed ebony cat dozing in a bed of violets on Jeremy Swamp Road, and I know this is a grandson or great-grandson of Tigger.

If you have a female and decide that a batch of gay fuzzy kittens would be an addition to the family, you may find a suitable male. Most veterinarians advise a

Amber helps with the mail.

second breeding a day later to be sure of a pregnancy.

The kittens usually arrive in sixty-five days, although the pregnancy may last for as long as seventy-one days. The prospective mother cat will behave as usual until the last week, but must be fed added calcium to prepare for the kittens to come. This is a good time for vitamin supplements and extra tidbits. When the cat begins to pace around, it is also time to fix up the nursery so she feels at home in it. A big carton is the best. (What would we do without cartons?) You cut a door in one side, leaving enough of a sill to keep the babies from crawling out. Torn newspapers make the best lining, so the mother can push them around, and when she has the nest to suit her, you can lay a baby blanket over the papers, plus a towel which can be taken out and washed.

When the kittens are born, a hot-water bottle wrapped in a soft towel is a help to keep the newborn babies warm until the whole family is settled in. As each kitten arrives, tuck it in the box, close to the hot-water bottle, while the mother is bearing the next one.

The mother cat usually cuts the umbilical cord herself, but if she fails to do so, you can cut it for her with blunt scissors, but be careful to cut about an inch and a half away from the body. Occasionally a nervous mother cuts it too close, and a hernia is the result.

There must be an afterbirth from every kitten, and if it does not come you may draw it out, if you are a courageous and deft person. Otherwise I hope your veterinarian can make a hurry-up house call.

Of course you may also take your cat to him beforehand, especially if it is a first litter and you have already promised a kitten to certain worthy friends. But the security of being at home is worth a great deal to your cat, and you will personally benefit by being present to help with the miracle of birth.

When I think of the homeless alley cats who find a damp cellar-hole and have their kittens in a pile of debris, I wonder once more at the mysterious stamina of nature. These kittens will be nourished by a semistarving mother, and survive to hunt garbage tidbits. They will have one heritage, the will to live.

So it is with the huddled masses in the ghettos. In a country with an oversupply of food, it is increasingly hard to understand why the innocent and helpless cannot be fed and sheltered. But the experts are not solving this problem very quickly!

Now back to your privileged kittens. They should be weaned by eight weeks of age. If the litter is too big for the mother to manage well, you may give supplementary feedings to the smallest ones before weaning, and if so, you need a formula. An easy one consists of 1 cup of whole homogenized milk, 1 egg yolk, 1 teaspoon of dextrose, 1 teaspoon of lime water. Or you may get a special preparation from your veterinarian.

You can feed this by a nursing bottle, at room temperature or a bit warmer. Use a doll's nursing bottle if the kitten is very small. The kitten will take about a teaspoonful or a bit more five times a day. You will know he has had enough when milky bubbles foam around the mouth. After feeding, if the mother cannot give the kitten a rubdown, you will have to do so. This encourages circulation and elimination.

By the time the kittens are twelve days old, their eyes will open, but they should not be exposed to strong light until they are about a month old. If the lids are gummy, you rub them gently with damp warm cotton followed by a rub with dry cotton.

When the kittens are old enough to be on their own, you will have a difficult time letting any of them go. But if you cannot keep them all, you can use selective judgment as to who carries them off.

Perhaps Mr. and Mrs. Brown turn up with two small children. The Browns couldn't care less about a pet, but the children have nagged. One child grabs a kitten, squeezes it, hauls on the morsel of tail, makes loud noises and tosses it in the air while the parents talk about the current heat wave. This bodes ill for the kitten. The main care will be left to the parents who are *not* interested. The obstreperous child is not going to be trained. The Browns will soon report the kitten is nervous and hides under beds all the time and won't eat the catfood. Also, she scratched the boy when he wanted to play games with her.

Another couple turns up because Mrs. Abbot is dying for a kitten. Mr. A. says cats are all right in their places but no cat is going to claw the furniture in *his* house.

A third family sits quietly while the children drop down to kitty's level and gently reach out small damp hands. The father wants to know exactly what kind of diet is best, and the mother asks if extra inoculations are necessary. They go off with the best kitten in the litter, while the Browns and Abbots remain catless as far as you are concerned.

By the time the kittens go to new homes, the mother cat is ready to rest, for she works hard rearing the babies. I have heard of only one cat who struggled against being bred and was forcibly bred anyway. When the kittens were due, she slipped out of the house and bore them in an old iron kettle half full of water. I feel convinced that in some mysterious way (who can ever really understand nature?) she knew these kittens were not normal, so she drowned them at birth.

We once had a cocker puppy born with a cleft palate, and the mother at once pushed that puppy to the corner of the nursery before we even discovered it. Just how she knew something was wrong is another of nature's mysteries.

When you part with a kitten, send along a favorite toy and a finger terry towel that smells of home. After all, when we go to strange places we take a suitcase full of familiar belongings. I have one friend who even takes her own soap when she goes traveling. If the kitten is used to one brand of kitty litter, send a bag of that along too. Also give the new owners a card with the diet list.

I am reminded of Margaret Stanger's supermarket story. She stood between two men, both with carts full. The first cart was piled with a dozen varieties of catfood.

"I am returning it," said the harassed man. "She can't decide which brand she likes best."

"Well," said the second man, waving at his cart, "I've got a dozen cans of nothing but tuna here. Mine has changed her mind about the brand!"

Cat lovers admit that a dog will eat anything, right or wrong, but that a cat is likely to starve unless the food is to her taste. So I imagine that even alley cats pick over the garbage and only consume what seems best to them. In any case, a kitten will settle down more quickly in a new home if the first supper is a favorite food.

Chapter 12

Amber is a private person. This seems contradictory when I think about how she helps the workmen who come to keep the house together. I decided when I first had her that she was the whole world's intimate friend. But when the summer guests began to arrive I found I was wrong.

Because of our experience, I would never advise anybody to try to show off a kitten or a cat. I had very beloved guests coming and had given them glowing descriptions of Amber's charms. So gay, so affectionate, so warm and so on, for two pages in my letter.

The meeting was a disaster. Amber took one look and hid under the sofa. After an hour or so, she emerged and skittered to the bedroom and got under the bed.

"Timid, isn't she?" said one of the visitors.

After another half hour, the small apricot face appeared in the doorway and Amber flew to a window sill and crouched behind the draperies. Her hair was literally standing on end.

"Does she *ever* let you pet her?" asked my friend.

I made the mistake of reaching out a hand, and Amber flew past me to the bedroom again, as if she had never seen me before.

There was not much to say so I said nothing. A few days later this friend admitted she thought cats were all right in their place but she turned cold when one came near her. This friend would gladly lay down her life for a dog but has *that feeling* about cats.

The next day a couple came in and sat visiting. Amber tiptoed out and began to sniff the gentleman's shoe and he put one hand down and she rubbed against it, purring her jet purr. She ignored his wife, who was also a cat lover and had lived with cats all her life.

"What a lovely affectionate cat," said the man.

His wife looked hurt. Amber never even went to that side of the room, but spent her entire time making up to the lovely man.

It is the same situation when small children come. Amber chooses one and follows that one around, purring happily. The others send her to the haven under the bed.

I no longer explain to guests that Amber wakes me up in the morning by purring lustily in my ear and sand-papering my face with that rough small tongue and then rolls over, spreading her toes in happiness because I have finally come to life, even groggily. I do not mention how hard it is to write a letter with a cat sitting on the paper, or to wash dishes with a small nose hanging over the dishpan, or to be sure the shower water is not too hot when she gets in the shower with me.

Typing may not be easy when a cat is sitting on the keys, but it is not lonely. When someone doubtfully asks me if Amber is companionable, I simply say that she is!

People who do not understand cats are not going to understand anything about them, and people who do never need ask.

But everywhere I walk, I have to be careful not to step on that five pounds of mobility. When I sit down, I look where I sit in case she is there before me and I might squash her. And I have to be prepared to stop anything and hold her and cherish her because suddenly she feels lonely. If I happen to be cooking, I turn off the stove and tuck her under my chin and rub her ears and assure her that I still love her just as much as I did an hour ago.

When she feels perfectly secure, she jumps down and chases a moth or swings on the Venetian-blind cords once more. And I turn on the stove again and hope what I am cooking will turn out all right.

Analyzing a cat's reactions is probably like doing an endless puzzle, but I can never stop working at it, because it is so fascinating.

I *think* the reason Amber loves workmen so much is that they are busy doing interesting things and never attempt to invade her personality. She can pounce on a discarded washer or a bit of rubber tubing, and when they reach over to pet her, it is in a casual way. I *think* that with strangers who come in and sit down, she is self-conscious. And if they jiggle keys or dangle the catnip mouse in the air, she is not sure what their motive is.

She definitely does not like to be swooped up by a stranger. But she loves Faith Baldwin and Margaret Stanger and Millie.

There is one final thought about people-cat relationships. Nothing in life is static as far as I know. Even the giant blue boulder on the beach at the Cape has changed subtly in the years I have been its friend. Impact of wind and storm and ice widens the fissures, smooths the rough places. My relationship with Amber grows deeper and richer as we face the vicissitudes of life together (which may be a cliché expression but which fits). She understands more of my curious human ways and I now know what she tries to communicate. Every day we make new discoveries. Also I observe my cat-phobic friend reaching out a hand to rub Amber's ears and just happening to find the catnip mouse to pull along the floor!

Last week a friend said to me that I ought to live my own life. Why not board Amber and take a few trips? Why should I be so tied down? I thought about it on the way home. I had been away about two hours, and as I drove up to the house, a small figure was perched on the nearest window sill and a lonely voice uttered a faint miaow. The expression in those two golden eyes would have done credit to a tragedienne.

Now I knew very well that Amber had been dozing comfortably on her pillow all the time I was gone until she heard the car motor. But when I went in, she dashed across the floor, giving a last desolate cry before the purr motor went on. She had, she intimated, suffered intensely and why did I abandon her?

Ten minutes later she was chasing a moth and definitely leading *her* own life!

So I sat down and watched her leaping incredibly high in the air and thought about people and pets. For many people, a pet is something to have around, to feed and keep in good health but something which is never, under any circumstances, to interfere with any plans of the owner. That is, to me, a pretty one-sided relationship.

It is one quite foreign to me. I feel a responsibility to the living being who shares my life. I do not consider Amber as a toy to be discarded at times, then picked up again. I have always longed to go to Greece, but I think that when I looked at the Parthenon, I would see in the midst of that magnificence a small apricot-colored cat pressed against the bars of her cage, left behind in a world she could not understand.

After all, nobody makes you have a pet. If you cannot bear to leave a dinner party early in order to be home at a decent hour, you do not have to own a pet at all. To own and be owned by a pet is one of the few voluntary occupations left in this atomic age.

As for me, as I write this, I feel rewarded because I suddenly have to write with one finger since there is a beautiful kitten with her paws on the keys and purring madly because we are together. Who needs the Parthenon?

Chapter 13

Since Amber is so exquisite, she is photographed nearly as much as a starlet. This has taught me a lot about the best way to take pictures of a cat. Our last experience was especially difficult. A fine professional photographer came from Worcester to take color pictures for a feature article.

As he walked in, past the sign PLEASE DO NOT LET THE CAT OUT OF THE DOOR, he saw Amber, a golden silhouette against the background of Mill Pond (this was on Cape Cod).

"Who is the kitten?" he asked, unslinging a camera.

"My Abyssinian."

"I never saw one like that!"

"Well, it is a rare breed."

Photographers remind me of Alpine climbers; they carry almost as much gear. This one was tall, rugged and handsome and did indeed look as if a few Alps would be no problem.

"I'll just take a few shots of her," he said happily. "Is she friendly?"

Amber went right over to him when she heard his soft musical voice, and she reached out one apricot paw to touch his moccasin. It was, once more, love at first sight. However, it was unfortunate that she was having a relapse from her first heat and by the time he had the camera ready, she was rolling on the floor and moaning. Hoping for the best, I picked her up. This outraged her. She landed back on the rug and rolled and sobbed. Even lying down himself, my friend could not focus on anything but a cat in torment.

As he said after two hours, all a photographer needs is patience. My own gave out after I had chased Amber all around the room, offered countless tidbits of chicken, blown the soundless whistle and tossed the catnip mouse. I used half a box of tissue mopping my face.

"Let's try her on the typewriter," he suggested. "I hear she sits on it when you work."

I laid bits of chicken on the carriage. Amber scooped them up instantly and was off like a jet. I finally got her back and held her.

"Could you hold her a bit *easier?*" he asked.

"If I don't squash her, she won't be here," I told him.

Meanwhile Millie, my beloved neighbor, had dashed out to pick the last of the pink roses and had arranged them in grandmother's silver teapot on the Shaker stand by the fireplace thinking the photographer would want to take a romantic picture of the author sitting in the armchair.

Not at all. What he wanted was a picture of Amber

Amber cares more about today than days to come.

in her harness, posed on the top step going down to Mill Pond, with the sea in the background.

But Amber flung herself down and rolled and got her small face covered with dead grass.

"I wish I could stay all day and take pictures of Amber," he said regretfully, "but I have to go to Provincetown to photograph the Pulitzer Prize-winning poet."

As he left I sat down. So did Amber. She was all over her relapse and in the next hour assumed one elegant pose after another—on top of the sofa, on the chair by the roses, on the window ledge overlooking the sea, and playing leaping games with a pencil she took from my desk.

"All I hope," I said to Millie, "is that the poor man doesn't find that poet has a cat!"

Even under normal circumstances, I think the best way to photograph a cat is to keep the loaded camera ready and not pay any obvious attention to the model. Then you might be quick enough, if you make no sound, to take a snap of the kitten busily scrubbing her paws and scouring her ears. You might catch her peering out of a blue sheet in the unmade bed, provided she doesn't know you have that little black box anywhere near.

You might even catch her leaping after a moth or looking down from the high shelf where the Balleek plates are displayed.

A movie camera would be even better. Cats are full of surprises. As I have said before, the typical image of a cat dozing by the fire isn't exactly a true one. Perhaps the typical image of a horse galloping wildly isn't true either, for I imagine horses do stand around sometimes!

Amber may sit by the fire briefly, but the next thing I know she is clinging to the top of the family-room window, chittering away at a squirrel who is eating something too near the house.

Her acrobatics at Stillmeadow are spectacular. The windows are twelve-over-eight small panes and the dividers between the panes are narrow. Somehow Amber keeps a precarious toe hold with her front paws and manages to put one hind foot on a lower divider. The leftover paw swings loose in mid-air. A tightrope walker would envy her balance. And I would love to have it all on film.

She herself now seems inclined toward literature. Since I began writing about her, she has watched the typewriter with fixed attention. As I have noted, in the beginning she jumped up and down on it whenever she had a chance, with sometimes disastrous results. As of now she types in the same manner as I do, tapping the keys lightly and staring at the carriage. When she hits the space bar she bounces with pleasure. She no longer tries to catch the ribbon or chew the keys as they pop up. In fact, her only problem is that she cannot as yet spell as well as I can.

Chapter 14

Amber and I have lived together for a year and a month as I write. I cannot imagine the house without her. On those dark days we all have, I may sit gloomily staring into space. But not for long. Amber skims in with a small ball of aluminum foil which has become a treasure. She tosses it in the air with one swift paw, pounces, withdraws and stalks it, loses it under the bureau and flattens herself as she pokes it out. Her intensity is something to envy. Few of us devote ourselves so whole-heartedly to any project. And always when I watch her, the darkness brightens.

Sometimes she takes a pencil from my desk and chases it all over the house. What I admire most is that the pencil, which really hasn't much life of its own, suddenly takes on a personality—she is being the fugitive pencil as she is also the pursuer. When she is tired of it and I pick it up from the back kitchen floor, I really expect it to jump in my hand. But for me it is lifeless and all I can do is sharpen it.

The house itself has changed since Amber came into

it. Almost all of the drawers are ajar so that if she slips in she can get out again. And since the day I opened a kitchen cupboard and found a worried Abyssinian in with the pots and pans, I keep that cupboard door partly open.

In fact if I do not see her for twenty minutes, I hunt for her. A cocker spaniel or an Irish setter is always visible, but a small cat may be inside the television set or on top of the refrigerator. Cartons and brown paper bags must be carefully examined. I once almost put Amber out for the trash man. When a large grocery bag began to vibrate, I realized my mistake.

When people ask me whether it is better to have a cat or a dog, I always say, "Both." Each in its individual way enriches life. They give you more than you can ever give them. My own idea of happiness involves two or three cockers, two Irish, three cats. When I see advertisements for Cartier's eight- and ten-thousand-dollar pieces of jewelry, I realize anew that I would prefer one small kitten and one bouncy puppy to any amount of diamonds and sapphires to pin on my bosom.

However, I realize that if you live in a city apartment or in a house near a throughway, you face limitations other than noise, dirt and polluted air. We did have several cockers in a New York City apartment in the past and managed one litter of six who were born under the sofa despite our efforts to persuade the mother that the linen closet was all set up for her whelping.

But I would not advise this procedure for anyone less besotted. The grown cockers went out four times a day on the leash. I spent more hours toiling through Central Park than any athlete puts in when training. During blizzards or hurricanes the dogs used their paper bathroom, but this did not provide the necessary exercise. Of course very small breeds do not require as much exercise, but even miniature schnauzers do need to go out of doors every day.

No matter what your city schedule is, you always have in the back of your mind a nonelectric clock measuring the time you have to spare before you must get back to take Honey for a walk. If I ever got home late when we lived in the city, the ancient elevator man Albert would hold the elevator for me until I scrambled back out with my dog. At such times he steadfastly ignored all pushed buttons on the other six floors and creaked us down as fast as possible. Fortunately, we moved to the country and fenced in a quarter of an acre, and this problem was settled.

A normal kitten gets enough exercise in the apartment or house. A dog does not leap to the top of the window, then skim to the chest of drawers in the bedroom and aviate to the back kitchen counter. Amber exercises madly until she finally folds up in a relaxed furry ball on the top of my typewriter. In good weather when she goes out with her harness on, she enjoys eating a certain kind of grass, chasing ants and moths, and smelling the roses. But when she has to stay in, she is not underprivileged.

From this point of view, I would consider a cat better for confined living. Also, the people in the next apartment can never complain that they hear barking in the middle of the night.

If you live outside of the city in a reasonably uncrowded suburb, you may not have the exercise problem even with dogs. In that case, a dog may head your Christmas list. If there are small children in the family, a puppy has advantages. A puppy will play any time the children feel like playing; a kitten plays only when she herself feels like it. Also, a puppy will endure a lot of rib squeezing which a kitten cannot abide.

A dog will do almost anything to bolster your ego, but a cat is interested in her own and not yours. I notice with Amber that even some of my adult friends have their feelings hurt if they want to dangle a string and play games when Amber is through with games for the time being and impolitely yawns in their faces.

"All right if you don't care," they will say.

Amber and I have no problems of this kind. When she feels like playing, I stop whatever I am doing and we play. When she wants to tuck up on a pillow, I never urge her to chase a toy mouse. If I am in the middle of a manuscript and she feels lonesome, she leaps on the desk and scatters the pages until I stop and gather her up and rub her ears and smooth the downy apricot underchin and utter those sentimental words only another cat lover would understand.

Since I believe many of us live too much by routine, I find this arrangement very satisfactory. Too often we feel we must organize every minute. Time dominates us and we find we are very tired. If every day is regimented, tension builds up.

Now that Amber manages our schedule, I have given up dividing the day into hours and half hours of chores and work. I seldom look at the clock to be sure I am on schedule for I know that I shall not be. Perhaps I have lost a half hour in the middle of the day when

Amber decided to take a nap in my lap. How could I disturb her? Sometimes at night I miss a favorite television show because I cannot get up to turn it on without interrupting her exquisite sleeping form.

But I can always watch how she tucks her paws under her delicate chin and folds the slim tail completely around her downy self and feel the quick small heartbeat under my hand. I hear the soft throb of that mysterious purr, and put one finger on her throat to try to discover just where it comes from. Then when she opens her topaz eyes and looks long and deeply at me and increases the vibration of the purr, I feel a sense of wonder beyond description.

Sharing life with Amber grows more rewarding daily, for there are fringe benefits from the sharing. Now I know when she walks with a certain rolling gait it means she wants breakfast but is in a mood to have me feed it to her in a teaspoon. A pale, barely audible miaow indicates that it is ten minutes of ten and I ought to get up and visit with her. If I have been up until one thirty and do not leap out of bed at her suggestion, she starts scrubbing my face (don't we always wash in the morning?) and paddling spread paws on my neck.

Most of life we spend trying to understand someone or something and often never are able to communicate. But with dogs and cats and other animals and some birds establishing communion seems easy. Amber listens attentively to everything I say.

It goes like this: "I have to get the mail now. I won't be gone any longer than I can help."

Amber makes any sea- or landscape look better.

Amber is already in the kitchen window ready to watch me drive off, and looking so desolate I almost decide to let the mail go!

This cannot be explained because of a time pattern for I seldom go for the mail at the same time. When I go out to dinner, I explain how long I shall be gone. She listens mournfully and then goes to the living-room picture window and sits on the sill.

If I tell her we shall go for a *w-a-l-k* as soon as I finish a page more at the typewriter, she jumps from my lap and leaps to the trestle table by the front door and waits.

It is fortunate I never try to deceive her for the candid steady gaze of her eyes would penetrate any trickery. For this reason I do not tell her ahead of time that we are going for a walk and then whip her into her carrying case for a jaunt to Kim, the vet, for a check-up. I wait until I can pick her up casually without saying anything. Then she understands this too and begins to squirm and make sobbing sounds.

But the communication between cats and those who belong to them (what cat owners do not?) goes beyond any words. The best argument for ESP is to have a cat. I may, for instance, be working at the typewriter and stop to think that I might fix the flounder fillet for Amber's supper. Amber is probably asleep on my lap or on the pile of manuscript paper on the desk, but instantly she is wide awake and skimming to the kitchen, where she sits on the counter by the refrigerator, waiting for service.

This, also, has nothing to do with time sense, since it is a random thought I may have at any moment. But random or not, I find myself getting the flounder out and putting it on to cook while Amber begins to purr and watch every movement. I resort to more pedestrian communication when I mash it up.

"It will be hot now. You'll have to let it cool."

Amber's pink tongue licks her chops, but she makes no move toward the fish until I test it with my forefinger and suggest that if she eats around the edges first, the dish will be cool enough. Then she takes a tentative bite and begins to eat.

Or sometimes I am sitting quietly reading and remember I have to go to a party before long. I look up to find Amber sitting on the sofa looking stricken. Her eyes are wide with disbelief. (Are you going to leave me alone again?) I begin explaining, but her mournful gaze never wavers, and when I finally get up to go, she jumps to the harvest table by the door and reaches out a pitiful paw toward me.

This reminds me, by the way, of the cheery souls who say it is easier to have a cat than a dog. Dogs bark and when they are puppies sometimes tear things up when they are left alone, whereas you can leave a cat any time. A cat doesn't care. I have no idea how this myth started.

My cats have all been miserable when they are on the wrong side of the door. Reason tells me that Amber, after she hears the car drive away, goes back to take a nap or toss pencils around.

But when I come back, the sight of that desolate small face pressed against the window screen makes me wonder if I couldn't have managed to stay home. The intensity of her gaze and the quiver of her mouth are evidence that she herself thinks it is pretty silly for us to be parted.

If a neighbor happens to drop in while I am gone, I am often told there was no sign of my kitten at all. Amber tells me, in her own way, that she couldn't care less who else comes and goes or how many cars drive up. She wants to hear a particular motor and a special voice.

Perhaps the most spectacular exhibition of ESP, to return to that, is of a cat named Percy who lives in an apartment house, nine stories up, and instantly senses when the owner comes in nine floors down and goes to the elevator. I do not argue about this.

There are many things we do not understand about the reasons for behavior of animals or mankind. I do not know why suddenly Amber feels she wants to get in a bureau drawer and jumps up and down trying to pry the drawer open until I give in. Once in, she pokes her face at me, smiling and purring. Does she want to get away from it all, as the saying goes? Or does she sense that a noisy truck is going to drive up and four large rolls of carpet will slide across the floor?

Why do we both one day feel tense and nervous, and ten minutes later a sonic boom shakes the house until every picture on the walls is crooked? Sometimes on a cloudy day Amber begins to pace restlessly, back and forth, forth and back. I now know enough to shut all the windows just in time before a thunderstorm descends with no warning.

When Amber stands on tiptoe at the front door, peering through the screen, I hurry to brush my hair and put on some lipstick before that unexpected carload of guests arrive!

Nobody needs radar if there is a cat around!

Amber is very sensitive as to how I feel. If I am depressed after reading of one more tragic "incident" in the world, she gives up her own pursuits and runs to me to rub her cheek against my face and obviously try to comfort me. When I lost a very special friend in an automobile accident, she simply glued herself to me, looking at me with saucer eyes and purring in a different register from the usual happy one.

And when I broke my wrist, she was obviously more upset than I was—with the result I had to be gay, no matter how frustrated I was. It was actually good therapy. Her expression as she sat watching me try to brush my hair with my left hand holding the brush always made me laugh.

One friend reports that her cat "tried like crazy to be a nurse" when someone was ill in the household.

The attitude toward death is the same with most cats. When one friend of mine died, the family cat simply disappeared for two days and was finally located huddling under the bushes, wet, hungry, bedraggled. This same beautiful gray cat vanished when seriously injured, obviously feeling he should retire to die alone.

W. H. Hudson the naturalist, who loved cats, said, "Cats are mentally near to us, their brains function even as ours do." I feel this reaction to the inescapable fact of death is shared by animals and humankind, for most of us have an urge to go away from it as if, perhaps, that might make death go away and things be again as

145

they should be. I also know a good many people who want to shut themselves away when they are ill. "Just let me alone," one of them says. Another remarks, "I don't want anybody around bothering me."

Both cats and we ourselves are unable to make peace with death and react in much the same way, denying it as best we can.

Chapter 15

Amber is now fully grown, although strangers always say with admiration, "What a beautiful kitten!" She will always be small and slight, probably never weighing as much as six pounds. But her coat has a deeper apricot tone so that at times it seems almost to give out light. The narrow wedge of her face has changed subtly so that she looks mature: looks more solid and her eyes seem even bigger. She has finally gained enough weight so the ribcage is fairly well upholstered. Her paws are bigger and the pads are like black raspberries. Her tail is no longer a quivering string but a firm length of seal brown.

In any situation now she stands on her own feet. If something upsets her, she firms into a tight ball and hisses fiercely. She is less apt to retreat from anything frightening. Her curiosity has increased, if possible. Her nose pokes into everything that comes into the house, from grocery bags and cartons to laundry packages.

She now comes when called, no matter how busy she is or how sound asleep. I did not train her to do this.

When I called her in the beginning and she came, I assumed it was an accident. I had planned to use the routine for dogs, which is to give a tidbit and much praise when they come, until the pattern is established; I would begin with her harness on, pull it lightly as I called, then give the reward. But I never got around to it, and suddenly I discovered she had trained herself. I can stand in the middle of the living room any time of day or night and call her and she comes dashing to me from the wing (on the Cape) or the back kitchen at Stillmeadow. She never looks for a tidbit. She is the only cat I have ever had who invariably would come when called, just as my cockers and Irish always have.

Perhaps this is not unusual, but it is in my experience. I may go all through the house looking to see where she is and there is no sign of her small person. Then I call "Amber! Amber!" and she materializes from some secret nook.

This past summer was the hottest in my area since records had been kept. This may have been the reason my nonshedding cat began to shed fluffs of apricot fur, giving me a chance to study individual hairs. Each has about two thirds of the glowing apricot color (the fanciers call it ruddy). Toward the tip is a pin point of grayish white. The top is a rich seal brown like her tail. This type of coloring is called ticking, although I have no idea why. In any case, the effect is luminous with the apricot shining through, accented by the ticking.

The shedding made the following typical:

"Yes, I do love you, but let me finish my grapefruit and coffee. Then I'll brush you."

Amber sits by the tray looking at me.

"It won't take me long, but I do want to finish my breakfast."

Amber looks at me.

"Amber, I wait on you day and night, but I do have to make a decision now and then. You go and eat your own breakfast."

Amber looks at me.

I put down the tray and go for the brush.

The purring begins and increases in volume as I brush and brush and brush. Cold coffee isn't too bad, considering. And after all, she only gets brushed five times a day!

I begin to worry about the barn cats in Connecticut. Perhaps they run through enough brush while hunting to lose some excess hair, or roll in the grass. I am sure nobody gives them sweet butter or oil to help prevent hair balls. If I put it out, it is a treat for ants and other insects.

The cooler days of fall stop the shedding, fortunately, and Amber's coat is satiny again.

One new achievement for Amber this season is figuring out how doors work. Luckily the doorknobs at Stillmeadow and on the Cape are so hard to turn that it takes both of my hands to manage them. After which I kick the door open.

I came in one day to find Amber swinging desperately on the living room doorknob, trying to make it turn with both front paws. She braced her hind paws on the door itself, which has a slight molding. Her tail was balancing the act by switching from side to side.

Another time the door was ajar and she was standing

bolt upright trying to push it open with her nose. She had one paw in the narrow opening and used it to pry.

Some of the doors in the 1690 house have the old hand-wrought latches. Amber tried to solve this by leaping in the air and landing with all five pounds on the latch. She did not get the latch up, but accomplished her purpose because I stopped working and took her out for a walk.

If a window is not raised high enough for her to sharpen her claws on the screen, she makes herself into a ball and heaves on the sash with all her strength. This also works, because I open the window until there is room enough for her to make extra holes in the screen.

She really enjoys having Kim manicure her claws and when we get home spreads her paws happily and polishes them off. If I am too slow getting her to Kim, she sits on my lap and tries to clip the tips herself. This results in my making a phone call, getting out her carrying case and starting off.

If she could run on the beach on the Cape, she would never need a manicure, but I would be minus a kitten. I admire the freedom my neighbor's cats enjoy—Smutzie and Tinker can roam at will; they weigh three times as much as Amber and really are more than a match for any wandering dog or coon. Often, however, when the family is ready to go back to Brockton after a week end, the cats are just not around! In that case, the family sits down and waits until the cats are ready to come in.

One habit that has grown on Amber is the desire to drink only water from the faucet. This is the same water that comes from the well and with which I fill her clean water dish. But when she is thirsty, she goes to the sink and sits, looking steadfastly at the faucet. I have to turn it on just enough to produce a small drip. Delicately she tiptoes toward it and turns her head to one side and drinks as the drops fall. An outside observer would comment on how mistreated my kitten is —not even a drink of water for her! But this just tastes better.

This summer her interest in television widened from watching the weatherman who uses a pointer to Johnny Cash, the country singer. She sits, spellbound, with wide dreamy eyes. I am also an addict of this remarkable performer, and I am sure my eyes have the same look as hers. I do not know whether it is the movement of his hands on the guitar or the sound itself which enraptures her, but in any case Amber is a Johnny Cash fan, and I imagine this might surprise him.

During most musical hours, she dozes, or scrubs herself, or chases an errant moth.

We have, on Cape Cod, what we call sour bugs which get in the house somehow during damp weather. They are small oval grayish bugs that just appear and wander around aimlessly. They never seem to eat anything or to have any purpose; they just move across the rug or crawl up a wall. Amber's reaction to them is strange considering that she is so excited about a moth or ant or fly. She tiptoes past them, not even putting out a tentative paw to examine them. Perhaps they do have a strange smell. But anything else that moves catches her attention instantly.

I happen to have a phobia about these bugs and cannot ignore them, and it seems to me I never sit down to relax but that one small bug appears on the beige rug, just going back and forth. Amber never helps me dispose of one. As she watches me scoop the creature up with a tissue, her gaze is fathomless.

The people who say a cat has no expression have obviously never lived with one. Amber has no trouble expressing any emotion she feels, and all without raising a paw. Her whiskers quiver with excitement, her eyes widen and her shell-pink ears prick forward when something surprises her. When she is melancholy, she can look like Niobe. When she is pleased, she smiles. She flexes her lips and has a beaming look. The purr throbs in her throat at the same time, and if she is ecstatic, she spreads her paws. But the smile comes first.

Amber seldom gets angry, but when she does, she reminds me of a small jungle tiger. Her whiskers flatten, her ears vibrate, her pupils dilate, and she reinforces this with a sharp hiss from between clenched teeth. She never hisses at me, but sometimes with others she seems to have a dire need to defend her personality. I am divided between feeling apologetic because she has lost her temper and being thankful she is not too passive! Which shows what contradictory creatures we all are.

Only a cat lover would understand that when Amber looks wistful I melt like a candle in hot sun. She reminds me of the lily maid of Astolat. She bends her head slightly, her golden lashes droop, the corners of her mouth curve downward, her ears are straight. I may have been at the typewriter too long, or there may be a rabbit outside the window she wants to chase, or she may feel it is time for some bits of steak. It is my business to find out. I always manage to.

Amber has developed one gift which is unusual, in my experience. When I suggest a walk, she levitates to the harvest table, quivering with excitement. She holds her head forward so I can slip the collar piece on. The strap is comfortable for I use the same recipe as for collars on a dog. If I can slip two fingers between the leather and her chest, it is loose enough but still safe. But when I fasten the strap, she is in a hurry. She manages to utter a squeak and purr at the same time. Her message is plain. I am slow and fumbling, which I am, but she loves the idea of going out so she would not want me to give up trying to get the small fastener closed.

I would like to suggest to the manufacturers a harness that fastens on the top instead of under the stomach, or even on the side. I have to hold up her left leg and at the same time bend double to see the tiny hole the strap goes in.

I was thinking as we took our walk today, and while she chose just the particular grass tip she wanted to nibble, that all of us, in some way, are subjected to harnesses, but if they offer safety and security we should be grateful. Certainly Amber adores hers.

I also wished we could adjust as gracefully to the end of something as Amber does. She would like to stay out indefinitely, tiptoeing around or lunging at the yard rabbit, but when we have to go indoors, she follows me and waits for me to open the door. Then she trots in and stands while I unfasten the harness.

When I go back to the typewriter, she bounces onto my lap, suggesting that I should spend my time holding her and appreciating how wonderful she is! I am reminded of a friend who once said she never would have a cocker because they are too affectionate. I would never advise an Abyssinian for such a person.

Amber and I are satisfied with each other. We like to share everything. And I do not find anything so important that I cannot stop it while I hold her against my cheek and tell her for the millionth time that she is the most beautiful and best. Nor is she ever too involved with a dish of minced steak to forget me. She stops and makes her air-borne way from the counter to my lap. She gives me a few sandpapery kisses, and then goes back to finish off her steak.

And when I am ready for sleep at night, she sits on the foot of the bed, waiting for me to say, "Amber, I love you," before she folds herself into a furry ball and purrs herself to sleep.

Amber, I love you.

Conversations
with AMBER

by Gladys Taber

PARNASSUS IMPRINTS
Orleans, Massachusetts

SOME PEOPLE LOVE CATS, some love dogs, some love other people. Some, alas, love only themselves! I love cats, dogs, people and occasionally myself, although I do have to work at the last one.

My belief is that the capacity to love depends chiefly on how wide our hearts are, and this can be unlimited. I have talked it over with Amber, who tells me she believes in using up all her love on me and this keeps her life busy.

She has no idea of leaping to a visitor's lap, purring, "Where have you been all my life?" So there is one large area in which we differ and which none of my conversations with her have affected one paw-length. Otherwise we are compatible in every way.

We began our life together when she was six weeks old and my sixteen-year-old beloved Irish setter, Holly, had just died. We had two strikes against us, for she should have been with her mother until she was eight weeks old and I was dazed with grief. Neither of us was bursting with the joy of life. She also had a few problems, such as worms and ear mites. I was exhausted from sleepless nights and trying to lug a sixty-five-pound Irish back and forth to the veterinarian. I thought my back was permanently strained.

Then my daughter, Connie, simply walked in the door with a small carrying case, which she put beside me on the couch. When she lifted the top, I saw a minute apricot ball inside and wide topaz eyes looking up at me from a pansy face.

An impartial observer could have predicted right at that moment that Amber was indomitable, for she stayed composed while the family tried to cope with the first case of hysterics ever known in our life at Stillmeadow. And when the sobs diminished and I gathered the morsel in my arms, Amber settled in as if she had come home, which indeed she had.

Amber is an Abyssinian. Both parents were champions with careers, but she was not destined for the show circuit but to be a companion for me, a housemate. Instead of collecting blue ribbons and silver trophies that would tell how beautiful she is, she has had to depend on me for daily reminders of that, and I have never grown tired of telling her.

The cat fanciers call her color ruddy. Actually the undercoat is pure apricot and the top ticked with seal-brown. The tail is also seal color, and a delicate splash of seal comes from between the pointed ears toward the brown-pink nose. Amber has the typical dense short coat of fur and high pointed ears. Her golden eyelashes protect wide round eyes that vary from onyx at night to golden in sunlight. Her paws are small, neat and satiny. At top weight she is five pounds, smaller than standard, which runs seven to nine pounds. The whole effect of an Abyssinian is of delicacy, grace and swiftness. She has the fluid movement of a cougar or puma when she leaps from the floor to the top of the bookshelves or refrigerator in one easy spring.

My dear friend Olive commented on one special feature as we sat one day by the open fire, sipping iced drinks and having the windows open with our usual inconsistency.

"You must admit," said Olive, "Amber has a very pugnacious chin."

"Well, your Siamese doesn't," I said. "He's the only Siamese I have ever known who has no courage."

"A complete coward," she agreed.

When Amber sailed into my lap, I felt the strong bones of her jaw. Above, her rose-petal mouth was demure, her pale golden whiskers no thicker than a spider's web. But she definitely did have a pugnacious chin!

While I brushed her (high time, said her tail), I used a magnifying glass to inspect one fluff of fur. I could see that the ticking was actually double, with a lighter touch between the seal tip and the apricot down undercoat. This is rather like the marking of a wild rabbit's coat.

Amber has two methods of communication in the ordinary course of our life. First there is the language of her tail, which expresses all kinds of moods. If I am talking to her as she basks in the sun, she answers with a slow undulation of the tail to let me know that she is listening. A stray cat outside the window starts the tail lashing furiously back and forth. An unknown sound at the door produces a circular swishing as a warning. When she folds the pointed tip under her chin and wraps her paws around it, the message is clear. It is like turning off an extra-dull television program. No more of that.

Her second language is the purr. Amber has three sound layers of purr. First, a soft tentative whisper while she decides whether combing might be a good idea. Second, a moderate middle-range purr, which is a sign of approval. Third, a throbbing sound as I reach for her breakfast dish.

11

When I feel her throat, the vibrating beats on my fingertip, and I realize once more what a mystery nature provides. For no matter how hard I try, I cannot purr! That special little sound box belongs to felines and to nobody else.

Occasionally, under great stress, Amber produces a thin miaow, but it is not audible enough to summon help if she needs it. However, when she once slipped out to attack two enormous raccoons, she swelled double in size and uttered a combination of a scream and a growl as she flew at them. The coons could have killed her in a minute, but that sound affected them like an A-bomb. They fled as fast as they could. Amber dashed after them. At the end of her property she let the scream diminish and resumed her own shape as she came back to the house, switching her hips in triumph. By then I had also stopped screaming and sank feebly on the couch while she polished her whiskers and rumbled back into a purr.

It is interesting that a variation of the growl-scream comes when we are at our veterinarian's having her nails clipped. Amber actually wants them clipped, since they regularly grow too long and curve under. Outdoor tree-climbing cats wear their claws down, but Amber's grassy yard and deep wool rugs are not effective. Our Doctor Kim is gentle, swift, cajoling as he clips the tips. But she feels she must make a drama of the occasion and consequently produces a wail and a hiss alternately. She adds to the theatrical effect by flinging her arms in the air to give the impression that she has eight limbs instead of just two arms and two legs.

"Now, Amberino," says Kim cheerfully, "I am just going to make you comfortable again. One more paw, please!"

I admit that Linda, the doctor's assistant, has to go to the next room to muffle her laughter, and I would be with her except that I have five pounds of furry eel to hold steady.

When the ordeal is over, Amber subsides into her carrying case with the relieved air of someone who has just survived a terrible crisis. One last moan emphasizes her feelings. She may be a quiet, soft-spoken cat but you would never call her inarticulate.

Soon after Amber came to live with me I began to make notes of our experiences, and eventually there were enough to fill a small volume. It was 1970 when my book about Amber came out. It was a book with which I'd had one major problem: I could not think of a title that fitted. I talked it over with Amber in the middle of the night when she plopped down on top of me to be sure I was still there. We discussed it again as she ate the butter from my breakfast toast. It was also a subject of concern to the editorial board at my publisher's until finally Tay Hohoff, my own editor, said, "Look, we have to remember that Amber is a very personal cat."

"That's the title," said one perceptive man, and *Amber, a Very Personal Cat* was recorded on a Library of Congress card.

Since that date we have lived a lot and shared many experiences. A kitten brings a special magic to a house but it cannot compare with a mature relationship. And since Amber and I live alone, we have had ample time to explore our own personalities and reach a high level of understanding. I have never been able to talk to myself for comfort. Although I am a verbal person, I do not find the furniture or even my beloved house itself a satisfying audience. I need an active listener and Amber is a listening cat. Unlike people, she never interrupts. She never criticizes me for what I say. But her speaking tail responds when my voice is deep with sadness. Her ears stand like small sails when I am excited. And when I am in a philosophical mood and speak thoughtfully, she turns that wedge-shaped head toward me and the wisdom of past ages seems to be in her eyes. Then when I fall silent she resumes scrubbing her immaculate face.

Amber reflects my mood instantly. For instance, she is not a football addict, but when a game is tied 24–24 and one field goal will determine the winner she leaps into my lap and her whiskers quiver at my excitement. And at such moments she does *not* tell me she wants another dish of minced beef.

If I am despondent, the look of anxiety on her face makes me pull myself together. And when my thoughts are racing like windblown clouds, I can always depend on Amber to listen. In fact, she is a better listener than some of my friends, who really do not pay any attention when I want to discuss how many shades of grey there are in the sky and how many on the land on a cloudy January afternoon—or when I have a flight of fancy about solving the malpractice problem for doctors (if the amounts awarded were not so stupendous, the suits would diminish, I think). And I have only one close friend who does not mind if I feel like reading a Keats sonnet aloud.

Actually I do not think we are a society of listeners in this confusing era. In a group most people talk all at once, but there cannot be a meeting of minds when no two people are even on the same subject.

This seems strange, since communication is the basis of our civilization. When language began, mankind was on the way from the cave to the skyscraper. Yet nowadays we seem to be forgetting how important it is.

Amber pays considered attention to whatever I say. Her answers may be a shake of the lissome tail, or a quiver of the golden-silver whiskers, or a spreading of beautiful paws or at times a polite yawn that speaks plainly, saying it is one o'clock in the morning and it is bedtime, even for us night people!

But if I have trouble sleeping and get up at two or three, she wakes instantly, ready to listen again to any kind of nonsense I may have dreamed up.

She purrs!

Yesterday I discovered that a new neighbor had come to call. Afterward she telephoned. "I wanted to ask you about a trashman, but I knew you had company and didn't want to disturb you."

"I didn't have any company all day," I said.

"Well, I thought it was odd because there was no car in your yard, but I heard you having a conversation with someone."

"Oh, that," I said. "I was just talking to Amber."

"I guess she must have walked up from the beach. I haven't met her."

"Do come again," I said. "Amber is my Abyssinian cat." There was a silence. I knew what she was thinking. Writers are supposed to be odd, but whoever thought they might hold conversations with a cat? This one must be really queer.

When I told this to Amber, her tail rotated, her ears flicked and she began pawing on the pages of my book. Her message was definite. "Forget about new neighbors. Why don't you stop digging into that stupid book and talk to me?"

"Cats are supposed to be independent," I said. For answer she flipped a page with a long delicate arm, thus losing my place in a very thick book.

Over our snack of sliced red apples spread with cream cheese, I explained that humans have a great many conventions. Singing in the shower is acceptable. So is singing along with records, even if one cannot carry a tune. But walking around doing housework while chattering away to oneself raises the eyebrows of any neighbors who happen to overhear.

"Amber," I said, "I am an eccentric. My favorite teenage protégé told me that once when I was describing the meanings of various colors. And I guess it's true."

She licked the cheese from another slice of apple.

"For instance," I said, "if you tried to cuddle up to a raccoon, your own species would call you eccentric. Normally cats and coons are not best friends."

She cleaned up another apple slice, then paused to wash her face, which was frosted with cream cheese.

"And perhaps in prehistoric days, if a primitive man mumbled to himself in the forest and his tribesmen heard him, they would have crashed through the forest, fully armed with

15

stones, to kill whatever enemy he had encountered. Then they would probably have bashed his own head in!"

As for me, I would certainly have been tucked away in the family attic in the early days. I not only talk to a cat who seems to answer in some strange way, but I talk to pieces of furniture and to plants and to my faithful old automobile (encouraging words often make her jerk into mobility). The truth is, everything on this planet has personality to me and I feel some kind of response when I talk to it. Fortunately Amber accepts this as natural. And it encouraged me no end when scientists decided that plants do better if they are praised or encouraged or sympathized with. I knew this when I was a small child picking wild flowers.

But plants seldom answer back, except in cartoons. Amber, however, finds it reasonable that I converse with her and has no trouble responding in her own mysterious language. All that troubles her is that she cannot make sense of those squiggles on the page of a book.

Put away the book, apples and cheese plate and tell me how wonderful I am!

Lately, experts have been studying what they call nonverbal communication between humans. Such a silent language is not new to those of us who have had families. One look from a husband may mean, "I want to go home. I have a big day coming up." Or, "I wish you would change the subject while everyone is still on speaking terms."

A look from a wife says plainly, "You do *not* want another drink." Or, "Please rescue me from X. He is getting to be too much."

A mother says without words, "I wish you would stop fidgeting."

A child indicates with one shrug that both parents are being too silly for words.

There are infinite possibilities. In fact, the experts now go so far as to say that the way a person sits or walks conveys a message (usually sexual).

People who live with dogs or cats also understand nonverbal communication. The other day a friend dropped in for a drink. I had an extra glass, filled with ice water, on the table by the sofa.

"What's that for?" she asked.

"Amber likes to drink out of a glass here on the table," I explained. "And she wants ice in it."

"How do you know that?" my friend said.

"She told me so."

At which point Amber popped up onto the table, dipped her tongue in, drew it out and lifted the ice cube with a small paw.

It happened that the next day I was in a hurry at breakfast and I filled her glass with water as I poured my mug of coffee. She went to her glass three times, whiskered the rim, drew back, stared at me, sat down. Finally I got up and checked the glass. The tap water was lukewarm and no ice cube in it. I fixed it at once, of course. She then drank a third of the glassful.

"You told me," I said.

I was reminded of my darling Irish, who had a passion for ice cubes and on hot summer days sat by the refrigerator door until I stopped work and provided a couple.

Amber expresses her opinion on all sorts of things. If she does not like her current meal, she hunches down by her tray, lashes her tail and turns a woebegone face to me.

"Take this junk away," she says definitely. "I don't want lamb again! I had it yesterday."

When she is pleased with herself, she parades around the house as if there were flags flying and bands playing.

In the years that we have been together, Amber and I have had many conversations on many subjects. No matter whether she is busy sharpening her claws on the forbidden green armchair or pushing a velvet nose in the spaghetti sauce, she will always stop and listen when I have some thought to share. And she will let me know how she herself feels. I have jotted down most of these conversations because they express the experiences we have shared. Happiness and sorrow have walked through our door; laughter and tears have companioned us. Amber has grown up and I presumably have grown wiser. But we have walked together and found something new in every day to be grateful for.

2

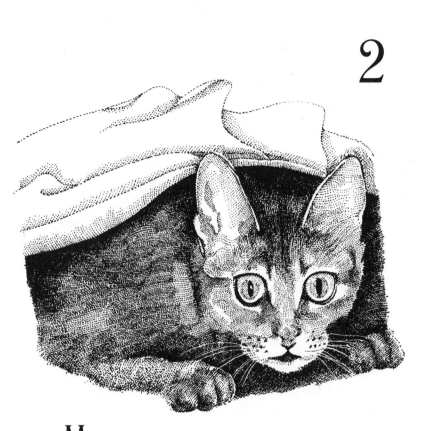

MONDAY IS NOT MY FAVORITE DAY. Amber gets me up with difficulty.

This may be why last Monday she finally gave up and fell asleep on the pillow. I slipped out gently and went to take my shower. I was still trying to adjust the faucets so the spray was not boiling or an avalanche of ice water when a triangle of nose poked around the bathroom door.

Amber stalked in and jumped to the washbowl.

"Miaow, miaow, miaow!" She sounded distraught.

"What's the matter? I'm right here."

"Miaow."

I stepped into the shower and drew the curtain. Amber

leaped to the windowsill, which is right beside the shower stall. She reached a paw out to claw at the curtain. Saucer eyes were wide with sheer disapproval.

"I'll be right out," I said. "I am simply taking my shower."

Braced on her haunches, she used two front paws to claw. By now steam was rising. She retreated to the top of the toilet seat, glaring furiously and uttering her wildest sound. She kept it up until I hastily turned off the faucets and got out.

Immediately she was dove-quiet (although nobody could call a mourning dove quiet, I must say). She jumped past my toweled, dripping figure, put her face around the curtain and got inside the shower stall herself, wading in leftover water. She stayed there until I went out the door, when she pranced after me.

While I dressed, she purred her loudest, rolled over on her back, spread her toes.

"Is all this because you were hungry?" I asked, pulling on my slacks. "I am not that late!"

A blissful cat purred away.

"No, or you would have dashed to the kitchen," I said. "You did not want me to take a shower—did you want the water cold enough so you could have one too? You were definitely not scared, you were just cross."

I have plenty of time to wonder, for she has been acting this drama every day of the week since. All I have to do is say the word "shower" and she starts objecting.

On the other hand, the moment I pick up the leash and doll-size harness, Amber leaps to the trestle table and offers a slender neck. It is not easy to fasten the buckle while she is pushing my hands, purring, making a windmill of her tail. Lifted out the front door and lowered to the green grass, she stands motionless. The world is so big, she is so small. She looks up at me for reassurance as a tentative paw bends the first blades. While she figures things out, I begin our conversation.

"The world *is* amazing out here, but you don't need to

worry. If any stray dog turns up you will be scooped into my arms."

I am thinking as she tiptoes ahead, "O! so light a foot ne'er wore out the everlasting flint." I too am suddenly awed by the vastness of the planet. I do not notice this when I dash to the car to keep an appointment. All I wonder then is whether the car will start. Now the infinity of the sky, the expanse of the pine woods, the stretch of lawn we walk on—all seem breathtaking. Even the Dawn roses over the split-rail fence seem so tall, the shell-pink blossoms bigger than soup plates. As Amber pursues the one kind of grass she likes best, I begin to see how many varieties grow in our own front yard. No amount of nibbling gives me any idea of the best eating grass, but she has no trouble at all deciding.

She leads me on a wavering course.

"Amber, how do you know what to eat? You love mushrooms but never stop for a small one by the outdoor faucet. Who taught you which is which? Your parents were champions and never had a chance to run outdoors. They spent most of their time in cages en route to cat shows. But you—you only make two mistakes."

She gives me a doubtful look.

"I mean baby's breath and sea lavender. You know you always throw them up but you insist on gulping them down anyway. Why?"

The chickadees scold from the bushes. She ignores them. A cardinal (always nervous) flits past and she hauls at the leash. She quivers all over. This flash of scarlet would be worth chasing right into the juniper.

The ilex bushes have just been trimmed. Amber is enchanted, so I twist off a small stem. The fragrance is spicy yet delicate. The polished dark-green leaves feel cool. While Amber pats them and sniffs happily, I rub a few leaves against my cheek.

"Amber, you teach me so much," I tell her as I struggle

to unwrap her leash from the lower branches. "How easy it is to ignore the familiar. Ilex dates back, I think, to Rome, and it has been a favorite foundation planting in this country since the early days. In the Victorian era it was pruned into dreadful shapes (still is, sometimes) or trimmed as square as a box."

Amber manages a U-turn of her leash and loses all interest in ilex. She wants to get to the mint and says plainly that I am too slow in unwinding that leash.

"All right, eat the mint," I say.

She does not eat the mint but she nibbles edges of the spicy leaves and rubs a clump with her chin. Amber's sense of smell is a whole world in itself and the range is remarkable, from an open rose high above the fence, which she stands on tiptoe to enjoy, to a jar of spaghetti sauce being opened in the kitchen.

While she plays with the mint, I keep thinking about the ilex. Only at this moment, thanks to Amber, do I really see, feel and smell it. Yet ilex has been around in my life since my childhood, when Papa planted a row of it too close together, in his usual exuberant way. (Who else would go to the grocer for a can of asparagus and come home with a whole case?) He was always pruning that ilex, chopping out entire branches and uttering his ultimate curse, "Confound it!"

But in those days I walked past with my head somewhere in the stars. Today my Abyssinian kitten has opened my eyes (and nose) to ilex, so from now on I shall have a new pleasure in life. And it is not far away in some exotic land either but right by the front door. Glossy branches will come inside for a winter bouquet in the big white ironstone pitcher. When I trim them, some of summer's fragrance will sift into the room.

There are always intelligent, otherwise normal friends who tell me that a dog or a cat is too much trouble, too much responsibility! I never argue, but I do feel sorry for them. I have yet to find any worthwhile relationship in life that involves no trouble, no responsibility. We are always faced with balancing the rewards against the problems.

When I think about it, I realize how much my dogs and cats have helped me for so long, and I feel that the love and joy of living we have shared cannot be measured—no computer could cope with it!

Now, although the family is dispersed, leading busy lives elsewhere, I am not alone because of Amber. From quarter of nine in the morning until after midnight, Amber is always busy keeping me company.

Even at night when I try to do a crossword puzzle, there are two imperative paws flat on the page just as I am about to fill in some peculiar word. So of course I stop to admire the delicate precision of her paws, give her a brushing, get a fresh ice cube for her water glass.

When I read, I often miss a line or two because she is turning the page for me ahead of time.

When you are alone, getting a meal is not very cozy, but when I fix supper Amber stands on the counter supervising and purring, and I give her a lesson in how to cook properly.

She always watches television with me. If my favorite TV program bores her, she snuggles. She prefers weather reports, with a man poking a stick around a colored map, or a forward pass in a football game. She also, incidentally, enjoys trumpet music and the way Seiji Ozawa conducts the Boston Symphony, but opera sends her to her lounging chair to give herself an extra bath.

As for household chores, bedmaking is her favorite and my defeat. But it is more fun with a cat under the covers pawing the sheets the wrong way than trying to get them even all alone.

She does not like the vacuum cleaner any more than I do. I have battled this difficult device ever since carpet sweepers went out of fashion. During vacuuming, Amber naps on the

23

pillow in my freshly made bed. It is a safe retreat from the noisy intruder.

Dusting is better. A dust mop can be chased, stopped, retired. Dishwashing is worth careful observation, although the water is too hot to dip a paw into.

The one time she invariably abandons me is whenever I clean out the refrigerator. She does not like that wave of icy air billowing out, so I do the refrigerator in isolation and find it lonely. Therefore I clear it out only when the contents cascade on me when I open the door.

Fortunately on Fridays we have our best friend Millie, who comes to help, and Millie does all the hard things we do not manage. Friday is Amber's favorite day because things are *going on.* Rug corners get turned up, dustcloths fly. The washing machine is going, and a quick-thinking kitten can peer inside when it is empty. Then when the washing comes off the line, a helpful paw is available for folding.

Sometimes Millie's husband, Ed, drops in. He is a special friend of Amber's, so she runs up to him to have her chin rubbed, play in his cap, poke around his shoes where his own cat has been. Then Millie flies by and Amber goes back to her housework.

Millie and Amber have complete understanding. If I am at the typewriter, I overhear bits of the conversation.

"All right, Amber, I'll dish up more food for you."

"Look, Kitten, can't you find something else to do while I change the bed?"

"Now I am going to *shut* the door on you while I air out the living room. You can go out on the leash later."

"You have already scratched that chair down to the stuffing. Can't you leave it alone? We don't want to do it over right now."

"All right, I'll leave the big paper bag on the floor so you can hide in it. But don't forget the time I thought you were in the other room and started to lug a bag to the trash can with you in it!"

24

"As soon as I dust the Belleek pitcher you can get back on that shelf."

"Amber, I am airing your litter pan, so you can't use it until it gets some sun for a change."

Amber's final help is to walk on fresh wax just poured on the floor.

Millie never picks Amber up; both of them are basically reserved. However, on Friday morning Amber is always in the kitchen window, watching for Millie at exactly the time Millie is due. And she reacts as I do when Millie flashes out of sight.

"Going to be pretty dull around here," says Amber plainly.

Amber lives surrounded by love. Cats who are not loved make do. They have an inner resilience most dogs lack. They establish their independence and lead their own lives. But sometimes a cat who has been neglected, abused, abandoned finds a human with a compassionate heart. Such cats overwhelm their saviors with devotion! If you adopt one, he may spend some time under the bed or behind the washing machine, emerging to eat only when nobody is around. But the next thing you know, you must walk carefully or you will step on somebody's tail. Somebody sleeps on your pillow. Somebody wails pitifully if a closed door is between you.

Amber herself is nearer to me than my shadow. Even when she is folded up in sleep (and cats sleep a lot more than dogs), she suddenly explodes into activity and flies to my arms just to be sure I still love her. In the midst of being airborne after a moth, she changes flight pattern to crash-land on my shoulder.

"Yes, Amber, you are beautiful. Haven't I told you so yet today?" I say. "And of course I still love you."

"I just wanted to be sure," she tells me.

When I have to go out, I explain, "Amber, I am going to dinner but I shall be home early. You take care of the house."

As I drive away I see a melancholy face at the window.

And when I come back she acts as if I had just returned from Mount Everest.

I always tell her just where I am going and how long I shall be gone. Non–cat people might think me crazy, but I know she senses my schedule. If it is going to be a brief trip her mourning is moderate, but if I explain that I will be gone a long time, she plants herself in front of the door to keep me from leaving.

This reminds me of a cat belonging to my dear friend and editor, Tay Hohoff; he instantly knew when the elevator in their apartment building started six floors below, carrying the one and only home to him.

I know cats who see children off to school and then go about their own affairs until the precise time the school bus drives down the road—then these cats are at the gate. When my friend Jimmy DeLory was a boy, he had a cat who followed him halfway to school every morning, patiently turned back, and was always there to meet him at the end of the road in the afternoon. It discouraged Jimmy from misbehaving and being kept in after school!

Amber has no desire for a loving association with another cat or a dog. She is frankly jealous. Once when a very small dachshund puppy came to call, I made the mistake of admiring him. When I finally fished Amber out from under the bed, she indicated that she was packing her bag and leaving me for good.

"I do love you more than anybody else," I said. "I was just being polite." This was not an out-and-out lie; I was being polite. But I was also enchanted by that silken miniature.

"When visitors come," I said, "they should always be greeted warmly, even if you don't like them!"

Amber gave me her desolate look, usually reserved for utter starvation.

"Social grace is a very important quality," I went on. "I admit a good many humans lack it. But I think you should try to acquire it."

No answer, not a tail flick.

When neighbor cats turn up and press earnest faces on the glass in the front door, Amber's response is attack. "Enemy invasion" is her opinion.

A long time ago a good friend stopped in with Moby, her miniature schnauzer. Amber rocketed through the air, giving an amazing jungle howl. Fortunately the guest still had his leash on and his owner saved him with a flying swoop of her arms.

A few other similar experiences changed my ideas of remodeling Amber, and I settled for shutting her in the bedroom when necessary. My dear friend Olive has a gentle, rather timid Siamese male whose name is simply Boy. She used to visit us in the days before she bought a nearby house, and when she did, Boy stayed in the guest bedroom, door tight. Amber stayed in my bedroom, clawing at the door. Whatever she said to Boy had an effect, for one evening he managed to open his door, put his nose to the crack of her door, and proved the voice of a Siamese tops any sound in the world. Luckily, the latch held fast.

Olive's miniature schnauzer holds herself aloof. At thirteen, Trinka believes in peace except when a strange man starts to clean the windshield on her own car or raises the hood to check the oil.

However, strange things can happen. One weekend Olive came for a Cape Cod weekend in the midst of a nor'easter. My daughter, Connie, was here too and we all decided to go out for a quick dinner before the main part of the storm hit. We left Trinka tucked in her security blanket in the chair by the fireplace. Amber was tearing around in my bedroom. Boy was speaking about the outrage from behind his own closed door. We sloshed to the car and drove off for a fortifying steak in the village. I left the lights on for the three who had to stay behind.

On the way home the road seemed extra dark. No lights in any windows anywhere.

"Has everybody gone out to eat?" Connie asked.

Coming into our driveway, I remarked, "That outside light has gone out again. Bulbs don't last the way they used to."

Then, when we opened the door, the house was black as a coal pit. So we knew the "electric" was off. The only sound was the banging of the screen behind us. We had not gone to dinner with flashlights. A cigarette lighter flickered long enough to show us that all the inside doors were wide open.

But absolute silence lay like doomsday.

"They have killed each other," I whispered. Connie fumbled for a candle and lit it.

Two perfectly groomed, quite undamaged cats appeared, yawning. Trinka was still dozing in her usual place.

We could not understand it. We still discuss that night with wonder. What brought about such a change? Had the storm itself become a mutual enemy? Was it the black dark swooping down? Was it because the humans were not around?

We might have done some research by walking out again, leaving them with no closed doors, and then listening from the stoop. We might have tried this in the daytime and at night. But Olive shook her head.

"I think we'd better not begin experimenting," she said.

So we just rejoiced in the new atmosphere of peace.

Most cats and dogs can and do make friends. We were used to Tigger's doffing his dignity to sleep in Honey's arms, ebony cat and sun-gold cocker both very happy. The cockers chose best friends among themselves too. Esmé, the Siamese, accepted the whole bevy without complaint, although when Tigger brought her the best and biggest rat from the barn across the road, she ignored his gift. He finally gave up trying to win any thanks from her and laid his prize in the doorway to my bedroom.

When Olive took in a starving, sick kitten, she expected problems with Boy. She planned that as soon as the waif was well she would find a home for him. But now the two resemble

David and Jonathan. They play together, hunt together, sleep comfortably together on the big bed.

Then when they come to the Cape, the car is hardly unloaded before a neighbor cat appears on the terrace to welcome them. He has a happy home, especially since his owner is a writer and provides a comfortable lap for long stretches of time. He also has an amiable dog in the family for a companion. But Seaweed wants cat friends, there is no doubt about it. He likes Boy, but his special pal is the ex-waif, Spunky, now handsome, lively and fond of all tumbling, chasing games.

So I have to admit that Amber is not so eccentric.

"But Emily Dickinson, who was a great poet," I sometimes tell her, "always preferred being alone. And she could be as solitary as she wished. She became a legend in her own time."

Amber stares at me with onyx eyes. One delicate paw taps me. Number-three purr pulses in her throat.

I get the message: "I am myself. I am not anybody else."

"Want to go for a walk?"

"That makes sense," she agrees, leaping to the table for her leash.

"Well, I am not typical either," I tell her. *If we were all alike, it might be a dull world* is my final thought as we go out to smell the roses.

Seaweed is an interesting person, competent, sure of himself but determined to be part of life at Topside when possible. He is fortunate that the two cats who own the house do not mind another companion. His own house is across the road and up a short distance, but he can be seen as soon as he appears around the bushes. I find even his way of walking fascinating —somehow he reminds me of a bank president on the way to a conference. His markings are somewhat like a patchwork quilt, but his dignity is Fifth Avenue.

Having fun visiting and enjoying a few cocktail snacks was never surprising. The incident that established Seaweed on our special list was the day last week when he took his usual route from his home, skipped across the road because a car went by, crossed the back yard, planted his stocky body at the glass door and was let in. Whereupon he marched to the hall, went down the cellar stairs and used the litter box. Then he came back upstairs and went back out.

I consider this one of the most remarkable episodes in my cat observations. Did he simply want to establish a right of domain? How was he so sure just where that litter box was, since he had obviously never spent a night in this house? Did he hope he was welcome enough to "use the facilities," as we humans say? And, practically speaking, why did he travel so far without stopping on the lawn, since he is an outdoor cat much of the time?

In the end I decided any normal, ordinary cat can keep any human being in a state of frustration.

ONE REASON AMBER IS SO HAPPY is that, al-
though I study her daily, try to understand and even teach her,
she is never experimented on. I am not testing her. We are two
individuals who live together, reaching out to each other, accepting each other's faults and peculiarities, sharing love and
enjoyment.

While I admire the incredible skill and knowledge and
unflagging patience of the animal experimenters, I would never
be one. I know how important they are; they are laboring to
solve all the mysteries of all the species up to and including
man.

But I cannot look at our world that way, for to me every

living creature is an individual, not typical of his kin. There are resemblances, of course. We spend a lot of time deciding in our own families whether "Suzy is exactly like Aunt Abigail" or "That's Papa coming out in her" (which is often said of me) or "Johnny is Uncle Ed all over again."

Physical resemblances can be startling. A small child can look like an exact replica of her great-great-grandmother—except that in the daguerreotype the clothes are so different.

However, no two individuals, even twins, are duplicates. You cannot make Xerox copies of people. The same is true of birds, animals and, for all I know, fish. The one species I can think of that may be an exception might be worker ants, who appear to have a mass personality, although I wonder, when I watch them laboring away like Egyptian pyramid slaves, whether one ant may be smarter than another, or one might not be ready to quit the whole job!

I have read about Washoe, the chimpanzee who, under controlled environment and with incredible labor on the part of her trainers, has learned to converse in sign language. Speech is not possible for her because the vocal cords are not constructed like a human's. But her skill with gestures and sign language has been a remarkable discovery.

Another chimpanzee, Lana, has learned to punch buttons on a complicated computer (like a telephone switchboard) and chooses the right one to press with a powerful finger so as to bring a banana sliding out. She can also turn on a television set or call her trainer just by pushing the right button. What she cannot do is go outside, for the poor thing is never allowed out of her special laboratory room.

Both of these animals can do many other human acts. In fact, they are smarter than I could be, for I am sure that I could never figure out a bit of sign language no matter how hard I tried. I also have trouble with all kinds of push buttons and would never earn a single banana. I do have several friends who could master these skills quite easily. On the other hand, they all have difficulty writing a letter.

My theory is that just because a few carefully chosen animals or birds can acquire so much human behavior, it doesn't mean one can generalize about their whole species, any more than if some Martians experimented with a man from earth who turned out to be Einstein. They might expect millions like him. What a shock it would be if the next subject turned out to be a person like me, who could not cope with the simplest adding and subtracting!

My second conviction as to experimentation is that laboratory studies cannot result in a complete analysis of a living creature. The one way, I believe, to delve into another being is to live with him or her, putting away all complicated testing machines, forgetting compilations, not trying to teach human achievements (we are so egotistic, aren't we?) or to chart behavior on a graph.

What I observe about Amber is what she herself is like naturally, how she feels, what she wants to teach me about her own complex person. During our long conversations she listens because she enjoys knowing that I am talking to her alone and not to anyone else. When company comes, she is capable of jumping on my lap if she thinks I am conversing too long. A firm paw and a nudge say plainly, "Talk to me for a change!"

I do believe all animals like to learn, but not under regimentation. The friend who tells me all cats are dumb and don't give a hoot about people has never been owned by a cat. Being owned by a cat is different from owning a cat and simply having it around. And we know that children living long periods in institutions may seem retarded but will flower when a loving family adopts them, handicap and all.

With all this in mind, I am never tempted to give Amber a training course. I am the learner as I live with her.

My feelings about categorizing living creatures apply to humans as well. A current best-seller has divided my own species into neat files according to age, based on interviews with 119 individual men and women. It is easy to look up in the right chapter and find what stage you are undergoing. This makes interesting reading, but I have gone along with my life for many years without having such a guide. And I feel that the author's conclusions are like the experimentation with the chimpanzees. I cannot believe all cats are alike, so why should I agree that all human beings must go through exactly the same stages at given times? Since this gifted writer is also an individual, I suspect that most of her conclusions echo her own personal experience in living.

All creatures have life patterns but with infinite differences. They may change, but not on a schedule. Why do some buds on my Peace rosebush open at different times, given the same amount of sun, temperature and rain? Why is every rose slightly different in color if you look closely? Why are the petals never exactly the same?

And why does Amber suddenly decide she wants a dish of chunky soup, which she has scorned for some years? If I comment on this, she widens her eyes.

"I just like this now," she indicates.

People seldom suddenly decide they "just love" an item they have abhorred all their lives. Only occasionally will a friend say, "I have *learned* to like turnips!" Whereas Amber, as a cat, has never, never tried to learn to like anything. Then suddenly right out of the blue, as the saying goes, she has a full-blown passion for a certain food that has never interested her before. I have discussed this often with other cat people; none of us can figure it out. Their cats never start asking for a different label on the cat-food cans. These people imply that Amber is certainly eccentric, with the implication that I am also.

Sometimes a friend comes out with it: "You are a bit odd in some ways yourself!"

It is true that laboratory animals can learn to eat foods they would not get in a natural environment. And off the record this sets me to wondering who first persuaded cows to enjoy molasses in their hay. It is also true that every species has certain foods which are, to them, life sustaining. Grass eaters, meat eaters, fish eaters, insect eaters all follow inherited life patterns. But those creatures that live with mankind develop as many human patterns as they *feel* like.

What is not true is that home animals know instinctively what their stomachs will put up with. Why should Amber eat baby's breath or sea lavender when she throws it up immediately? Why do my friend Charles Schlessiger's cats eat S.O.S. pads?

For that matter, why do children eat lead paint? As a nonexperimenter I have never tried a few flakes. Can lead taste sweet? Or is it merely because it is there?

Some experimenter could do a book on the natural likes and dislikes of living creatures; perhaps one has and I've missed it. Amber would be a difficult subject. All I can say is that she likes plain salt but not seasoned salt. Wild cats may get salt from something in their prey, especially if they catch fish from salt water. Other wild four-footed animals will chew the ends of oars into splinters because of the salt residue from the rowers' hands. My Canada geese must get some salt as they preen their feathers after a long swim on the sea inlet. I have no guess as to what most land birds prefer. Some of mine eat only berries and seeds; others want insects. Robins dig for worms, chickadees love sunflower seeds, quail love cracked corn and lots of it, goldfinches adore thistle, cardinals prefer an orange or a grapefruit cut in half and impaled on a nail that sticks out of the top of the fence post.

Most birds like suet and peanut butter (which needs to be mixed with seed to prevent its sticking in their throats the way it does to mine). None of the birds I have will eat the tiny rape seeds, although mixed birdseed is full of them.

Blackberry, my skunk friend, never turned down anything but especially loved cream, chicken, tuna, beef, lamb, vegetables and fish. He was not a house dweller, he was wild. He had never been in a house; he had his burrow under a bayberry bush. His natural diet was insects and grubs, with an occasional tulip or hyacinth bulb, dug up as fast as planted. Moles were good fare, possibly field mice. Consequently I could not see why a sophisticated, varied human diet gave such joy. But it was obviously good for him, since he was plump and deeply furred with a glossy black coat striped widely with ermine. He could amble faster than any other skunk I have ever seen. He could also drive off a friend who came at times to the split-rail fence. Blackberry kept this other skunk at a distance until his own dish was almost empty. Then he would stop stamping and threatening and uttering his curious birdlike sound and would simply watch quietly while his friend finished the meal.

Skunks are mammals, so his love of cream and even stale milk stirred a memory of nursing days. But his mother never served macaroni and cheese!

Experimentation with animals flourishes in our era and I know it will provide a great store of information, some of it leading to discoveries about our own peculiar species. And nobody will ever pay any attention to my thoughts about it, except perhaps a homemaker who has kittens and puppies tumbling around the house, or a farmer's wife who helps with the chickens, pigs and cows.

At this point Amber invites me to go to the kitchen and leave this odd box alone. A nice fresh flounder fillet would suit her. She helps unwrap it. Just in case, I take a piece of leftover steak from the refrigerator. Her eyes are blank. I get the message.

"We had that *last* night," she reminds me.

Sometimes I like to indulge in fantasy. While Amber and I were considering this whole matter of science, I imagined myself as a subject of experimentation by a select group of mastermind dogs and cats. Amber would be the head official for one reason: she was not born to take second place in any way. The staff would be Holly, my Irish; Dark Honey and Little

Sister, cockers; and Tigger, the Manx cat we used to have. Esmé, my Siamese, could be chief critic of the whole affair. She was always so verbal!

Testing my intelligence would be discouraging. No amount of sustained effort would enable me to navigate on all fours, nose down, and follow a scent, not even of a skunk who leaves a musky odor when he plugs along. Sniffing of deer or rabbit tracks would be a lost cause. Even the obvious trail of a bobcat's smell would only leave me with a scraped nose as well as a lame back!

I should perhaps explain here that among those of my own species I am noted for my sense of smell, often being compared to a beagle. But in the fantasy my animals were not impressed.

"She couldn't track a dead fish if I dragged it from the beach right to the doorstep," Holly said. "She has to see it to begin carrying on."

Training me to hear a prowling wild animal outside the house at midnight would be a second failure.

"The only way she ever knows enough to look outside is when I tell her," Amber stated. "I can jump from a good sleep and rush to a window, but unless it happens to be a couple of raccoons fighting, she has to be waked up by my jumping on her."

Test three for mobility would go from bad to worse, as Holly noticed. Nobody would use a stopwatch to time my speed running half a mile on the beach or swimming halfway across Mill Pond. No use trying to race through brush with me. "You would just go back and find her stuck in some briers," the Irish said.

The cockers hated to admit I can't even chase a ball and fetch it in my mouth. Neither can I heel properly on a leash. Can't make a decent hole in the ground with my paws or climb a fence to get on the other side, either.

Amber was even more discouraged. "No matter how I paw at her ears, she cannot fold them flat or lift them forward.

No wonder she can't even hear a twig fall. Once a bug got into one of her ears and we had real trouble. I have pushed her ears around a lot trying to teach her. No luck. Can't train human ears to be practical."

The cockers and Irish spoke in unison for once. "No ear flaps either. Field running needs flaps."

The group was not making a written record, but if they had been, I would have scored nothing but zeros.

Ears drooped, tails sagged, whiskers were motionless.

Tigger had been quiet, like the gentleman he was. But his jade eyes looked thoughtful. "I showed her how to locate a mole burrow," he said gruffly. "I showed her how to poke a piece of long grass into the hole and wait to pounce when it moved." Big blunt paws folded under his square ebony chest, he sank down on the hearth. "All she did was tell me how wonderful I am," he said modestly, "but she wouldn't try it herself!"

"I've been showing her for a long time how to jump from the floor to the top of the bookcase," Amber put in. "She did make it to the top of the low stool once, but then she fell flat on the floor. Of course, she has no tail to balance with."

"I manage without a tail," Tigger said. (Like all Manx cats, he has only a stump.)

Esmé interrupted. "Tail or no tail, she is afraid of heights. The rest of you weren't around when I climbed to the top of the tallest tree in the yard. I was a very young kitten then. She couldn't even use the ladder by the back door. She had to get the farmer from up the hill. He climbed right up, hand over hand."

Amber gathered herself together, her back legs thrusting like a rocket, tail swinging, arms full length. She landed in the middle of the high shelf where the Belleek tea set lives.

"Let's think this all over," she told them. "I fear we may have to stop this experiment. There is no sign of progress."

"I told you so," said Esmé. "Either we have to get a better

subject or do over our program with a different approach."

"I resign," said Holly. "I don't want to hurt her feelings. Nothing is worth that to me."

The cockers put their heads together, breathing heavily.

"But it may be our fault," Little Sister said. "I missed scent discrimination at the Obedience Trials that time when I knew exactly what I should do—bring back the one object she had touched and let the rest alone. But I never brought that wooden dumbbell. I sniffed a lot but I never picked it up."

"Why not?" asked Holly. "I found that part of the test a cinch. Never missed."

"Possibly because she had *painted* a fresh number on the dumbbell the night before and all it smelled of was paint."

There was a brief silence.

"So what?" asked Holly.

"So she had *made a mistake!* The test couldn't work because of human error. I'll tell you what she did. We went home—a long, long way. Then she scraped the paint off, scrubbed that dumbbell, put it in the sun and dragged me to the back yard to try it again, again and again. So I won the Utility Dog at the next show and got some ribbons and stuff."

The implied suggestion that the experimenters should begin all over again fell on deaf ears, whether they folded back flat or hung limp.

"I hereby declare this group dissolved," said Amber from the Belleek. "And after all, even without training, as far as I am concerned she is the best to live with of any human I ever saw."

"Where is she? Why doesn't she come home?" asked Holly.

So they all resigned and went to watch through the picket fence to greet this untrainable human, who, with all her limitations, was the heartbeat of their lives.

That ends the fantasy, but leaves a bit of truth as most fantasies do. To each his own!

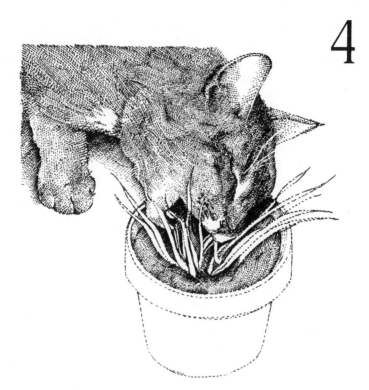

I LIKE TO STUDY conversational patterns, and when I had my Siamese cat, Esmé, I learned that when cat people get together they are as single-minded as vegetarians, or kelp and soybean addicts. For they can talk for hours about what their cats will and will not eat. Once you meet a cat lover you will pursue his or her cat's food predilections endlessly.

"Joseph will only eat X brand of tuna. If I get any other brand by mistake I have to take it back."

"Sam likes mashed potatoes but will not eat carrots."

"Petunia loves any kind of tuna fish but never touches crab or shrimp."

I usually keep quiet, for Amber probably has the most unbalanced diet known to catdom. Because of an early illness, her insides are what used to be called "delicate." Her basic food is baby food. When I buy it myself, or wait while Millie gets it for me, any new shop clerk eyes us dubiously. We do not look as if we had babies. Explaining that this bagful of strained beef, veal and lamb is for a cat results in looks of utter amazement. Amber also eats minced beef, lamb and chicken, but for vegetables accepts only asparagus tips (I must admit that I get tired of eating the stalks all year round). When I make one of my classic beef stews, she sorts out the carrots, potatoes, onions and so on and eats just the beef.

Under no circumstances will she have any traffic with an egg, although I have cooked eggs dozens of ways for her because I was brought up to believe eggs were *good for you*. But if I open a can of lasagne or ravioli she laps up so much of the sauce that I have to add water (not according to directions) so that I won't be eating plain pasta. She also adores fresh flounder fillet but disdains haddock.

The chops we like best are what I call lamb steaks. They are not as elegant as the thumbnail size or as expensive. But one of them does nicely for us both.

Last night a noted television performer commented on commercials and said that Morris might be a finicky cat, but if he were not fed for ten days he would eat any old kind of cat food. This statement only shows that this man does not know cats—and in fact he raises horses, which seem to be easy-feeding creatures. Let him get a cat!

I have no idea of trying starvation on mine, for I have enough trouble keeping her weight up to five pounds. If she turns down her meals for even two days, her bones begin to stick out.

She also has a throw-up mechanism very much like the one so many children have at an early age. She loves liver but it comes up instantly. As a result, I eat it only when I go out.

I used to panic when she lost a meal, but our beloved Dr. Kim told me long ago to feed her again right away. This has worked miraculously, except for liver, to which she has an allergy as bad as mine for caraway seeds.

I often wish I had known Kim when the children were babies. My one and my housemate Jill's two did get upsets, but in those days one withheld food while the poor small ones squawked like baby birds. Obviously in the baby stage the throwing-up mechanism sometimes triggers for no reason, and it does not mean the poor child should be starved!

There are so many cat foods on the market they cannot be counted, and I am always surprised when a television hour preaches the virtues of three or four different brands in succession, with small bits of the program popped in now and then. Amber occasionally dips into a can of cat food, but only for a small taste.

Having raised cockers and Irish for a long time as well as always having had a cat or two in the kitchen, I might sum up my experience in feeding animals. I have found that both puppies and grown dogs will eat what you decide is best for them. The only one who didn't was Silver Moon, a very special cocker who made a circle of discarded carrots around her dish. But she also had to have a glass of tomato juice every morning. She was the one exception out of thirty-five.

But I have never persuaded a cat to worry about a balanced diet. Esmé, the Siamese, wanted chicken, chicken, chicken and once sent a non-cat guest into hysterics when she landed right on a platter of succulent fried chicken (she preferred dark meat). Tigger, the staid banker-type Manx, supplemented his diet by eating the insides of mice and moles (all kinds of grass and grain bits).

In addition to her regular menu Amber gets a good lap of vitamin syrup, which she eats from the tube. She also chooses the best kind of grass in the lawn or nibbles from the pot I keep for her on the kitchen windowsill.

I get a great deal of mail from anxious cat owners on the subject of diet, and my answer is simple.

"Your cat will tell you what he wants. Supplement his meals, if possible, with some of that gook in the vitamin tube. Then don't worry. Leave a pat of warm butter on his (or her) tray; it's better than spreading butter on the paws, where it gets all mixed up with fur."

Getting something down Amber's small throat when she does not want to swallow it brings out the tiger, cougar and leopard in her, all combined. A pill, for instance, is not welcome. Kim casually hands me an envelope of pretty pink or pale yellow pills whenever she "comes down" with something.

"Give her one quarter of a pill twice a day," he says.

" 'Give' is the wrong word to use," I remind him.

The pill always turns out to be the size of a pinhead. A quarter piece is barely visible. Simple. I tuck it in the middle of a morsel of fresh flounder fillet while I chat with Amber about how delicious it is. Result: the flounder vanishes and the pink or yellow dot stays on the plate.

I have an antique mortar and pestle that is fine for pounding dried herbs and such things, and I once spent some time pulverizing one quarter of a pill in it. I did manage to remove a bit of powder and immerse it in lamb baby food.

"What's wrong with this?" Amber asked, shaking her whiskers. "You had better take it back—it isn't fit to eat!"

During one desperate period when she had a gum infection, I was supposed to rub a cherry-colored liquid on the inflamed gums twice daily. My dear Erwin (the neighboring teenager, who called himself The Help) undertook to manage. We wrapped our small victim in a bath towel from which only a face emerged. One of us propped her mouth open while the other coped with an agitated whirling towel. Sometimes we made contact between a few drops of the liquid and her mouth. Usually we wiped up cherry liquid from the counter, and Erwin went home with a shirt spattered with what looked like blood.

His mother washed his shirt every day until this era ended.

My own feeling about the whole subject is that the manufacturers of all cat medications should realize that a cat can smell anything: all pills or liquids should be absolutely odorless or else they should have the delightful perfume of cod-liver oil. The manufacturers who produce the vitamin syrup in the tube should be awarded a medal. As Amber happily laps the vitamin glob, I can always stop breathing (I too am very sensitive to smells).

Fortunately most cats are naturally healthy! Free-running outdoor cats do sometimes get worms or ear mites, and they should also have distemper inoculations. These are things the veterinarian can cope with quite easily.

Meanwhile, the folklore about cat care goes on. I get considerable mail from cat owners asking if milk will give their kittens worms. And one wrote me that if you put bluing in the milk, your kittens will not have distemper!

Garlic was once used as a cure for worms. Now garlic is a marvelous gift to mankind, I think, and must be good for almost anything. But though I am pleased when Amber helps herself to a dab of spaghetti sauce, I doubt whether it could destroy worms!

In this era of escalating food prices and world hunger, food has become a major crisis in most families and also a main subject of conversation everywhere. There were hard times in my family often as I grew up, but thanks to Mama's skill we ate well enough to suit a gourmet. What I learned then was never to waste anything. Mama was always ahead of her time, and she invented savory stews and casseroles out of odds and ends long before they were fashionable. In her own childhood, for instance, a recipe might call for a dozen eggs or two cups of heavy cream or a cup of pure first-run maple syrup. I found an old newspaper ad for eggs at a dollar for a few dozen. Early recipes calling for a dozen egg yolks meant that the whites were discarded. But Mama never wasted an egg white—it went into angel food cake or a soufflé. An extra yolk ended in a sauce.

She was a pioneer in saving vegetable juices for soups or gravies, and the minute fruit softened, jams or marmalades came to the breakfast table. Leftover bread crisped into croutons or bread crumbs (I know she never bought either one ready-made) or went into creamy bread pudding or a cheese bake. The bones most people tossed into the garbage were simmered with herbs and onions to make stock or broth.

I kept Mama's pattern, but during the affluent era Connie used to come home from college, run to the refrigerator (they all do) and stare in horror.

"Mama, what are you doing with one cooked carrot in a bowl and a tablespoon of peas in a saucer and half a cup of mushrooms in waxed paper?"

"Don't you throw anything away," I would say, "and leave those chicken bones alone!"

I am always reminded of a friend just back from a village in India who cried when he found his wife throwing out a handful of dead lettuce leaves.

"Can't you understand that just one of those lettuce leaves would help a starving child?"

"We can't mail the whole head of lettuce across the ocean," his wife said.

"But if we saved all the wasted food in this country," Dave told her, "we could feed so many people."

Explaining world food problems to Amber is a lost cause, of course.

We do not waste any of her own leftovers, however. Everything goes out in a pan with the lamb trimmings, bits of cheese and extra salad scraps for stray cats and raccoons and of course for any passing skunk. Our trash can has no nourishment in it for bird or beast.

"So you see, Sweet, you must eat every bite of your chop," I tell her.

Her only complaint is that I no longer leave a faucet dripping for her. Since we have wells at both places and live in water areas, this might seem silly. But my cousin Rob has told me the water table is falling all over the country, and we must conserve water or the planet is doomed.

Learning to conserve is the basic lesson for this age and not an easy one for an extravagant generation. I compromise on the water problem by standing near the faucet while she drinks as many drops as she needs; then I turn it off.

"Conserving a cat's water," I say, "may seem odd, but you notice, Amber, that I no longer leave mine running all the time I brush my teeth. I shut it off between brushes."

She settles for a last luscious *plop* before I turn the knob.

Then she takes a drink from her own glass in the living room, polished off with a swig of flower water from the rose bowl.

It all works out, she suggests, but the best water comes dripping from a cold faucet!

Amber is always interested in food, but one subject that stifles her with boredom is the care of cats. When I am answering letters about it, she sits yawning on the typewriter table, now and then reaching a seal-dark arm to poke at the W key, the one that sticks midway to the top.

"It is wrong to carry a kitten by the nape of the neck," I explain, poking her paw away. "A mother cat carries very young babies that way for one reason: It is the only way she can. And it is only when they are a few ounces in weight."

Amber couldn't care less, as the saying goes, since she has no kittens.

"A kitten's neck bones are delicate; so is the throat," I am typing as I talk. "A human grabbing a cat by the nape of the neck can damage the throat or even strangle the cat."

Amber manages a small purr as she knocks the pen from the table and decides to pursue it to the most inaccessible place under the desk. After I move some furniture and sit down again, I am through with mentally carrying kittens and am ready for the next subject.

"Amber, please don't claw all those papers up," I say. "I have trouble enough sorting them."

"As for declawing," I type, with her tail swishing my face, "nature gave the cat claws to climb with. They provide a good handhold but also a balance. They belong to the whole animal. Trim them regularly but don't remove them altogether."

Amber, now on my shoulder, is holding herself steady with her own claws.

"Time to go to Dr. Kim for a manicure," I remark.

Most cats try to do a home clip on their curving claw tips, but it is not easy. Some owners, with the use of professional nail clippers, can manage. However, if you clip too close, you may cut blood vessels and a flood of red will result. I have the proper clippers but not the courage, so we wait for our friend Olive to come or we go to Dr. Kim's.

Now and then a kitty will work on a log on the hearth to control the growth, or even use a scratching post, but none of the cats in my life ever would.

Amber gets restless at this point and wants to sit on my lap and claw my work pants.

"I have to finish this page," I say, "and then we'll have supper."

My typewriter clacks on. . . . All kittens should be checked by a good veterinarian, given inoculations, examined for worms. Gift kittens from pet shops may have various ailments packed in with them, but even those born in the master bedroom should be popped onto the doctor's table; it doesn't take long and helps to ensure a long healthy life. Outdoor cats should be regularly checked for ear mites, fleas and worms, which they pick up from wildlife or from any of the neighbors' pets that run loose.

During shedding season cats swallow dead fur while polishing their coats. Amber manages to disgorge small balls of apricot fuzz on her own—always in the middle of the night, and coughing like a Model A Ford. Some cats need a dose of prescription medicine from the veterinarian to get rid of hair balls. But daily brushing and combing can take care of this problem for the most part. It also helps if a little butter is available. If a cat is exposed to fleas, either out of doors or by a visiting fireman, a trip to the doctor is better than a remedy from the drugstore. A steel flea comb is extra insurance. These are sold where pet supplies are marketed. Experts have mixed feelings about flea collars—some favor them, while others distrust them. I'm glad that Amber doesn't need one.

"I hope you'll get supper," Amber remarks. She says this by running to the kitchen door, back to my workroom, back to the kitchen.

"Let me just finish one sen—" I am off to save a starving kitten.

The question of spaying or altering cats is much written about. Spaying is a topic I have never discussed with Amber. I doubt that she would understand my concern. She herself was spayed long ago and clearly never gives it a thought.

Keeping a cat safe in the house during the romantic period might be possible if she were shut in a padlocked closet. A determined cat can open an ordinary latch by swinging on it, or work a doorknob around, or find a crack in the baseboard right over the cellar. But she doesn't necessarily have to work at all, for more often than not someone leaves an outside door ajar, or its latch is loose, or a window screen is tired enough to give way, or the mailman lugs in a package. Or the children forget to watch for the shadow of a silent Juliet slipping out behind them.

"Gee, Mom, I never even *saw* her!"

I never wanted to risk having Amber produce a family fathered by some passing tomcat. And, after planning just which champion Abyssinian would be the father of Amber's first babies, I learned that the doctor had discovered she had a large cyst. Not motherhood but an operation would follow.

I save my thoughts on neutering and spaying for cat and dog owners who write asking my opinion. My thoughts are brief but definite. Unless an owner plans to keep and care for the offspring of the cat or dog, it is imperative to spay females or neuter males when the veterinarian advises. From the time I was very young and brought home a paper bag full of newborn kittens someone had thrown out, I learned what can happen. Nobody can count the number of homeless, starving cats roaming city alleys or of puppies finally picked up by animal rescue crews. If an owner can accommodate the extras (I have one friend who manages seventeen cats, half of them charity cases) that is fine. But few can accommodate a horde.

Siamese and Abyssinians may have only one or two babies in a litter, but domestic shorthairs have a basketful. Our cockers varied from two to eight, although four or five is more customary. An Irish is happy with thirteen.

At one time we had thirty-five cockers, two Irish and three cats, but theoretically we were running a kennel, and on forty acres of country land exercise was no problem. Most of the time we waded through dogs and cats in the farmhouse. This was ideal since we had time to housebreak and obedience-train them, which was a pleasant change from canning tomatoes.

But in an apartment in the city or a small house in a town, numbers must be limited and free puppies or kittens are not easy to find good homes for. It is plainly better not to bring them into the world to be destroyed.

"But altered dogs and cats get fat and lazy," I hear frequently.

There is no truth in this. Overfeeding and lack of exercise cause these conditions. Neither is there any personality change in neutered animals. Their natural emotions do not change. Their intelligence does not diminish. And they do not grieve over the lack of offspring. The owners may, and they may project their own feelings onto the animal, but it is human beings who subconsciously worry about having babies or not having them. This is especially true of women, whose life was once meant to be devoted to childbearing.

In the wild state, too, the survival of a species depended on increasing the population at a rapid rate. Life expectancy was short and extinction always threatening. But now the figures as to the homeless, unwanted, starving kittens and puppies are in the millions. So owners should consider carefully before turning Lassie or Pussy out to roam when in heat.

This is most important for cats, whose time of coming in heat varies; no calendar can mark the date. And some of them breed early, while some breed just as the owner decides it is all over—nothing more to bother about.

The fortunate dog and cat lovers who can manage one or two litters are to be envied. There is nothing quite like seeing a few ounces of kitten appear, damp and warm. The first squeak at coming into an alien world is followed at once by the basic urge all living creatures have—to eat! In a jiffy the tiny blind faces turn toward the mother, and a new life-giving supply of sweet milk is at paw's end. It always brings to the watcher a sense of mystery and of the miracle of life itself.

If the last baby born seems weak, the mother begins licking the tiny body, rubbing life into it, working especially on the throat. The more vigorous ones get a brisk going-over, but the least one gets a real massage. One wonders how the mother, faced with a tangle of squirming morsels, realizes that one of them is in trouble.

Nature's wisdom keeps the eyes sealed during the transition between that inner security and the new world. Sometimes one milk-blue eye opens first, then suddenly two wide blank eyes begin to focus. From then on it is a short time until puppies or kittens are popping from the playpen or nursery box and the mother takes time out for a good run and a check on the kitchen. The littlest one may whimper, the rest fold into sleep.

It is hard to imagine any owner who could gather up the whole bundle of warm eager babies and have them destroyed or, worse, toss them out to starve to death.

Thinking about this, I mince the best of the lamb chop for Amber.

"Nobody has to have a dog or cat or any pet," I tell her, "but once you get one, you have a responsibility. They are not toys. Actually the richness of any relationship depends on caring."

Amber dives into the lamb—her favorite edible. She doesn't poke the bits around with a paw; she seems to breathe in the juicy bits.

"At least you do not worry because you've never had any kittens," I say. "So far as you are concerned, the sun always shines!"

5

IN SUMMER ON CAPE COD the air is warm with
the scent of sweet fern and salt, the gulls glint against the pure
turquoise sky, the clouds seem to follow their own reflections
on Mill Pond. It is a season for wild blackberries and fresh-
picked mint in a tall icy glass. And it is a time for summer
visitors. Jill's son, David, comes with his family, then her
daughter, Barbara, with hers, and finally my daughter, Connie,
with the grandchildren.

This year, on the brink of the visiting season, I decided
to have a word or two with Amber. "Settle down in my lap,"
I said. "We have something to discuss."

Amber felt a monologue coming along and arranged her
tail neatly.

"We're not islanded," I began, "but part of a family. You remember last summer when David and Anne and their three children, together with an extra girl from Thailand and a very large, ebullient setter named Tomato Honey, all spent five weeks in that cottage down the road? Tomato Honey was named because David remembered the days when I used to make that special preserve at the farm and he loved it. So Tomato Honey is her registered name. You had to get used to a whirlwind blowing in, a bevy of youngsters, all dripping from Mill Pond. Finally you gave up hissing and swelling and hid on the top shelf of the bookcase."

Amber listened, eyes wide.

"Now Barbara and Val do not have a dog or cat as yet because they are flying too much in the course of their careers. Ellen, their daughter, is at Yale in law school—no pets allowed. But Davy, the son, who's about to graduate from Haverford, tells me he will have a big dog, probably a golden retriever, as soon as he lives off campus. And they are all likely to be coming to see us this summer."

Amber poked dreamily at her brush—and got results.

"But let's consider the subject of *another cat* in the family. As Connie's mother, I feel sad that living in a New York apartment has meant no pets for her and Alice and Anne, but now my granddaughters are old enough to help out—seventeen and fourteen. When Connie is teaching at Barnard and gets in late, they are back from school. So they could keep the kitten company. Eventually they will have a cocker or two and, if they leave the city, maybe even an Irish. Meanwhile they could now have a *cat*, which I hope will be an Abyssinian.

"They do need something. Now since they spend more time with us than the other children do, both at the farm and on Cape Cod, it means that if they do have a kitten, it will be with them whenever they come, right in your own territory—probably sleeping with Anne but listening to Alice when she practices her violin.

"This kitten will be a resident. I want it understood that

she will *not* be mine. Your exclusive position will never be menaced. If I love her, as I am sure to, you must realize it will have no effect on my cherishing you. That is timeless.

"Let me put it this way." I laid down the brush because my wrist was tired. "Alice and Anne are not mine either, but I love them without diminishing a whit my love for their mother. You have been able to concentrate your whole heart on one person, but the mystery of love is that it can spill over and only deepen. Even the greatest psychologists, Sweet, cannot explain this."

The July sunlight glowed on apricot fur as she turned over to have her stomach rubbed.

"When they come with that kitten, I know you will be furious—I was about to say you are only human, but I won't. We shall take practical steps. A good many necessary lessons life teaches us, and one is that No is inevitable. Your No will be to stop hissing, getting your claws spread out, fur upended, tail spinning. You will stay in the bedroom while the invader quiets down and explores the rest of the house, fortified by a snack and a game with a catnip mouse (not your own). Later the bedroom door will open a crack with one of you on each side. She may yowl while you make your tiger sound.

"Then she will retire from the battlefront to the den with Alice and Anne while you establish sovereignty. Extravagant praise for you. The next step involves tolerance of her breathing the same air. Finally, the only problems in the house will be that Anne has lost her sneakers, Alice needs time to wash her hair again. Connie's purse has vanished and we are overdue at the Lobster Claw for dinner.

"When they leave, you will walk lonely through the house as I do." I gave her a final pat. "Now that this is all cleared up, I'll do a lamb chop for supper."

"I was ready to stand by the refrigerator to suggest it," Amber said.

———————

I don't usually favor pointing out people's faults, but that discussion of Amber's jealousy led me to think about the whole business of getting along with people. As always, once she had finished supper she was ready to hear my views on still another subject. I took a fresh cup of coffee and tried to explain how I felt.

I have noticed that my friends—and family—often begin a talk by saying, "Of course I don't mean to criticize, *but* . . ." This means that I will stiffen up and try to listen patiently because even though I know that arguing is less successful than the siege of Quebec, always agreeing damages my thin self-esteem. Further, I know that defending my behavior never, never persuades the critic, who inevitably *knows better.* The best reply is a gentle silence, which may make the critic uncomfortable. Whoever first said a soft answer turneth away wrath (is that in my Bible?) was about as wrong as anyone could be, for a soft answer invites a prolonged explanation of everything you have done wrong!

My special refuge is to think about something else as my flaws are explained all over again—all for my own good, as I know. I think about the weather or the flight of the cardinals in the yard—so light, so easy, delicate as falling leaves—or, more practically, what we might have for supper.

This involves discipline, and discipline is never easy. For I may begin to list my own faults and weaknesses as long as the subject has been brought up. And that list is encyclopedic and more depressing than anything the friend or family can think of.

I really believe in praise and feel it is the worst shortage we have in this era. A few words of praise ease the heart and there is always—yes, always—something to praise in anyone you meet. For instance, a very rude and bored lady clerk responds to being told that her blouse is a lovely color or that her silver medallion is so interesting—all of which are not lies. Then, instead of sending me scuttling off like a scared rabbit, she takes the shelves apart looking for an extra pair of curtains that may or may not be in stock.

What does it cost to be polite? Certainly no more than to find fault. I remember the filling station youngster who looked as if he wanted to wind the gas hose around the neck of every customer, but who did wash the back windshield for me.

"Thank you very much," I said. "I'll have easier driving all day."

He dropped the long brush and stared at me. "Nobody ever says thank you any more," he said.

This impressed me so much that I wrote about it, for it started a long time of thinking for me about social behavior.

So now, Amber, I want to begin by saying that you are not only beautiful but absolutely wonderful. As my companion, you are perfect. When I am sad, you comfort me; when I am happy, you fly through the air needing no wings. When I cannot bear to get up in the morning, your purring in my ear and your patting my cheek with a thimble-sized paw help me decide the day won't be too bad after all. When I work, you are ready to poke the typewriter keys to show me how easy it is. When I have to go out, I always know a small triangle of face will be in the window. You are seldom more than a few feet away from me unless you get shut in a bureau drawer or are sleeping on the top shelf of the bookshelves. If I read too long, an interruption such as a velvet arm reaching out to flip the pages over is always welcome.

However—and what would we do without the word "however"—I do want to discuss something with you seriously, now that you have eaten all the asparagus tips and I have made do with the stalks. This has to do with that subject of social grace.

A great many people come to our house just to meet you. In fact, yesterday a very nice couple turned up all the way from Oregon.

"I don't read books," explained the husband, "but my wife does. I do like cats, though, and since my wife told me about your book about your cat, we came to see Amber."

So what did you do? You hissed at the wife as she tried to pick you up and then all we saw was the vanishing tip of a velvet tail. Now all you had to do was sit and be admired. I wouldn't ask you to purr, for I know purrs are for personal loving. But you could at least have stayed in sight for a few minutes.

As you know, this is not an isolated instance. And no matter how much I try to cover up, I can't. You heard, from under the bedspread in my bedroom, what that frank woman said.

"My, what an unfriendly cat!" she said.

I couldn't explain that you are a passionately adoring cat with me, since that would have made it worse. I could not apologize for your putting me in what can only be called a spot, and I spent a miserable hour with the man who doesn't read but loves cats and his wife, who came many miles to meet you. All that kept me sane was wondering why putting someone in a "spot" always means a disaster? As any TV commercial can explain, Wisk or some other detergent will banish spots—and leave no ring around the collar either—but the spots you put me in, Amber, are not so easily dealt with.

The worst problem is when parents bring rosy, energetic small children who are enraptured at one glimpse of your beautiful apricot fur and onyx eyes and your smallness (five pounds is a nice toy size). Children at any age move like lightning and so they often cut off your retreat. They get small stubby hands around your stomach and squeeze hard as they sweep you up.

Your behavior at that point is deplorable. You not only hiss but spread your paws into clawing position. Your tail swells to balloon size. Your whiskers stand out quivering.

Now I do not mean to criticize you, but it would be a big

help to me if you would make a small change in your life-style. If you could bring yourself to greet guests quietly for just a few moments, maybe even allowing one pat per person, it would make life a lot less difficult for me.

Actually, I do not mind your being exclusive and I have a feeling that, were you starved for affection, you would welcome any stranger who opened the door. And after everyone has gone, I enjoy your snuggling in my neck and purring the high-level purr. Perhaps if you were a lap-sitter on any old lap that was available, I would not feel quite so cherished as I do!

But I am confused about your whole attitude, for any workman who turns up finds you poking under the sink with him or chatting with him in the bathroom as he takes the insides of the toilet apart.

"Got a nice cat there," I hear. "She ever have kittens? I would certainly like one."

Then why cannot you exhibit a little social grace toward other visitors?

Amber, please try to be less fiercely aloof when guests come. When I am trying so hard to be welcoming, at least do not hiss.

Now we have come to an understanding about this, I shall toss that shabby felt mouse for you and toss my own thoughts in the air with it. I think a great deal about love (and certainly tell you endlessly how I love you). Love is the foundation of living. The Bible has more about it than I can remember. Love has more facets than any other emotion the heart experiences. Without it there would be no poetry or music, no truly great men and women to give light to the dark of history. And we are told that God so loved the world, he gave his only begotten son, that little peasant babe born in a stable who lived to be more important than any emperor or king in all the centuries.

(Your ball is under the sofa? I'll fish it out.)

I want to think about something that love involves which is often forgotten. Love involves responsibility. Too often people in love do not want to accept this. Why not? Responsibility is a heavy word and can be a heavy burden. But without it we do not have love.

If I say, "I love you madly," it should mean that I will put up with you when you are difficult. I will forgive you when you hurt me, will share your sorrows, comfort you, sustain you. This is an enormous job.

Put it simply. A fire in the fireplace is heartwarming, glowing bright, but it involves having someone ready to lug more logs in from the woodshed, poke the wood, clean the hearth. No fire keeps burning without being tended. Even a candle will not send a soft light unless a match is held to the wick and the excess wax is carefully scooped up as it drips.

I must remember that I have responsibilities to those I love. These responsibilities may be dull, time-consuming, a nuisance, but they are there. Otherwise that word "love" is as thin as a piece of carbon paper.

(Your ball is under the television set? I'll get it, but why do you always toss it where it is hardest to reach? Why do I crawl around retrieving your toys all the time? Because I love you—that is why.)

You too feel responsibility, although some people say you are just a cat. You protect me from all sorts of dangers, such as that field mouse who got in from the cellar, the moth zooming around the corners, the coons in the yard. You bring your favorite toys to plop on my pillow. You tell me when anyone comes to the door—not by barking, of course, but with tail lashing. You turn the pages of my book with a helpful paw. If I am absentminded—as I so often am—and the house gets cold, you sit by the register to remind me to turn the furnace up.

If I am happy, you go about your own affairs, but if I am sad, you leap onto my chest and start snuggling and purring a comfort purr. You give me the gift of sharing my feelings, day or night.

So perhaps I should not object if you fail to observe the social amenities with strangers or guests. Instead I should think about all the times I myself fail to give enough to others, fail to have enough patience, enough understanding, enough compassion.

(I do have to say, however, that if you roll that ball under the refrigerator one more time, it will stay there. Or if you put it under the middle of my bed. I cannot move that bed again. You will have to settle for that miserable felt mouse that does not roll. My responsibility as a ball chaser is limited because, after all, I am only human!)

Now we shall stop this one-sided conversation on a note of my deep appreciation of the fact that you always let me talk and you listen. Very often when human beings are together, there is no listening. It is sometimes difficult to finish a sentence—it simply disappears in a tangle of voices. Everyone wants to talk, nobody cares to listen. The result is that whosoever is impelled to speak raises his or her voice. If there is a group, I usually think of a hen yard invaded by a random fox. I then try to wrap a bit of silence around me—at least I myself do not add to the noise. But you have the magic gift of listening, and your comments are quiet—a flick of your tail, a widening of your beautiful eyes, a velvet purr or at most a faint miaow not as sharp as a mouse squeak. Moreover, whenever I speak to you, you do not ignore me—you don't go looking out of the window or skipping out to have a snack in the kitchen. You keep your pointed shell-pink ears attentive.

What a treat!

A walk in the peach-gold glow of the summer sunset, while both of us listen to the mockingbird practicing trills from the tip of the wild pear tree, is the best end to such a serious conversation.

An important part of loving someone, of course, is learning to accept that person's individual qualities, but the mystery of personality is one that will never be unraveled—or so it seems to me. Individuals inherit from their own species, as well as from the environment. They develop by the impact of circumstances. The location, the climate, the period in history all shape them. But every single living creature continues to be an entity.

A child born in remote Africa, a child native to Switzerland, a child breathing his first difficult breath in the smog of a city in America—they all face the journey from birth to death along different highways. They all, however, have one similarity: They are human beings, although no two are exactly alike.

Parents cannot understand how this can be, but they are aware of it. "I can't get over it," a mother says. "We raised them the same way. But Jerry and Bob are different as night and day."

"Well, Jerry gets that stubborn streak right from you," the father says.

"So Bob never gets anywhere on time any more than you do," says the mother.

A lot of energy is spent in most families tracing the worst traits in the offspring to the other parent.

People are fumbling with the mystery of personality, but they usually end by turning their thoughts to something easy like whether or not there are flying saucers!

Naturalists fortunate enough to study birds discover that, although the nestlings may look alike, one fledgling gets out of the nest first while another is timid, more dependent and gets the small end of the worm. One takes to the air as if flying were wonderful. Another tips back and forth at the edge of the nest, retreats, staggers, tumbles out squawking and may even fall. The distracted parents, especially the mother, swirl around, scolding, cajoling.

I myself was fortunate enough to see a pair of Canada geese on Mill Pond, right below my window, teaching their babies how to swim. One parent led the procession, one was rear guard. I could not tell which parent led. The puffball babies splashed in between. Some paddled with determination, some partially submerged at times, the least one in the rear obviously only longed to be under a mothering wing and the rear parent kept nudging that one along. All of them churned up the water.

The leading parent swam with head swiveled around to watch every moment. The father and mother moved effortlessly, tall, graceful, proud but obviously nervous. The children seemed too tiny to belong to such stately parents.

But no two reacted to the desperate adventure in the same way. Personality was already emerging. I watched until they all reached the shingle a third of the way on this side of Mill Pond. I longed to get down the steep bank, fish out the tiniest one and carry him myself, a mistake parents so often make in my own species.

The Canada geese were wiser. Somehow their offspring had to learn how to live in their own world. And nobody drowned. But I could pick out the one who would someday lead the flight when that long triangle makes the annual journey, while we landborne humans listen to the wild, moving farewell.

Amber hears it and it means something to her, although I cannot explain what. She listens, she watches, her tail comments.

"The geese are going over," I say. "I pray for happy landings."

Since they mate for life, I feel an extra anxiety. Sometimes when a group swims across Mill Pond, I see one alone, an outsider whose mate is gone. No matter how I count, there are nine in the group where there should be ten.

In the animal world I have had the closest opportunity to study the personalities of newborn puppies. As they fumble blindly toward their first meal, every one is already a different personality. One is gentle, one is quick, one is slow but determined.

Cats are just as surprising. One family of our barn cats all look alike, grey with white markings. The young are small copies of the mother. But there the resemblance ends. The timid one hides behind a rock or peers through the hedge. He wants to eat alone. The brave one, of course, is trying to get in the kitchen door. One small one rubs against the nearest human, purring.

I never knew Amber's siblings, but Connie saw them when she went to bring Amber home.

"She's the smallest, Mama," Connie said.

"That's the right one then."

Timid she never was. (Her character does not reflect the general character of her breed.) She is passionate, fierce, always sure of herself, always independent. She is a lap-sitter only with me, quite indifferent to the advances of most other people, who admire her even though she hisses at them if they try to cuddle her. She is possessive and jealous with regard to me. She has a few people she cares for but is seldom demonstrative with them. She has a special feeling for Connie, which may mean that she remembers Connie as the one who brought her from the cattery cage. She will play games with Anne, but so would a tiger cub in the jungle. She is charmed by Alice's violin. Otherwise she is remote.

Heredity gave her the beauty of a champion, environment shaped her in many ways, but her inner self, I feel, is something especially her own, inexplainable. I doubt whether any of her forebears were exactly like her, and as for environment, her home with me is the same as that of all my cockers, Irish, cats. Yet she is completely different from all the rest.

During the first part of her life the house was full of children, parents and visitors. Moreover, the family has always been animal-oriented. But this did not make her a party girl. From the first minute I picked her up, she established ownership of me exclusively. Now that we are alone most of the time, I notice she is happy to have Millie come and follows her around helping do the housework and getting in the way all the time. She is secretly fond of Olive but wary, since Olive is the one who clips her claws when we can't get to the veterinarian and who pokes a pill down a reluctant throat when necessary. But when other people come, Amber leaps to the shelf and settles in the midst of the delicate Irish china, preserving a good distance from anyone in the house, as I have said.

And even I, who have known her all her life, can never understand her completely. In the end, the only individual I can really understand is myself, and even this is questionable. After all, I am the one creature I have lived with day and night since my first wail at arriving in the world.

But how many human beings can study their own personalities or analyze themselves objectively? Those I know seem to nourish an image of what they wish to be and then insist that this image is reality!

When I think about my own personality, I can trace outcroppings of heredity. I know there are bits and pieces of my parents in me, such as being nonaggressive like my mother but in a crisis feeling my face flush as Papa's did and anger exploding like a volcano. Or my ability to see two sides of any coin, as Mama did, but then suddenly reacting like Papa—to him, there was only one side, the right side. Like my mother I tend to love most people and all animals. My father shared his endearing charm like June sunshine but loved only a few humans and one Irish setter. In fact, after Timmie, the setter, died at fourteen and I got a cocker puppy, Papa said I had betrayed Timmie and never changed his mind about this.

But although I clearly recognize how like I am to both, and realize how much my environment has also shaped me, there is still that inexplicable third part of me that cannot be accounted for but that marks me as an individual personality. Why is it there? What created it?

So the more I live with people and animals, the more I wonder about the mystery of living beings.

When I discuss this with Amber, she pays no attention.

"Amber, much of you I do understand," I say, "but there will always be part of you I cannot explain or analyze."

Amber never interrupts me except by pushing the sofa table drawer open and poking at her brush.

"But let me tell you," I say, "I admit that you understand me so well you know what I am thinking before I say a word. Yet a part of me is as much of a mystery to you as it is to me."

She indicates I have talked enough, pawing the brush out and rubbing her pink nose against my chin.

Thinking is all right up to a point, she suggests, but doing is better!

WHEN A TRIP TO THE VETERINARIAN is due, I take the carrying case from the closet around midnight, when Amber is asleep on the white pillow on the upholstered chair by the fireplace. Amber is like the princess and the pea. The legend has it that the real princess was identified when someone put a pea under a pile of mattresses and the minute she lay down she screamed with pain. Amber is most comfortable on top of layers of softness. She would wish my best cashmere sweater on top of the pillow.

My bed itself is comfortable and the electric blanket nice and soft, but if I toss my best woolen slacks on one corner and add a robe, Amber folds up there, on top of everything. During cleaning day a pile of soiled laundry on the bed is always topped with five pounds of kitten so Millie and I can't get at the washing until her nap is over!

The carrying case is luxurious with its plastic viewing top and cozy bedding, and she rides quietly in it for the five-hour trip from Cape Cod to Stillmeadow. But when it comes out by itself with no typewriter, cartons of manuscripts or suitcases, Amber vanishes. So the first hazard in going to the doctor lies in getting a mini-tiger into the case and battling to include the tail.

She knows instinctively (here is instinct again) where we are bound. With gloomy resignation she crouches in the carrier. In fact, she is so still that I keep looking in to be sure she is there. Once at the doctor's we sit in the waiting room, which is always full of scrambling dogs, howling cats, anxious owners. The biggest dog, on a heavy chain, hauls his owner across the room to us and sticks his nose in the air vents of the carrier. A frisky puppy tries to climb on the top. Amber makes a small ball in the farthest corner. After all, she is an old pro. A few dogs who have had obedience training sit quietly beside their owners and just tremble slightly.

The owners vary from the handsome man who is overdue at the country club for a golf luncheon to a weathered fisherman whose eyes squint from looking at far horizons. There are always elegant ladies carrying their miniature poodles in blankets embroidered with Cheri's name, and next to them a couple of shabby young men with ponytails and ragged jeans and sandals that do not quite fit.

The inevitable small boy with tear-streaked freckles has his puppy in a cardboard carton and the patient is not too ill to claw holes in the sides. When his nose pokes out he is stuffed back in. Next to Amber and me sits a very pregnant young woman with a golden retriever puppy trying unsuccessfully to sit on her lap. My feeling is that she should go in next no matter whose turn it is. And then the small boy, before his carton falls to pieces.

My definition of America is a doctor's waiting room,

especially when it belongs to a veterinarian. Look what happens in that waiting room. Instant friendships blossom like roses in June. The poodle lady comforts the ponytailed young men. She herself once had a puppy who swallowed furniture polish and he survived all right. One of the young men fishes a bottle from his blazer.

"That's the white kind," she says. "I am sure there is no ammonia in it."

We go the rounds, getting acquainted, and true democracy works better here than it usually does. By the time the big sliding door to the treatment room opens and the doctor calls, "Who's next?" the country-club man has given up his turn, as has the about-to-be mother. The poison case is next, although it should have been last. The cat who fell from the roof follows. By now everybody is on a first-name basis and sharing all their troubles.

Amber and I go in last, since her problems are minor. Dr. Kim gets out the nail clippers. Amber is already regressing to the jungle. As always, she seems to have eight flailing arms and legs, together with at least two lashing tails and a healthy scream.

"Well, Amberino," says Kim, "not much wrong with you!"

His hands are slim, with long fingers suggesting a musician. The wrists are supple too. But these hands could lift my Irish setter and carry her up the hill to the hospital as if she were a feather. Now they move like lightning flashes with the clippers, and one tiny apricot paw after another takes less than three minutes.

"If they could only understand," says Kim.

Amber does understand. Her claws bother her when they are too long. She puts on a show only to establish her independence. As her audience, we do not behave well, for her show is hilarious. We laugh.

Today Kim checks Amber's ears while she flattens them

against her head. He listens to her heart and as a final insult takes her temperature.

"Perfect," he says in his light, easy voice. "Right out of the book!"

Back in the carrying case, the tiger turns into a demure small princess. The wild, spreading paws fold up, the tail diminishes, the last hiss subsides.

When we get home, her remark is easy to understand. "Took you long enough to drive back."

Then she leaps to her tray on the kitchen table and paces until a dish of minced lamb or beef helps her get her strength back. It comes back with a rush and she whirls around the house, almost flying. She has a speed that would get her a ticket from any police officer. As I restore myself with hot coffee, I see only a blur of apricot marking her flight.

The ultimate goal is my lapful of purring, kneading (how good the paws feel now) peace.

"Now, Amber, we must have a serious discussion about the way you carry on at Kim's. I admit you do not claw me or bite me or even scratch the doctor. We've seen him mopping the blood from his hands after some other cat has clawed him. But that cat might have had a broken leg. You don't even hurt anywhere. Next time I want you to be a lady—a gentle, demure lady."

How easy it is to give advice! But how difficult to practice self-control ourselves. Who am I to feel superior? Our previous trip to Kim's was some weeks ago when Amber obviously suffered what Victorians called a malaise. The weather was so bad I tried home nursing before venturing out. She decided not to eat. She was not, she said, in pain. She kept on bird-watching and occasionally took a paw to her pink felt mouse. But minced lamb, chopped chicken, beef—even asparagus tips—had no appeal. When I made a ham sandwich for my lunch, she even ignored the tidbits of her favorite pink meat (not on her diet list).

So off to Kim's the minute the rain let up a bit and we could make it to the car. This time Amber was reasonably polite to the doctor.

"Temperature absolutely perfect," Kim said. "Ears the cleanest on Cape Cod. Mouth and throat fine. No sign of her intestinal problem—let's see, the last one was during Watergate."

"But she won't eat and she doesn't leap around. She doesn't even try to catch the typewriter keys!"

He looked thoughtful. "Is everything all right with you?"

"Well, no, it isn't. I've been upset lately over some problems one of the children is facing—a situation I can't help with."

He popped Amber back into her carrier. "That's it," he said. "Remember, Amberino is a very sensitive cat. If you are upset, she will be too." He handed a small bottle to me. "I know you can't get pills into her, but see if three drops of this twice a day will go down."

Trying to be gay when one's heart aches is quite a job, but for Amber I would probably try to crawl across the Rockies. So I talked it over with her on the way home.

"Dear love, things do work out, usually. And if not, we must remember that it was my own ancestor who first said, 'What can't be cured must be endured.' I apologize for loading my troubles on you."

I put on my favorite John Denver record, "Sunshine," and instead of sitting with my head in my hands got back to work. It wasn't long before a small inquisitive nose poked onto the typewriter carriage. John Denver's music, the click of typewriter keys and the second-degree purr blended comfortably.

That day Amber finished two jars of beef, three servings of minced chicken and one of asparagus tips. She gave herself a conscientious scrubbing and took one of her skipping tours of the whole house.

This gave me something to think about. I began with the

shopworn cliché "No man is an island." Each of us affects those around us, willingly or not. There is, I believe, some kind of aura that emanates (if an aura can emanate), intangible but actual. When we consider two beings who love one another, this intensifies.

I am dependent on Amber in many ways, but she is also dependent on me for much more than food, warmth, a cozy lap and brushing on call. She expects serenity.

I think of two people who love each other. There must also be mutual dependence in the relationship. Often in a crowded room a look flashes between them, as distinct a signal as the Chatham light on the Cape for ships to steer by. Some of the glow in their look brightens that room.

We are mutually dependent is the message.

This is a pretty serious thought because it adds responsibilities to each one. In this era of Women's Lib, the emphasis is so often on the independence of woman, the complete separation of the sexes. The danger is that life will become a battleground. Since I do not believe in war, this saddens me. Real happiness to me involves depending on and offering dependability to another.

"I don't know what this is all about," Amber purrs. "Let's go out and check on the cardinals and that silly mockingbird."

"All right. But I promise you I'll see to it that I do better about giving way to depressions."

As we walked, the sun came out and mysteriously my heart was singing.

The first time Amber was ever seriously sick was when she was struck with what seemed to be a bad case of intestinal trouble—of course in the middle of the night. The next morning I rushed her to Dr. Kim. He gave her a calm but very careful going-over.

"Has there been any serious trouble at your house?" he asked me. "Is anything wrong?"

"Why?"

"Well, she has an attack of colitis," he said, "and it could be caused by tension."

Then I remembered that a group of friends had spent the previous evening at the house. To say it was a disturbed group puts it mildly. This was at the climax of Watergate. Voices were at top level.

"I guess it was Watergate," I said.

So when we got home, I went around singing "Happy Days Are Here Again," and whenever someone dropped in I welcomed the visitor with a request. "Don't mention Watergate. It made Amber sick."

"Makes me sick too," was always the answer.

The closeness of an animal to the family is not always understood except by people who are owned by one. But I should have had more sense, for in the past whenever there was trouble in the family our cockers and Irish collapsed. Fortunately in our family we have never had shouting conflicts as some do.

I have come to believe that dogs and cats reflect the owner's personality. They are even more dependent on the emotional atmosphere than are children, who are, in my experience, more independent. When I am asked what to do about a nervous, high-strung or even uncontrollable pet, I always find that the atmosphere in that particular house is tense, difficult and usually noisy as well. The best remedy for the animal is to calm down the humans.

Sounds are extremely important to animals, for their hearing is more acute than ours is. Voices raised in anger really hurt their ears. (They do mine, too.)

I note sometimes that the voices of humans change even after maturity. When my own vocal cords get tired, my voice grows slightly husky. In the past few weeks, Amber has added something new to hers. The delicate miaow becomes a chirp, a single note much like the sound my mockingbird utters when he wants service at the birdbath (nobody ever washes as much as he does). Amber's chirp means there is something she does not like, such as my absorption in a book. The strange part is she adds a firm purr, meaning that she still loves me. This dual chirp and purr always gets instant results.

Amber is most vocal before I get up in the morning. Cats and dogs, I know, have a better sense of time than I have. Amber never gets me up too early, but if I have been up until 1:00 A.M. and am really not alive at our usual rising time (which is more often than not), she will wait patiently until exactly ten minutes of nine and begin purring her loudest purr right in my ear. Then she starts kneading my chest in an authoritative fashion and follows that by rubbing her head against my cheek. As a last resort, she nibbles my hair. This always gets results because I begin to wonder what is in the hair spray used at the beauty parlor. Suppose she got a layer of lacquer in her flower-petal mouth?

So the day's conversation begins.

"I'm up! You're right—it *is* time. But I haven't been away anywhere except in the far country of dreams."

"Purr, purr, purr," Amber offers.

When I sit up groggily (how I hate morning!), she rolls over and presents a feather-soft stomach to be rubbed. This is the only time she ever goes so far to persuade me how vulnerable she is.

Lately we have changed one detail in our morning pattern —another example of how important it is to widen the horizons of understanding. It came to me, after one of our visits to Dr. Kim for the theatrics of nail clipping, that she might associate being swooped up as a prelude to being popped into the carrying case.

So recently I began carrying her under my arm not just from shower to bedroom but also from bedroom to kitchen, *every* morning, singing cheerily, "Breakfast coming up!"

Loud, emphatic purrs accompany us, along with my off-key singing. Carrying can lead to something desirable, she now admits! It no longer even means she will be shut in the bedroom because a strange dog or cat has come to invade her domain.

I admit that my ego has been bolstered by this new pattern. And as usual I relate this small happening to larger areas. Forming happy habits in a family might often make life have less friction. Take, for example, the door-slamming of the very young. This has always been beyond me. Perhaps the in and out, slam, slam, out and in, slam is a subconscious assertion of self. In my house it is just as easy to close the doors as bang them.

Now back to the subject of time. When the unfortunate "spring forward, fall back" periods occur, Amber and I are both upset.

"Now, Amber, it is *not* going to be the time you think it is. Let me figure: we lose an hour—or do we gain it? So if we get up at ten of nine it is not going to be ten of nine. Do you follow me? It is one of the government's ordinary mistakes. But this is our country; we have to go along."

We have problems for a while. For the first few days we leave our clocks according to our own time, although I change my watch so I won't turn up at the wrong hour for a luncheon date. Then we face the fact that Amber is hungry and lonesome an hour before rising time. And by four thirty in the afternoon I am ready to get supper (even though the clocks say that it is only three thirty).

During this period, if I sit up until one, I explain to Amber that it is only midnight but agree that a snack is in order anyway. She flies to the kitchen counter. A bit of minced steak or flounder fillet is acceptable while I have half of a toasted English muffin.

In the morning we discuss getting up. "Amber, man should not be a slave to clock time," I say. "I think our world is far too mechanical. Nature's own time is better. Nature's rhythm of seasons depends on no dial. But you and I live by the clock because other people in the United States do. Consequently it is now too early to get up, so plop down by my shoulder and turn off the purr machine."

After a last paw poke on my nose she gives in, but I know she has a lower estimate of my intelligence.

One of my most admired friends has only one flaw. I tell myself every man must have one, but I think this is a serious one. Bill thinks cats are stupid, ignorant and care only for themselves. Somewhere in his childhood he must have encountered a stupid cat. I never have. I have also never met a cat who did not relate to human beings if possible. Even the barn cats who visit the farm daily are anxious for affection. As for intelligence, anyone who has ever known a cat really well feels that this cat is superior to most Harvard professors in brain power.

Whether or not a cat can grasp the principle of daylight saving time is a minor matter.

So far as she is concerned, Amber is the one cat in the world. At the farm in Connecticut we have always been foster parents of the barn cats who come across the road from George's barn to spend their days around the well house, which is right by the back kitchen door. They come for two reasons: to get a varied diet and to be loved. George lives down the road and only stays long enough to care for his Black Angus steers. He has a full-time job in town, as many farmers now do.

The cats get warm milk at milking time, keep the inevitable rat population under control and bed down in the sweet-smelling hay. But sometimes they have their babies at our house, under the terrace where they have scooped out a warm nursery. A few are definitely wild and approach a banquet of chicken or fish only after the donor goes inside the house, but most of them are hungry for affection and try to get into the back kitchen. One lusty young male once made it inside by taking the screen from the door.

My granddaughters, Alice and Anne, take turns going out to play with them. The wilder ones watch wistfully. All of them completely refute the people who tell me that cats put up with humans only to get fed.

Our first house cats, Esmé and Tigger, used to accept the daily guests as part of the landscape. But Amber views them with a mixture of scorn and hatred. If one turns up when she is out on her leash checking her own territory, there is no détente. She attacks with more courage than sense, for anyone practiced in rat killing could demolish her in a minute.

Inside the house she sits on the counter by the back window, lashes her tail, hisses like a steam kettle, flattens her ears. Four paws are in launching position. That one time the male let himself in (we had to get a new screen), we were all down by the pond investigating the muskrats. When we came back, the kitchen seemed to be full of meteors as Amber and the intruder whizzed through the air. Everything movable was scattered around. After order was restored, the exile had an extra meal by the well house while Amber polished down her fur on the highest shelf.

But I wonder—neither cat had a single scratch, no ear was bitten. Was my little princess staging the third act of a drama? Did she scare the wits out of the poor male? Or did he have it in mind to take over as *the* house cat?

I never got a word out of Amber. But she needed a great deal of reassurance. Her ego was flat as a pricked balloon.

"Amber, every love is separate, special," I said. "Nothing could threaten your place in my heart. Even if that kitty moved into the house it wouldn't matter."

———

My first Abyssinian, Aladdin, looked much like her except that, being a male, he lacked the fragile look. He also was the standard weight—around seven or so pounds. But he was completely social in temperament. A houseful of cockers, Irish, two other cats, three children plus assorted adults were fine with him. Whenever a guest's lap was available, he was in it. He met people at the door. But eventually his social grace was his undoing, for at eight months, when someone left the gate ajar, Aladdin went out to become the only member of the family ever to be lost. Some passerby on Jeremy Swamp Road must have stopped to look at this unusually beautiful cat, opened a car door and welcomed Aladdin when he hopped in.

Weeks of hunting every inch of woods, swamps, roads, fields by everyone in the community, plus advertising, radio broadcasts, signs in the village post office and store, had no result. He left an emptiness never to be filled. Years later, through a series of odd circumstances, we heard about a family of cats in a village some distance away who looked remarkably like a picture of Amber that had been published in a newspaper column. Since true Abyssinians were unknown in our region at that time, it seemed obvious our Aladdin must have been adopted and lived to father a family and, I am sure, led a happy life in his new home. The knowledge eased our hearts.

Amber would never have made it. Any hardy soul who picked her up would have been clawed, hissed at, bitten. And I think Amber would have died of grief.

"So, Amber, I'll take your lack of social grace with some comfort," I tell her, even when I try to persuade her to be gracious to strangers.

For losing a dog or cat brings such anguish. I was reminded of this when Olive's Siamese, Boy, went out in the yard at her Cape Cod house one night at sunset and did not come back when called. He is a gentle, sensitive, home-loving cat with no sense of adventure in him.

This is a quiet, wooded area, strictly residential, the neighborhood inhabited by longtime families, all firm friends. The hunt began at dark and by morning a small battalion of searchers started out, organized into road patrols, beach walkers, telephone monitors and the rugged ones like Helen, Vicky, Olive and their guests plunging into what is called the puckerbush, bedded in poison ivy. The local chapter of the Animal Rescue League began their excellent radio alert.

Seventeen hours later Boy turned up. The search crew was battered, barely able to walk, scratched, battling the oncoming poison ivy attacks. Boy admitted he was tired, also hungry, but was otherwise in fine shape. The mystery addicts among the humans sat before the open fire having snacks and drinks, every one a Sherlock Holmes. The consensus was that somehow Boy must have slipped into a shed or garage with a door ajar and decided to take a nap, whereupon someone closed the doors and went off to spend a weekend with the children.

"But he never wanders out of the yard," said Olive.

"And nobody was away, so far as we know," said Helen.

Boy slept cozily on the hassock by the hearth.

It was strangest of all to hear for several days on the radio the broadcast message, "Lost, Mill Pond, Orleans, Siamese cat, male, answers to the name of Boy." Boy would be placidly eating fresh shrimp at the same time. It was a relief when the tape was cut off.

I remember another time Boy disappeared. Olive spends only summers on Cape Cod and goes back to New Jersey for the school year. Boy loves Cape Cod. He and his housemate, Spunky, the dying kitten Olive rescued on a stormy night, are supposed to be in the house prior to departure around Labor Day so they can be popped into the car at the last minute.

But Boy is psychic. One day at the end of summer it was especially important for his mistress to leave on time for the long trip. Car loaded, house ready to close, sandwiches tucked in, Spunky safely in the car . . . but Boy was missing from his favorite spot by the fireplace. Could he have slipped out during the car loading? A diligent search of the shrubbery, garden and neighbors' yards produced no results.

He is usually very good at coming when called but not this time. Every cat owner knows how many hiding places in a house a cat can find. Olive began in the cellar and proceeded to search the kitchen shelves, bedroom bureau drawers, and every piece of furniture with space underneath. As a last resort she opened the door to the attic. Her vocal cords exhausted, she managed a faint call and got an answer. It came from behind the wallboard of the attic walls. There was a crack between two sections.

An hour and a half later she had chopped a hole in the wall and was able to extricate the unwilling traveler. Later, when asked about the trip, she said, "I didn't get off as soon as I expected."

The Siamese had made his point about staying on Cape Cod. His mistress has been talking ever since about living there year round. There is no puckerbush in a New Jersey urban area and the juniper tree on her place on the Cape is so good for climbing!

Amber is not a bird catcher except for one bird that found its way into the house, but she agrees about the joys of Cape living, for the quail skip around right outside the front door, the sea gulls swoop down past her watching window, and baby rabbits take sunbaths in the sandy driveway. At the farm inland the wildlife is a naturalist's dream, but the woods and swamp and pond are not so close to the house. Even the bird feeders are farther off.

One problem with cats, in my opinion, is that collars are not safe. A collar tight enough to keep from catching on a tree branch or a bush is apt to strangle, but a loose collar comes off with the help of any sensible cat. A dog can be comfortable and safe with collar, tag and even a ribbon bow at Christmas. The neck bones are stronger; the whole construction seems different.

Collars with bells make me wonder how any cat endures the ringing in such incredibly sensitive ears. I remind myself that all humans are fallible and many mistakes are due to ignorance. The good intention to protect the birds seldom does much good, but at least it shows a wish to protect the birds.

Birds usually come off well since they can fly, although I have a couple of cat friends who are expert birders. I have never owned one. Mice, rats and moles are the natural prey. Occasionally a small garden snake is suitable. Moths and butterflies are delicious, so Amber tells me. But spiders are to walk around on tiptoe.

My own species, unfortunately, is the greatest predator on the planet. We have the distinction of killing our own kind as well as other living creatures. But mankind as such is relatively new and may develop beyond this in time.

If not, we too will be an endangered species.

During July and August careless motorists pile up casualties as they make time on their way to vacation. I think of our favorite barn cat, Mittens, run down on the way to her newborn kittens with a field mouse in her mouth. She was small but quite visible with her white paws. She was a bit slow from bearing her first family and from the field mouse, but she almost made it. The driver saved about half a minute by not slowing down and I wonder what he did with that half minute. The memory of Mittens's last look at me is what he left behind, along with the limp little body. Casualties of young children, too, mount up, along with those of old folk who cannot leap like giraffes—but think of the time saved by the speeders who live to boast that they made their trip in record time!

I do not talk to Amber about this. She accepts her leash because it is in her pattern. She will even jump on the shelf and knock it off to suggest a walk. I am the one who regrets it. My other cats could run free in our own fields and woods, but they were bigger, more solid and more knowledgeable. Besides, in those days thruways had not sliced our area.

City cats do well in apartment living. One favorite of mine named Shadrach led a very happy, very long life in an upper-floor apartment in Manhattan. He had a devoted following and his owner, Tay Hohoff, made him the focal point of the parties he loved.

Tay was pleased to know that Amber identifies the sound of my car motor, but what surprised me more was that my friend Blackberry, the skunk, also knew. Any other car sent him lumbering into the bushes. Mine brought a plump ebony-and-ermine-body hustling toward the auto. I do not know of a human who has this perception except my dear friend Jimmy DeLory, whose business is taking care of cars.

Most cat lovers have seen instances of extrasensory perception in their cats. Some cats save lives by rousing sleepers when a fire occurs. Some sense illness before anyone else in the family does. Some know immediately when there is a death, even far away. Although they cannot bark, they can scare burglars.

Amber speeds to tell me someone is coming into the yard. If I am in the opposite side of the house working and look up to see a small whirlwind spinning down the hall, I get up. She is never wrong and takes her responsibility as watch cat seriously. She also announces when an unexpected storm is coming or when a branch blows down.

No two cats are alike. Spunky is now a big athletic male, blacker than a moonless sky. I feel he must have a memory of his terror, for he makes a point of owning the whole establishment. He and Boy are devoted friends, but Spunky asserts himself by wild tree-climbing, swinging on branches, diving into thickets. Then he vanishes inside the house, causing frantic searches. Nothing that opens a crack is impossible. It is as if he needs to remind himself, over and over again, that now he is safe in a secure world.

Another black cat manages the household of my friends Millie and Ed. Sam is as athletic as Spunky and smooth as new satin. When he came as a kitten, he made history because he ate everything, including mashed potatoes and all sorts of leftovers. Those of us with cats as difficult to suit as a diner in a French restaurant tried not to feel wistful. However, he joined the club in due course and made a list of selective items.

"This is one cat we are not going to spoil," said Ed.

Now if Ed is at my house, he suddenly gets up. "Time for Sam's walk. He'll be waiting for me."

"If our next cat wants to go in and out in the middle of the night," said Millie, before Sam moved in, "I am going to put him down cellar."

"Sam got me up at five this morning," Ed remarks.

"I was up at six thirty today. Sam was hungry," Millie comments.

"Well, any person so charming is worth waiting on," I say.

The cat they had before Sam used to meet me when I drove in for dinner and escort me to the house. But Sam plunks into my lap as soon as I am in, snuggles briefly, then jumps down into my carryall bag to poke around before going to check the kitchen.

Six other cat friends all live in one house, along with two dogs and their owners, Gail and Jan. This large family came about naturally when it got around the neighborhood that Amity Hill was a desirable Camelot.

"What can you do when a poor cat has kittens under your back terrace?" Jan asks.

"We couldn't find good homes for any of them," Gail says.

The house is big, rangy, and even when full of guests does not seem overcrowded. The medley of animals all get along together better than most people do and even take turns when guests are served fresh jumbo shrimp. The first time I was invited for dinner, it was autumn and a fire burned in the great fireplace. The guests sat in a big circle around the hearth enjoying the elegant hors d'oeuvres—tiny quiches, creamy cheeses and spicy meatballs simmering in the Chinese wok. Finally Jan brought in a platter of the fresh shrimp with individual bowls for serving. Gail passed the sauce.

Just at this moment someone opened a door and a cat loped in. His stately progress to Jan's lap suggested royalty favoring his courtiers with a visit. What he really was doing was helping himself to the biggest, most luscious shrimp in Jan's bowl.

"Look, the cat is eating your shrimp," said one newcomer.

"Shrimp is the favorite," Gail said.

At once another cat slipped in gracefully, accepted admiration and settled by my chair on the side nearest the shrimp. When I held one out, this one did not grab but took the treat gently, ate neatly, put out an urgent paw for a second helping. Meanwhile at spaced intervals more cats joined the party. At that time there were six. It reminded me of those television parades of Miss America, Miss Universe, Miss Junior something-or-other. But the cats did not need a Bert Parks to run their show. They simply drifted around from shrimp to shrimp as if they had planned the whole placement.

It was obvious why the shrimp platter was so large—there was enough for humans and cats both. Afterward, the cats polished whiskers, sat on willing laps or moved to a cozy nook. One took off from my shoulder to a beam that spans the ceiling. His performance on the beam was a Flying Wallenda solo act and everyone deserted affairs in Washington, the Dow Jones average, the rise in crime and saving Rock Harbor from being just a marina to watch the agile leaps so high on that beam under an arched ceiling that grew more remote with every spin.

I later discovered these cats are what we call "happenstance cats." Most simply turned up. One felt having her babies born under the patio was a good idea, as indeed it was.

One had never recovered from experiences in a bitter world and was shy. Aside from all being what the cat fancy labels "short-haired domestic," their personalities differed, their original bloodlines were an enigma and the varied colors somehow made me think of a United Nations assembly—

except these four-footed creatures behaved so much better! The three dogs in this household conceded that they would stay upstairs until it was not quite so crowded. They missed the shrimp but had special snacks when the trays were carried out.

I told Amber what a wonderful time I had had, but she was busy going over my shoes, jacket and tote bag (one cat spent some time in it), and finally she needed extra assurance that I was not playing around with other cats or dogs.

I have some friends who say wistfully, "I wish I could have a kitten."

"Why not?"

"Well, I don't really have a good place to keep one. I have so much company coming and going—and three of my best friends can't stand cats—and where could I keep her litter tray?"

I assume this really means the speaker does not want the responsibility of a cat and should not have one. With Gail and Jan, they became a Rescue League simply because they could not bear to turn away from the needy.

"It's just a question of management," says Gail, quoting our Dr. Kim. When non–cat visitors come, there is no sign of a cat or a dog in the house—as I know, for I once went there and began to be afraid something terrible had happened. Separate quarters for the animals are agreeable. It is taken as a matter of course that dogs and cats get along so nobody tries to kill anybody. (This was true of our cockers, Irish, and cats also.)

"We will not have any more," says Jan, "but somehow we found one more kitten can always be fitted in."

"But taking nine animals to Kim's for inoculations," Gail says, "I think, is moving a menagerie."

Our own bevy of cockers, Irish and cats were not above nudging and pushing when we had a party and served everything they liked best. My Siamese usually got the juiciest shrimp. If Esmé felt like it, she skipped onto the harvest table while grace was being said and checked on the roast lamb or chicken herself. So I must assume that the behavior of our animals just reflects my own temperament.

In my category of cats, one that I never saw is unforgettable. This cat came out of the woods near Gertrude Holbrook's house on Cape Cod. Bedraggled, lost, he would not come near, so she took food out to him. Finally she somehow managed to catch him and put him in the cellar, away from the attentions of her black cocker. This cat had a piece of collar with part of a tag and she made out half of a telephone number in an off-Cape town.

Gertrude attacked the problem with her usual determination. After endless efforts she reached an understanding operator. "I have a lost cat here," said Gertrude. "I have no idea who the owner is and I have only half of a telephone number. Is there any way you could help me?"

"I'll try."

How much work this involved is staggering to contemplate. But eventually the call came.

"I have the name of a subscriber—the digits seem to fit. Would you like that number and name?"

"Would I!" said Gertrude.

She reached an unknown man on the mainland of Massachusetts. "Did you lose a cat on Cape Cod?"

"No, all our cats are right here. . . . Wait a minute. Where did you find this cat?"

She told him.

"It can't be possible," he said. "Two years ago we spent a vacation on the Cape, in that area, and our kitten wandered off. We stayed over, hunting and hunting, for days. Missed schools, jobs, everything, but we had to give up the cottage in the end."

"This may not be your cat."

"I'll be down to see," he told her. "I'll start first thing tomorrow."

The reunion was like a soap opera, Gertrude said.

In this instance I had to admit that one collar was justified. How this cat survived two years—winter, summer—is a tribute to the incredible stamina of this species. And his reunion with his owner is a tribute to the dogged determination of one compassionate woman plus a most unusual operator.

The theme of the Animal Rescue League broadcast was proved. "Don't give up—your pet won't!"

Amber was not interested when I told her this story. The concept of being lost was no concern of hers.

"Suppose you slipped out and a strange dog chased you?"

She purred. "First I would chase him. Then you would come and find me." Her wide innocent gaze conveyed this.

I changed the subject by asking her to explain why no two cats ever behave the same way. "Amber, you could tell me why this cat named Charlie always tips his water dish over. The owner has tried all types of dishes and cups, some of which he broke (imagine a cat breaking anything)."

Amber was attentive; the word "cat" was being mentioned.

"The poor lady finally bought a plastic gallon container, cut it in half, and put the bottom half on the sink for about a month. It was turned over every morning. Charlie likes to drink from a dripping faucet just the way you do, but water is becoming another endangered product. His owner cannot stand by the sink day and night. The lady wants my advice, and I must say this is a touchy problem."

Amber's answer was to tiptoe around a dozen oddments on the end table and poke her head in her drinking glass. The water level was too low; her whiskers would not go in. The one lap of water she got was *not* cold enough.

"Well, it took you some time to train me," I said as I went for fresh water and an ice cube. "I daresay Charlie's message has not yet been received. I wonder if he would like to swim?"

Cats have preferences as to dishes more than any dog I have known. In this way they are like people: some prefer mugs, as I do; some like small china cups; some want tall glasses, some short ones. Some want pottery soup bowls, others the old-fashioned flat ones.

Then there is that one wooden spoon, that certain ladle, that old cutting knife, the special French whisk that is the only one for a particular cook. It is all a matter of taste.

That one special cat who will eat only from a thistle-pattern cup or plate or a baby-food jar trained me long ago.

But Charlie is a mystery!

When I think of how cats train their human families, I am always reminded of an incident concerning my friend Martha and her family and cat. The cat liked to be out at night and would often either stay out or ask to go out to greet the full moon when it was bedtime. Martha and her husband and their two mothers lived in the house and were used to the cat's life-style.

One night their son arrived home at midnight on an unexpected furlough from the navy. The front door was locked, so was the back. He pounded, yelled, tried to find an open window, but he simply could not rouse anybody inside and faced the prospect of curling up on a chilly front porch until morning.

However, he was a very intelligent young man, as naval officers should be. He went to the back yard and stood under a tree the cat was fond of climbing. Raising his voice, he uttered the loudest miaow he could manage. "Miaow! Miaow! Miaow!"

Within moments the whole household had jumped out of their beds and scurried to open the back door. (The cat happened to be inside the laundry hamper on that particular evening.) As the son said ruefully when they let him in, "Only the cat could do it."

I wonder what a policeman on patrol would have thought had he observed a handsome young man miaowing loudly in a back yard—especially in the middle of the night!

IT IS A CAPE COD OCTOBER MORNING and the ocean outside the bedroom window is unclouded sapphire. The Canada geese argue about flight schedules as they paddle in the shallows. Are the young ones really ready to fly? They learned to swim such a short time ago.

I am still in bed, but Amber sits on my chest alternately kneading her paws and patting my cheek. Her purring is imperative, and if I pay no attention she will of course start chewing my hair. At this point I look at the clock, all the time knowing it has to be ten minutes of nine because Amber marks the hours better than the clock, which may stop running in the night.

"All right, I am getting up," I say with no enthusiasm.

"But remember—I didn't go to bed until one fifteen."

With the aid of purring and poking, I reenter the enemy territory of day.

"I'll be ready in a minute."

"High time."

Excitement explodes as I pull on my slacks (I won't pause for a shower this morning)—skips, leaps, trombone purrs, blanket digging, finally a turn upside down, arms dangling, apricot stomach exposed, tail flat.

"Come on, off we go to breakfast."

Small wedge of head tucks under my lifted arm as we go to the kitchen. On the way, we sing. Amber purrs like a motor. I vocalize. "Oh, what a beautiful morning. . . ."

Deposited on the kitchen table, Amber paces.

"I thought you'd never get up," she says plainly. "I am starving."

As she eats her junior beef, I sip my coffee and start a conversation about sleep because, as I remark, "Our little life is rounded with a sleep." (I'm quoting from *The Tempest*, not that Amber cares.)

Sweetheart, I tell her, you are more fortunate than human beings in many ways. For instance, when you are tired, all you have to do is fold your tail underneath, wrap up your paws and instantly fall into a deep sleep. You are so motionless I have to touch you to be sure you are still breathing. Now my Irish could drop off to sleep, too, off and on daytimes, but she dreamed. The banner of plumed tail beat the sofa, lips twitched, front paws paddled the air, soft whuffing sounds came and went. She ran in her sleep, obviously chasing rabbits or squirrels. Awake, she never caught anything, for an Irish setter's job is to stand and point when he or she gets close enough.

But you seem to be drowned in sleep. This means that at any moment day or night you can surface and start skimming around light as a feather. But let me tell you I have read that

Katharine Hepburn, the most vital, ebullient actress of our era, has a habit of flopping on the floor and sleeping seventeen hours or so. Then she springs to life and soon exhausts everyone around her with her sparkling energy. Perhaps this is just one of those fables about the great, but there must be a grain of truth in it, for it is not the kind of anecdote anyone would invent.

Sleep, which you take so casually, is a main preoccupation of human beings. Scientists spend many wakeful hours studying it. Books are written about it. And I have spent many drowsy hours at dinner parties listening to groups of friends talking about sleep until I yearn to go home and lie down. Last week, when friends were at our house discussing nothing else, what did you do? You went to sleep and never stirred a paw. It bored you—that is what happened.

I imagine you opening one onyx eye (it was night) and muttering, "I think that you all had better just shut your eyes." Simple.

But now we have been told that there are day people and night people. And we love to explain to anyone which we are, for it solves a big problem. I am usually interested in this subject, but sometimes I find myself drifting off into a faraway place (a very useful talent I have) while the talk drowses on.

Day people (please stay awake now) rise at six and charge through the days with banners flying. They accomplish. But at nine at night they fall asleep in the middle of the Boston Symphony as the climax comes with cymbals, thunder of drums, throbbing of bass viols.

Night people meet the day like wounded warriors on a battlefield. Some wives manage breakfast in a semicoma just about the time the children are trying to find their schoolbooks and the bus is due, husbands, already late for the commuting train or an appointment, are hunting for briefcases, the dog wants a run, the cat claws at the window screen. Or the women themselves must dash off to their own jobs if only they can get organized. People like this do not rate highly in the morning.

But like the Dow Jones average on a good day, they climb as the hours pass. By midafternoon, when day people start to feel limp, they begin to fly. So by the time the family is ready for bed, they are ready for anything but. The late show, or late-late show, finds them as alert as a runner when the starting gun goes off. If they are reading, they finish the book. When they do sneak off to bed, they are greeted by nothing more exciting than snores.

I was raised to believe it was immoral not to bound up at sunrise. Staying in bed after six meant that you were lazy, indolent, quite useless to humanity. Only lately, and with effort, have I come to realize I was born to be a night person and cannot help it any more than I could help having blue eyes and fair hair. But I still feel guilty when a day-person friend phones me at ten in the morning and speaks too apologetically.

"I know I shouldn't telephone you before ten," she will say. "I was up at sunrise—it was indescribably beautiful. I did my errands at eight and I have the laundry in. Are you up?"

I am too kind to ask her how she liked the late show when Jimmy Stewart gave that hilarious account of his African safari and told how he met the spitting cobra who bites first and then —"Ah, um, ah, spits extra poison on you to finish you off."

When the talk of day and night people diminishes, the next topic of conversation is likely to be how many hours of sleep one needs. Some lucky folk brag about sleeping only five hours a night. Those who need eight or nine say nothing, so they are easily identified.

Insomniacs say they have such trouble sleeping that they are often up at three in the morning heating milk or reading or doing chores. Those I know never yawn and God forbid they would ever take a nap. Some of them admit they doze off while watching television if the program is dull. Experts now state with conviction that most people do get enough sleep, some-how, at some time, for their own constitution.

A few rare persons, usually men, claim they seldom sleep at all!

Mama was a night person whose schedule was dominated by Papa, a day person if there ever was one. She solved it with no fuss, as she solved every problem. She went to bed when Papa did, but as soon as he began to snore, she tiptoed out to the sewing room and ran the Singer machine for hours. How do I know? I know because during those same hours I was up writing poetry by the light of a candle.

A conversation entirely devoted to sleep may end with a few more crackers and cheese, or fresh shrimp dipped in sauce, together with one last question: "Do you ever dream? Do you have nightmares? Let me tell you about the one I had last night."

I do dream and also have nightmares and, what is more, I always dream in color. Like my Irish, I move a lot, I think. The bedding is always half on the floor in the morning, although, Amber darling, I am glad I don't dislodge you from your perch on my hip where the electric blanket must be warmest. I listen with interest to other people's dreams, for they reveal a lot, but I usually keep mine to myself, feeling sure they have Freudian meanings I don't want to analyze. Even dreaming all last night that I was hunting for table mats for my dear friend Millie is probably significant. I think it had something to do with our searching all over the stores to find some that were not slippery on the underside, but no matter. It probably symbolizes something.

Now I shall bring this dissertation to a close while you make a small envelope of yourself on the white corduroy pillow on the sofa and drop into a peaceful dreamless sleep and I go out to clean up the kitchen, feed the birds, water the plants and wait for afternoon to feel lively and full of ambition.

In the fall Amber and I take a morning walk after the early chill has gone and the golden grass is warm and dry. Moving warily, she checks all the trails of those who came this way in the night—rabbit, wandering cat, huge strange dog (must have been large, the footprints are so far apart, the grass is a bit flat), a hunting coon (circle the bird feeder for this one). Where the quail have fed she paws the grass.

"Amber, did you inherit your sensitive nose from your ancestors who roamed the jungles? They hunted primarily by sight and sound, not smell, but they did need to smell the paths of enemies and to know where their own lairs were. But you do not really need such a supersense. Why do you have it?"

She is too busy sniffing our tiny resident tree toad, who lives in the parsley bed near the outdoor faucet. She does not offer to pick him up or chase him—just gives him a good smell-out. I have picked him up when he gets stuck on the brick steps. He weighs no more than a small leaf; his tiny arms are toothpick size. He has been around a couple of seasons now, and all he asks is a trickle of cool water sprayed on the soil on hot dry days.

One must suppose instinct plays a part in all life. If this little creature were a baby mouse, Amber would have a mouthful of mouse in about three seconds. Deep in her some ancient power only dozes, to wake any moment. But what really is instinct? A young kitten senses danger if a large dog pokes a quivering muzzle around the open door. A bevy of quail rise from the scattered corn I have tossed out for them and plow the air awkwardly when a human walks near. Instinct tells them about guns even if their whole lifetime is spent poking around in my restricted wild-animal haven. Even the tiniest puffball goes scrambling wildly to the bushes when my neighbor tiptoes across the lawn.

Night animals sense danger in the sharp light of day, and day animals seek snug hideaways at night. Nature helps by giving vision accordingly. My friend Blackberry had poor vision in the daytime, as all skunks do, but although it was some better at night, I doubt whether even contact lenses would do much for any skunk, night or day. His sensitive nose and lively hearing compensated.

Blackberry used to wait by the front step for me every evening. He would move his head back and forth, swaying his shoulders slightly when I opened the door. His eyes were shiny as jet beads, but it was his nose that identified me. When the warm, comfortable smell of his own human came to him, he lumbered from the stoop to lead me to his feeding station. His basic instinct that mankind meant danger was more than modified in my case because he would gladly have entered the house and smelled everything in it (curiosity seems to be another deep instinct in both birds and animals).

Naturalists have studied instinct in birds endlessly, but just how migration patterns are set up is still a mystery. How do the Canada geese know it is time to practice for the long journey? Is it a change in temperature or light, or a built-in sense of time itself? Also, they know instinctively where they will end that journey—if they are not killed en route. The long, wavering V of flight brings a new sense of wonder to human beings.

"The geese went over this morning!" we say.

"I heard the geese at dawn," neighbors telephone to report.

"Means early winter," predicts the farmer.

Amber and I hear the honking rising from Mill Pond, our salty inlet. She leaps to the windowsill, talking excitedly with her tail. Sea gulls can yell endlessly and she pays no heed, but something in her responds to the geese. I know they are arguing, and I long to interpret their language. Perhaps some do not want to start yet, and some think they ought to be over the ocean already. Surely the most imperative honk comes from the leader, and he will be obeyed when the cacophony diminishes.

I talk about it to Amber. "We shall be here to welcome them back, but you and I are earthbound. Wings are meant for flying, and we are destined to keep a safe landing place for their return. I have a feeling you understand better than I do."

So we watch the travelers mount the airwaves. I call farewell while Amber, motionless, lifts the delicate wedge of her head and looks and looks until the sky is empty. I pick her up and feel her warm purring self.

"I'm still here. Don't be lonely," she tells me. Then the impulse to go outside strikes her and she whips to the table by the front door and starts nudging at her harness and leash.

No matter what the season, Amber and I always end our walk with a sense of anticipation as we turn toward home. The little grey house with its deep-slanted roof looks so familiar, so rich with memories, so sheltering. Amber feels the same joy and runs to the door.

"We have been long away," I say.

Whenever she comes in, Amber establishes her domain by bounding to the kitchen table to be sure nobody has touched her tray. Amber is a snacker. In fact she could never eat enough to survive if she had to follow a fixed regime. Small bites during the day and also from time to time at night keep that special wolf from her door. Remembering this only cements my belief that no rules can fit all situations. Snacking is usually very bad for children, but some small stomachs may not have the capacity to stoke up three times a day. What they fill up on between times is another story. Even when they were very little, my granddaughters put away enough fruit for an orchard, berry patch or banana plantation without damaging their appetites a whit. They were astounded when a visiting child came with her suitcase full of candy and had no appetite for regular meals.

"She's going to have trouble with her teeth," said Anne, then age six, shaking her head. "And by the way, do we have any more of those plums left?" She had only had two bananas, one apple and some grapes in the hour since dinner.

9

I T WAS THE KIND OF DAY last Thursday that makes astrology plausible. For both of us. In the night Amber ate a few bites of some dried material in a winter bouquet. A friend had sent it to me and I could not identify it. So I discovered it was not edible when Amber threw up in the early dawn. I cleaned up the small bundle of what looked like baled hay.

Second, the telephone by the bed exploded in my ear at seven thirty.

"Is Liz there?"

"No, Liz doesn't live here."

"But I called the right number."

"Then your right number is wrong."

Third, Amber did not want the baby beef but admitted she was hungry. She preferred the lamb, except that we didn't have any. I found a jar of minced veal.

While waiting on her, I spilled my orange juice. Mopping up spills is not my chosen sport. Even after I washed the floor, it stuck to my slippers.

Finally awake, I investigated the guest bathroom because there seemed to be a brook running there. Amber watched with enthusiasm while I tried to rearrange the insides of the toilet tank. Company from the city was due that afternoon (the tank *knew* that). I telephoned Olive, who acts as my private rescue squad, and she repaired it temporarily with a coat hanger. Then she went to town and bought new fittings so there would be no OUT OF ORDER sign when the company arrived.

"Amber," I said, "with all the glory of the technological era, why doesn't some scientist invent a modern toilet tank?"

Even scientists must have bathrooms. Mine today are exactly like those in my childhood. The arm breaks just as it used to, the rubber ball sits lifeless, the water we try to conserve flows unendingly.

The day wore on, and I mean wore on! It took a screwdriver to open a jar with a twist-off lid. I would have taken some Bufferin if I could have coped with the cap that keeps children from opening the bottle. Any child who wants to eat Bufferin seems odd to me but can probably get that cap off. I, however, cannot.

All the mail I had sorted the day before cascaded to the floor when Amber located one fly above the desk.

There are such days in the life of any homemaker, I know. Coffee spills. Washing machines stop when the tub is full of sheets. A willing guest pours soap powder in the dishwasher instead of detergent. The fondue set vanishes and panning for gold would be easier than finding it. Half the light bulbs (long-life ones) die just as the dinner guests come in. Amber loses her favorite tiny Christmas wreath.

The only way I find to manage such a day is to give my full attention to something beautiful and ignore the mechanics of living. This is the best restorative. Usually I sit comfortably on the couch with Amber on my lap and concentrate on appreciating her as if I were an artist.

"Amber, sometimes I know you realize how beautiful you are. Your movements are proud, butterfly-light when you leap, fiercely graceful when you attack the old toy mouse. The lift of your head is arrogant, the whisk of that velvet tail is imperative."

Amber lets one arm stretch out full length, a princess accepting my homage.

"Then when you nap, you fold up as gracefully as a fan and tuck paws under chin, tail packaging your whole self. A drowsy purr completes the arrangement. I am sure the sight of a cat asleep would make the worst insomniac relax."

Today I have been studying her while she dozes beside me on the couch. Trying to think like an artist, I decide that the triangle is the basic design of her head. It is an upside down one, the apex being what Olive calls her "pugnacious jaw." The base stretches across the forehead. The slanting sides of the figure slope down to the rosy tip of the nose, slightly interrupted by silver-gilt whiskers.

Above the head, two triangles point toward the sky. An Abyssinian's ears are almost translucent, pink as a Dawn rosebud. A whiff of pale fur protects each opening. The ears are large in proportion to the head.

"Your ears are like full sails," I tell her. "I think if you got in the sea you would not have to paddle much, just go with the wind."

I suppose the eyes are elliptical or oval, but sometimes they seem round as full moons. The pupils adjust to light changes in a miraculous way—golden or onyx under apricot lashes. I can even imagine that her eyes, too, suggest a triangle at times.

The graceful neck, narrow shoulders, flexible slim body end at the haunches, which remind me of a racing filly's, long and powerful. The back rises a bit, adding more thrust where the slim tail joins. The lower half of the legs is flat—a wider base for springing and handy to sit on while bird-watching.

The infinite genius of nature shows so clearly in this small cat, it fills me with wonder. Combining the peak of practical use and incredible beauty is something mankind rarely achieves.

My half hour of concentrating on Amber has left me feeling that the world is rewarding and my troubles with a small D day not worth a thought. As I start to fix our lunch, I thank Amber for bringing a sense of balance to me.

Perhaps I have found a new recipe for all harassed humans, no matter who or where or when. All it involves is moving away from whatever problems pile up. The retreat can take any form. A country person may go out in June and ponder on the mystery of one opening rose. Think of who first saw a rose in the long-ago days, how a root produces new roots, green leaves, sap running in the bush after a below-zero winter. Why does one rose differ from another? What sense of timing brings the petals to open at one moment?

A city dweller may lock the door of the apartment—the repairman will not come on time anyway—and walk on the street. The whole world is there: countless people. Studying every face provides enough drama for the theater. Faces always reveal personality, clothes usually describe manner of living. Then thinking about what dreams are hidden, what joys and sorrows have molded them, brings a release from involvement in leaky pipes, refrigerators that keep defrosting, doors that will not shut.

For music lovers, the radio or stereo can take over to bring a new perspective to life. My own taste varies from Bach to

John Denver, from the Boston Symphony to country music. A dose of either is the best medicine I know of for depression.

Every home has room for a few books. Books can transport you light miles away from problems. One friend of mine always keeps a mystery at hand, another a favorite historical novel. Still another reads about mountain climbing when her own mountains are too much for her. I like all kinds of books but keep my copy of Keats by the sofa for the most depressing times.

It really does not matter what moves us out of our personal defeats. What is important is to block out the immediate and experience something different. We come back to find more energy to face a particular day or night or hour.

Often we are discouraged, too, because we have made mistakes. The more we consider them, the larger they grow. A whole day can be wretched. "It's all my fault," we say. "I was so stupid!"

Ralph Waldo Emerson talks about that when he says, "Finish each day and be done with it. Some blunders and absurdities no doubt crept in—forget them as soon as you can. Tomorrow is a new day: begin it well and serenely, and with too high a spirit to be cumbered with your old nonsense."

He must have had a few bad days himself!

Amber gets up and comes swinging to the kitchen.

"How about a flounder fillet?"

She stands on the counter, sniffing.

While I mince the flounder, the sunlight dapples her fur. It is an extra pleasure. Her coat is dense but does not obscure the fluent lines of the basic structure. Her apricot undercoat glows and takes over on legs and small head areas and under her chin. The upper coat is ticked with two tickings, the top autumn brown. It is soft but firm in texture so bits of fur do not drift in the air. It feels like warm silk.

Nature did a special job with all this, for if Amber ever got lost in the woods, I would never see her. Perhaps in spring

I might catch a flickering movement of her dark tail. In autumn it would resemble a stripped wild-rose cane. The apricot would appear as a fallen pink-gold maple leaf or two. The brown would blend into chestnut. I would be hunting an invisible cat, except that if I kept calling, no bundle of leaves would rush to me.

After supper last night I started a new book, but I was really still thinking about recipes for bad days. Surely anyone who can do crewel work or knit afghans has an escape into serenity. My attempts to thread a needle lead to frustration. But I am good at jigsaw puzzles. I do not recommend them for brief pickups, because once into a jigsaw you may let the next meal burn up and pans fuse with the burners. Escape time must be rationed.

I put aside the book and tried a magazine article. The author, a psychiatrist, explained that worry, frustration, brooding over quarrels all drain our emotional energy, which should be conserved as much as oil, gas or water. I find the word "energy" itself saps mine, but I agreed with his thesis. I tend to feel tired just hearing about some insult someone has suffered, especially as every repetition enlarges it.

It is certainly true that emotional energy can be overspent. Even the heart must have rest. Most of us know people who actually get hysterical when their emotions are kept at high pitch too long. Then there are those who develop "a case of nerves." Professional help may be needed for people suffering from waste of emotional energy.

Spiritual energy also needs replenishment. It seems to be the basis of the life-force. Without it we are not whole. Chronic anxiety, despondency, fear can result. Even Jesus went away by himself at times when his spiritual energy ebbed, conserving and replenishing it by quiet and private communication with God.

Christians have the wellspring of the Bible to draw upon and the restorative power of prayer. Most other religions have their own sacramental books and their own rituals of prayer or meditation. The renewal of energy may come from nature, or great music, or books. This is an individual matter. For some, great art brims the spirit.

"I never have a moment to think," said a friend.

"Take it anyway," I advised. "It's good medicine."

My observation of animals and birds leads me to believe that they instinctively conserve their own energy. A sea gull soaring overhead in the limitless sky suddenly plummets to the ancient glacial boulder on the Cape beach and rests, motionless as if carved. What he thinks I shall never know. When he is fully rested, he pokes at a wing, ruffles a bit. Presently he is off, wingbeats more powerful. My songbirds are bundles of energy, like perpetual motion. They dip, dart, whirl, gobble seed, flail away in the birdbath, wrestle with nest material. In throat-stretching song they establish their territory. But then they, too, drop, usually to sit on the split-rail fence and do nothing. Energy depleted, they wait until the life-force flows again.

A bird who gets trapped in the house or the garage, on the other hand, will waste every scrap of energy beating on walls, windows and doors and, unless rescued, will finally parachute to the floor, lids closed, heartbeats failing. Because of terror, he wastes himself.

I know people who do exactly that. But outdoor birds are wiser.

Animals, too, are sensible about this matter. Rabbits run marathons all over our yard until I get dizzy watching them. Then, for no visible cause, they turn off their energy, flop in the midst of a jump, flatten out. Powerful hind legs lie limp, heads sink. They, too, I think, need no government to pass energy laws.

Amber may do acrobatics all through the house, up and down, over and under, find brown paper bags to spin around in, toys, pencils, pens to fling into the air, pounce on, lose under the couch. She can be tossing letters and papers, or rearranging ashtrays with a busy paw. (Everything must always be in the same place.) She exercises herself and my typewriter keys until it tires me to watch.

Then suddenly there is a cessation of all movement. I waste some of my own energy looking for her because I cannot be sure she has outgrown her ability to hang by a drapery cord.

I do know better than to worry, however. I know a small bundle of apricot fur is folded snugly wherever instinct has dictated. The amazing thing is that it is not a slowing down, it is an instant signal from nature. It even happens in the middle of the floor, which is not her favorite place. She has chosen safe nooks in every room, even in the bathroom, but when this signal comes, she never puts one paw in motion to seek out a special hiding place.

She is used to my bending over to feel the warm beat of her heart, just to be sure. She may even open one eye. But her whole personality is about the business of *not* wasting her energy supply. She is replenishing it.

"Amber," I say, "presidents, Congress, business corporations, industry leaders, ecology and conservation groups cannot solve, as of now, the energy crisis that could mean the end of our planet."

She manages a small yawn.

"How did you learn all by yourself not to spend what you haven't got? How did you know that 'waste not, want not' is a truth, not just an old saying?"

Amber does not answer. She has an inherited wisdom that mankind lost somewhere in the long travel down the ages.

Saving energy is a new idea. It is awesome to discover that the supply is never infinite. Even newer is this idea that all living creatures have a limited amount. Physical energy, spiritual energy, emotional energy are all expendable if we never conserve them.

I can imagine what Papa would say to such foolishness. He

was a Niagara of energy and spent it with complete disregard of the laws of nature. For a scientist it was strange, but he never realized nature's laws might affect him.

Mama was wiser. When she reached the point of utter fatigue, she would stop and lie down.

"Just a catnap," she would say firmly. "I have a slight headache."

Looking back, I doubt that her head really ached, but in those days it was the one excuse always allowable for the so-called weaker sex. I think she needed to rest from the ceaseless activity in our household, letting the well of energy bubble up again. She occasionally sat down by the big window overlooking the wide quiet river, and even then I sensed she was easing her mind and heart and did not crash in with some minor problem.

Papa's reaction was different. "Grace, Grace, where are you? What are you doing? I can't find my best shirt!"

I now think he knew where the shirt was but he could not bear to have Mama—or me, either—out of his immediate range.

"No use wasting time," Papa said.

I had inherited his inexhaustible supply of energy but, like Mama, I also had to recharge. I simply said I had to study, went to my bedroom and dreamed over a book until my spirit was renewed. Papa associated any cessation of activity with idleness. Even today I get letters from his geology students who declare that they adored him but he had nearly killed them racing around on field trips. He never walked, he ran.

Papa would never have understood a man like Dr. Wyman Richardson, who wrote *The House on Nauset Marsh*. Not only a famous doctor, he was also a gifted writer whose account of his stay in an isolated cabin near the Cape Cod ocean has become a classic. One chapter describes what he called a do-nothing day. But he was really doing a great deal on that day. He was storing away feelings, observations, energy to carry back to his job. A do-nothing day would help all of us, I think.

The last time I gave myself a do-nothing day I spent most of the morning watching the birds and also observing my tiny red squirrel. I have an Audubon bird feeder with glass sides and a slant roof with a hole in the top no bigger than a half-dollar. Pouring sunflower seeds in is not easy; the hole is too small and really needs a funnel, which I lack. I depend on the chickadees to harvest the spilled seeds. But yesterday I looked out and saw that the feeder was full of red squirrel! I stared in amazement. I must be dreaming. Presently a minute point of nose poked through the hole, two shiny eyes stared back at me and then the whole furry body emerged, bushy tail and all. Stuffed with sunflower seeds, he sat on the split-rail fence, erect as a soldier. He was a living miniature. He stayed a long time, resting from his accomplishment.

I have no idea how long it had taken him to solve the problem or how many times he had failed. That hole is too small for the birds, who feed at a crack in the bottom.

But this morning when I got up, the bird feeder was again filled with squirrel. I stopped worrying about how I could get an imprisoned squirrel out of a glass-enclosed box without calling the rescue squad. No human could possibly haul him out of the hole and I didn't want to smash the glass with a hammer, but luckily there was no need.

I settled for dumping sunflower seeds in the yard while the chickadees bounded around lecturing me. A very small red squirrel watched smugly from a nearby branch. If I could only go close, I would be able to say I saw a squirrel smile!

Amber is more interested in our squirrel than in the bevy of plump quail in the yard. Perhaps she feels a kind of kinship. She announces his arrival with excitement, not animosity. He can see her on the kitchen windowsill and flicks his tail, drops a sunflower seed from his paws, twitches his nose but shows no sign of fear.

But if a car drives in, he vanishes. The darting motion is like a dance and he is airborne almost like a bird.

My dear friend Jimmy DeLory has a chipmunk who lives under the deck at his house by the lake. When Jimmy calls him, he pops up through a knothole in the flooring and seems to fly to land on Jimmy's big palm. He uses the hand for a platter as he scoops up his nuts. His tail flicks, too, so it must be a balancing device. His voice is a tiny squeak.

Eileen, Jimmy's wife, keeps plenty of nuts ready but tactfully never feeds him.

"Chippie belongs to Jimmy," she says.

When guests come, they watch from inside the glass doors of the kitchen while Chippie scampers up and down Jimmy's arm, chattering away. He eats an incredible amount. It is heartwarming to see the tall man and the wee creature enjoying their friendship.

My red squirrel is not much bigger than Chippie. I wish I could hold him in my hand, but Amber would have none of it.

"You can hold me," Amber informs me, "whenever you have a spare hand!"

I reflect that when people reach out to relate to animals, life is richer for both. At the opposite end, killing animals and birds is a sorry business. Shooting or trapping may give a momentary sense of triumph—man the powerful. But the limp body is only another victim; no more experience can come of it. Life has more to give than death.

10

AUTUMN HAS CHILLED INTO WINTER now, with pewter skies and crusts of ice along the roadside. Amber and I spend more time indoors. Even so, we do not have many dull moments.

Last Tuesday I was sitting at the typewriter deeply absorbed in my work. It was peaceful outside the window—a still, grey world with a few early snowflakes falling. A Mozart symphony on the stereo filled the room with music.

Amber had been in the bedroom, asleep in the cozy warmth of my pillow. As I turned my head I saw her tiptoeing through the doorway carrying something that looked like my favorite black dustcloth. But it was not a dustcloth. Two dark wings dragged the floor. It was a starling! Amber's pink nose and one eye were visible in the midst of the feathers.

My reaction was to scream. "Amber," I cried, "what have you done?"

As I leaped up, she paraded up to the desk and laid the bird at my feet. He was so big that Amber herself seemed smaller than ever. However, she was quivering with pride. I picked the starling up and she watched with interest as I rubbed his throat, massaged his body, examined his legs and claws. There was not a drop of moisture on the blackish feathers.

Suddenly, in a whir of wings, he was off again—straight for the living room, with Amber flashing after him.

"Amber, wait!" I shouted.

For once she was deaf.

"I'll get him! Just be calm!"

Who was going to be calm?

Ricocheting from the ceiling light, the invader hit the draperies. Amber got halfway up before he plummeted into the kitchen. I took time to run for a beach towel and almost tossed it over him as he hit the hanging lamp over the table. His next swoop had a downward curve, and instantly he was in Amber's mouth again and she started toward me, tail swinging with triumph. However, he was as big as she is, and with both his wings outspread all I could see of Amber was a tail tip. She loosened her hold a moment in order to get a better grip and —too late.

Once more I barely missed catching him, and the wild chase continued to the den, the guest bath, the wing. Cat, bird and anguished person dragging a beach towel must have been quite a sight. Freed again into the larger captivity, the bird suddenly did a skyline flight, bulleted down and somehow got *under* the couch. This is a convertible sofa bed and the space beneath is about an inch high. Amber could get her head in, but not her shoulders. As she wrestled with the space, the starling clawed his way to the other end. So Amber sped around the couch to get her head wedged in again at a different angle.

"Amber, let's go into the bedroom." I spoke as firmly as I could, but I was short of breath.

No answer. She knew what I planned and did a Flying Wallenda out of reach. Her whole self vibrated her message. "Mind your own business. This is mine."

At this point we three were in a cul-de-sac. The bird couldn't get out, Amber couldn't get in. I couldn't reach either of them. Would we be like this all night? I knew who would outlast the others—my delicate little cat. Her staying power is incredible in any situation.

The opening of the wing door seemed fictional to me, as did the appearance of David Gilmore. He had left my groceries in the kitchen but walked out around the house to the wing to have a chat. The sight of that big, broad-shouldered young man affected me as a sail affects a castaway on a desert island.

David could move out the heavy couch, and he did. Before Amber could whisk in, he grabbed the starling in one big hand. All his hockey playing paid dividends in his aim and speed. A moment later I again held our visitor.

It is a strange sensation to hold a winged creature in one's hand. Now that the wings were folded back, the whole bird was not much bigger than my cupped hands. The claws were so delicate as I moved them back and forth that I could hardly imagine them holding a branch in a wind.

When I stopped shaking, I remembered to praise Amber for bringing the treasure to me in the first place.

"Now what shall we do?" I asked her.

The starling was quiet in the warmth of my hand, and the shiny eyes looked at me as I stroked the head. If I put him into a box—provided I could find a box—he would suffocate or die of fright. I have no guest room to put him in, and if he flew around the house Amber would be flying too. But it was winter outside—well, let's be sensible, he is used to it. David took him gently and carried him out to the farmer's porch, as we call the breezeway in these parts. We decided to leave him for ten minutes and see what happened. If he didn't recover, we would call the Audubon Society. When we came back, he was gone.

Amber's frustration was so obvious she wasn't sure whether to let me comfort her or to stalk away, stiff-legged with outrage. David was very much pleased as he shoved the couch back into place.

"No problem," he said.

I was too shaky to bother with supper, but when Amber relented and marched into the kitchen, I gave her a dish of minced chicken while I opened a can of soup for myself.

"There went my afternoon's work," I told her.

She was too busy to answer, but her fur gradually flattened into normalcy. By the time I began to read a book I had to review that day, she was pawing at the pages, indicating that I had not praised her as she deserved.

The mystery of how the starling got inside the house is still unsolved. The only way he could have entered was down the fireplace flue, and a big fire screen stands there. It had not been moved. The whole episode took place at the end of the house farthest from my workroom, but I would have heard the screen fall on the brick hearth. And when she first caught the starling, Amber did not even knock a candle over. A bird in the house might be more usual in summer, when a screen might be loose or a door ajar, but the house was tight against the winter weather.

It was also a mystery that Amber wanted to bring this intruder to me although it was heavy lugging. I kept on praising her extravagantly, and she was obviously feeling proud as she followed me around. She was, she indicated, the guardian of the house, as indeed she was, for a distracted bird flying madly around can do a lot of damage.

The mystery was not in a cat's wanting praise for catching a bird, but that Amber was behaving according to type. She is not a bird hunter. When we go out, she nibbles her favorite grass tips while chickadees, mockingbirds, finches and whoever else is hungry flit just a few feet above her. In fact, her one previous killing was a rat that got into the farmhouse one night. She dispatched him with no sound and laid him in the doorway to my bedroom, where I almost stepped on him when I got up.

Cats are as individual as people. I have one lovely Siamese friend who does love to catch birds, and his mistress has tried every way to dissuade him. He is so timid he will run from his own shadow, as they say, but something rises in him when he sees a bevy of birds in his yard and sometimes he does catch one.

In any case, when I called Helen Beals, my dear friend, to report on the starling incident, she commented instantly.

"Did Amber tell you how it happened?"

Amber never did. She only spent some extra time scrubbing and polishing herself and then ate an extra helping of asparagus tips and broiled fillet of flounder for supper.

The starling must have had a lot to tell his companions as he too ate an extra supper of the birdseed.

That night as I got ready for bed I thought about the behavior of birds when they get into the house. They do not seem to seek an escape route. They simply go crazy and bang around. They never try to get back the way they got in—down the chimney when the cover has blown off or through some open window. They go headfirst against panes of glass, ceilings, pictures, walls, draperies. They dash against shelves full of fragile teacups or rows of books. They hit all the lamps, toppling the lighter ones. In short, they do not *think* at all. And no instinct leads them to any door that may be open. If they get into my garage, no amount of shooing will persuade them to fly out the big garage door. No, they are beating against the wood piled against the walls.

Any trapped animal I have ever known will sense the

whole problem. A dog will try to dig out, and usually does, or climb the fence, and usually makes it. Trapped in the cellar or a closet, a dog claws, bangs, howls right where the entrance is. An Irish setter can even get the latch open or turn the knob. A small dog works at clawing the door bottom and can make a good deal of headway before someone wonders where he is.

Perhaps the trouble with the birds is that they belong to the sky, whereas animals are earthbound by nature.

Anyway, my last comment to Amber was, "I'll call the carpenter to come and fix that screen over the chimney. It's one chore I am not likely to forget!"

Amber purred a top purr, stretched her lissome self and gave me a wise look.

"But we won't close the damper," I said. "Remember when it rusted shut and we built a huge fire and the smoke nearly suffocated all the guests?"

So calm was restored. Nevertheless, both of us were affected by the invasion of our privacy. I knew that the experience was stitched into my own memory. And the next day Amber kept checking the house just in case a bird might be there. The day after, she had forgotten it—or had she?

This led me to wonder about memory. So far it is one mystery left to the scientists, but they are working on it. They have found that if one part of the brain is removed, the ability to remember is lost. Head injuries sometimes wipe out all memory of the accident that caused them. A cerebral operation may leave the patient with no memory of anything except for a single moment.

My thoughts on this subject were heavy going for Amber. Also for me. I wondered whether instinct, which all living beings have, is a kind of social memory.

"How did you know," I asked, "when you saw that starling, just what to do? Do ancient memories from jungle days survive in your little head?"

Amber began kneading my lap.

"Now that's instinct," I said. "Or is it? Is it memory of the few weeks you lived with your natural source of milk?"

My own memories are a file, accessible at times but entirely unorganized. Sometimes a whole memory springs up, and I am sitting in my baby carriage being pushed down a leafy street. A lady in pale blue leans over me. I am wearing a flowered bonnet. That is all. Yet years later, when I smell blossoming lilacs, they smell like that lady. But memory is not perfect—was it lavender?

I can't remember a grocery order or the last name of someone I know quite well. I have incredible blanks as to zip codes, phone numbers and what I ate last Tuesday. But I instantly recall my first date, any event I was emotionally involved in or a perfectly unrelated remembrance of roses over a picket fence. My memories are set up like scenes, with color, sound and always smells. But they stop dead, like a TV show when it goes off, just a blank with nothing behind or ahead.

So I conclude that there is a memory button somewhere that something pushes, but for me that button is very independent. No matter how I try, I cannot make the thing work when there is one line missing, for instance, in a favorite sonnet, although often at one in the morning I wake up and it is there. I can battle to recall a name which obviously is in the place of no return. Hours later I tell Amber, "Melinda Morrison." This does not impress her at all.

Perhaps at times the memory machine is too busy recording the immediate and filing it away. Or could it be that some material is not so deeply embedded? The carbon copy in my typewriter always has some lines less clear than others, although the force of my thumping, I am sure, does not vary!

I cannot ask Amber about her memories. But when we go back to the farm, it doesn't matter how short or how long it has been: She dozes in her carrying case five or more hours, seldom ever looking out of the plastic dome. Then suddenly she stands up, peers out and arranges her paws for action. We do not need the sign "Jeremy Swamp Road." We know we have just turned into it. At the farmhouse she rushes through the house into the room where her litter box is. Then back to the kitchen, up to the counter where her food tray belongs. Third stop is the windowsill in my bedroom that has the best view of the bird feeder. Finally to the back kitchen to check the toys she left on the last trip.

On our return to Cape Cod she naps until we reach the pink highway bridge that signals the highway exit leading to our town. Now, if we have been held up anywhere so the trip is an extra hour long, she opens her eyes, looks up, and utters her faint miaow. "High time we got there," she says definitely.

"Just getting to the pink bridge," I tell her.

In the house overlooking Mill Pond, she acts as if we had never been away and establishes possession with easy familiarity: litter box in place, tray set out in the kitchen, toys in the pewter porringer on the living room table. She stops to stir up the bed until it provides a proper nest. Last, she checks the birds from the picture-window sill.

"Same old sea gulls," she observes.

I notice the only thing that upsets her at either end is if someone has moved any furniture. Her surprise and disapproval are shown by whipping her tail, prowling around the object, going back and forth from its proper location to its new spot.

My longtime study of her makes me believe that she has complete memory of both homes tucked in her small head. What is more, her mental map is not confined to the inside of the house. Outside, too, her chosen points never vary. Inland, at the farm, under the wisteria tree is a favorite place, for the birds nest under the well-house roof beams it shelters. By the sea, there is a corner behind the garage where once she saw a deer mouse. Then she drags me to the edge of the bushes where a path made by wild creatures invites scrutiny.

"Amber, you can't go in there," I say. "It's all poison ivy and too risky."

If someone like a raccoon has passed that way, she turns

her head and glares at me. "I want to be alone!"

How far back her memories go I shall not find out. When she came, at six weeks, she never tried to hunt for her mother. She did not act as if she regretted being snatched from a cage at the cattery.

Since her mother was a champion career cat and, besides, lived in the city, the two never met again. Would Amber recognize her? Our cockers and Irish always identified their parents on visits, so perhaps she might.

AMBER WAS HELPING ME sort the Christmas mail. When I put a brown paper sack on the floor for the discards, she made a graceful leap to the bag and disappeared inside. I stopped to watch it careen across the floor. One seldom sees animated paper bags. When she was through, she stayed there with her tawny head poked out.

I have heard so many tales of cats getting inside automobile hoods, into suitcases, into laundry bags—in fact, into anything with an opening—that I think in primitive days they must have lived in caves or burrows or scratched cozy nooks in a forest floor. I have been told that the cat species originally dwelt in trees, safe from groundlings but in a good location for leaping on prey. Certainly Amber is comfortable on the narrow arm of a captain's chair or the edge of the bathtub, or on a windowsill so narrow that part of her hangs over. But nothing compares with a grocery bag!

On the other hand (and with her there is always another hand to talk about), her trail through the house is laid out in midair, from tabletop to back of sofa, kitchen counter to Hitchcock chair, headboard of bed to dresser top. And even when she does condescend to walk on the floor, she never walks straight across the room. Instead, she follows a circuitous route that takes her much farther but is obviously much more interesting. She circles every piece of furniture and detours around the rugs, too, whenever possible. At this time of year she makes a side trip to sniff our small Christmas tree, which is standing near the picture window. It is a Scotch pine and makes that whole corner of the living room smell like a Maine forest. Amber loves the fragrance and also loves to bat at the lowest ornament, a scallop shell suspended by a gold thread. It hangs from a handy branch where she can reach it comfortably, which is just where it should be since it was a present for her.

The paper bag game palled in time for her to dive into the piles of mail and rearrange them. Some of the envelopes, I noticed, were addressed to Ms. I usually answer these last.

"Amber," I said, "you are the most liberated female I know. If you were a liberated human female, I doubt that you would feel the need to use 'Ms' to symbolize the obvious. Neither do I think you would care very much whether or not the word "man" was deleted from the language. If anybody ever introduced me as a chairperson, I would certainly feel as awkward as the word sounds. And as for 'Miz,' it reminds me of a bee buzzing too close."

Twelve more Christmas cards cascaded to the floor.

After all, I thought as I picked up the mail, a married woman who wants to conceal her marriage can call herself "Miss." And many professional women use their maiden names anyway. Nowadays, when some people marry five or six times, it probably saves a lot of confusion!

"Amber, you don't get called anything but Stillmeadow Amber. I myself like to be called 'Mrs.' "

I do not feel, I decided, that this means someone is casting me in an inferior role. It does indicate that my grandchildren will never have to wonder whether Gram was legally married or just had one of those arrangements.

It occurred to me that most crusades begin well—this one did. There have been many centuries in which women were not equal to men in law, in personal relationships, in pay for the same jobs, in advancement in careers or factory jobs, or even in the home. Not too long ago, when they married, the husband gained ownership of all property and all rights over the offspring. Men also controlled all governments, since only they had voting power. Luckily, most of this injustice is now past history.

There are still many changes to be made, of course, and they will be, unless the crusading forces lose perspective— which, alas, often defeats any crusade. The saying "For each man kills the thing he loves" seems true too often. Of course, now it should be "For each woman kills the thing she loves."

I have listened to some of the more extreme crusaders who talk as if they had forgotten that on this planet there are —have always been—two sexes. Mankind lacks the power of self-pollination that some plants possess. Future generations depend on both male and female beings. I would like to see the two sexes stop belittling each other and settle down to live as partners on this peculiar planet, sharing its blessings as well as its pain.

It is a lonely business being a human creature, and our species seems to be the only one on earth in which male and female are often in conflict. It is certainly time for men and women to be at peace with one another.

Yet even in everyday conversation we tend to emphasize the negative.

"What can you expect? He's a man," I often hear.

"Well, that's just like a woman," is another frequent comment.

This kind of opinion dates back, I suppose, to Cleopatra, who nevertheless managed very well as a woman.

In our era parents are responsible for much of the sex discrimination. A good many families still give priority to the boys. It's not surprising that the girls resent this. Left to themselves, children accept one another with less rivalry.

My grandfather was an exceptional man. There were four boys and four girls in the big mansion, and he offered them all equal education, even going so far as to send one gifted daughter to Rome to study opera. One girl loved hunting and grew up to be the best shot in the area. The concession to her femininity was that, when she shot her deer, she sat down on the nearest log and poured herself a cup of tea while she waited for a couple of men to turn up and help carry her stag out of the woods.

Farm chores were equally divided, except that the boys shoveled the manure—with over a hundred cows, it wasn't light work. But the girls helped with all the chickens.

Grandma was special. Unlike most wives of her generation, she did not run the house. She was usually seated at the grand piano in the parlor playing and singing. And it seemed to me, just from the way Grandpa looked at her, that he never worried about her not doing woman's work. The rest of the family felt the same way. I suspect that if he had not been able to afford a neat, rosy Irish girl who loved to cook, the children would have taken over the huge kitchen. Certainly the family roles weren't at all rigidly limited in that household.

When we visited Grandpa and Grandma's, I played with a bevy of boy cousins who never bothered about my being a girl. I did everything they did except climb trees, and that was only because I was (and am) afraid of heights. But not one ever told me I was just a girl. I waited at the foot of the tree and munched an extra red apple.

Today I feel great affection for both men and women. When I read the outpourings of the most aggressive feminists, I do begin to feel protective of that opposite sex. Besides, I love the old-fashioned social graces—I appreciate having a man open doors, rise when a woman comes in, carry the drinks, lug suitcases and all the rest. This makes me feel cherished—never, never insulted!

At this point in my conversation with Amber I got up to light one of the Christmas candles Helen and Vicky gave me. Outside the big window the sky was dark and no moonlight glimmered on Mill Pond. A single low star seemed to be poised just above the juniper at the corner of the yard. As I stood near the Christmas tree, the same star seemed to be shining on my little indoor tree as well.

In the fireplace a half-burned log shifted slightly and the coals brightened to gold for a moment and then faded to a soft ruby again.

It occurred to me that one of my main objections to the extreme feminists is that they seem to regard home as a prison. The theme of so many current books and articles is that the housewife is a poor, downtrodden little woman tied forever into her apron strings. The message is that she should escape her dull routine, get out into the world, have a career. Be creative! Only then will she find herself.

Amber yawned. Home is definitely where her heart is.

She knows that there is a lot of routine in housekeeping. But so there is in any job. In the days when I was a teacher, and also when I worked in a magazine office, I found neither was constantly exciting. The artists I have known did a lot of dull chores, even to cleaning brushes and washing paint rags. The businessmen I know use much of their energy on very boring matters and are always tired. An editorial office in a magazine is a grind most of the time.

Even the constant rehearsing of a symphony orchestra can be deadly, no matter how gorgeous the final performance is.

Opera singers endure drudgery ad infinitum. The life of actors involves about as uncomfortable an existence as that of traveling salesmen. Because of a storm, their plane may land at some remote airport or be grounded. The luggage is lost. The hotel reservations are mislaid. Mostly people who travel a lot complain about always being hungry and arriving somewhere so late that the restaurants have closed.

The ideal dream life just does not exist, I am sure.

The woman who finds herself stuck at home doesn't have to be pitied. A home can use any number of creative skills—and such a variety. Then, too, she may run her business according to her own plan in a kind of freedom not found elsewhere. If she feels like it, she can do the laundry at midnight—no overtime for staff. Or she can let everything go if she needs time off to finish a fascinating book. She can spend a long time on a gourmet dinner or put it off and serve an omelet and a good salad. She can pop out to shop when there is a special sale of imported sweaters.

Best of all, if she has been up half the night, she can obey the alarm clock long enough to get the family off to business or school and then sneak back for an extra bit of sleep while the breakfast dishes quietly soak.

Along with the belittling of women's lives at home, there is the feminists' crusade for getting the children out of it. Maybe these reformers do not mean to imply that taking care of the young is servitude but simply that it is limiting to "the self." The minute children are housebroken, some people are all for placing them in nursery school, day school or *somewhere* so that Mama will be free to lead a constructive life.

To be sure, for the woman who must work to help support her family or who is deeply involved in her own career, child-care centers are a blessing. They fill the place of the grandmothers and aunts and other relatives who used to help out in the old days. But some reformers recommend these programs for all children, no matter what the family situation.

I am divided between rage and pity at this concept. For one of the greatest joys in life is watching and sharing in the excitement of children growing up. True, I know a few women who "can't stand" children. They also dislike dogs and cats.

Granted that it is a big job to raise children properly. Puppies and kittens, too, can be problems at times. But the rewards are extravagant. The first word a baby utters is usually "Mama," and fortunate the mother who is right there. It takes the mind back to the first word spoken by that first strange creature who stood upright instead of traveling on all fours. The mystery of acquiring speech is still awesome. So is the moment when a puppy or kitten suddenly recognizes his or her own name.

Parents who share family life store enough happy memories to fill any empty spaces in later life. And I notice when the grown children in my family bring their own offspring to the old farmhouse, they unpack a goodly store of memories too. They are, in a way, trying to give the sons and daughters part of their own childhoods. The new generation love to hear that their mother ran away from home on her bicycle but came back in time for supper. And what happened the night the barn burned down. Or how Esmé, the Siamese, climbed the biggest maple and couldn't get down.

"Living is building up memories," I tell Amber. "And I like to think yours are all happy ones."

If I could have my wish, I would wish that every individual, man or woman, could find the opportunity he or she needs for personal fulfillment. Let the young girl decide to become an astronaut—or a garage mechanic—if this is her particular bent. But do not belittle the girl who dreams of becoming what the magazines now refer to as "just a housewife." Happiness means something different to each of us.

Thinking about happiness, I feel that perhaps we worry about it too much nowadays. This is an age in which searching for it is the overwhelming preoccupation. I call this the Ego

Era. And we search, not for a brief moment of happiness but for a constant, unending state of bliss.

I began to bother about this when I was talking to some teenagers the other day.

"I don't want to waste time on English," Tom said, shaking his tangle of hair.

"Why not?"

"It isn't fun."

"English is okay, but I—uh—hate math. It's—uh—like, well—uh—it don't make me happy to hang around figuring," Dick explained.

"It's pretty nice to be able to add and subtract when you get a job."

"Somebody else can push buttons—uh—on the calculator. Like I say, not me."

"Sure, and why get bored reading—uh—a lot of—uh—books and stuff? No fun. I want to go where the action is and, you know—uh—have fun," Jane said.

"Last semester I got out of one of those dumb foreign language deals." Bob sounded proud.

"Why do you all go to school anyway?" I asked.

"It's one stupid law. But you can cut a lot if you work it right," Dick summed up.

When I recovered from shock, I began asking around in my area and found that these teenagers were perfectly normal, healthy, bright youngsters. Rich or poor, from all kinds of backgrounds, they were united in the belief that they should never, never waste their time on anything that wasn't a fun game. Their goal was happiness and involved never doing anything that was not sheer pleasure. And pleasure—easy fun—was the only kind of happiness they could imagine.

If this philosophy of life takes over that whole generation and future generations as well, will mankind regress to the Stone Age? Will their descendants go around mumbling "uhs" but have no language for real communication?

When their parents and grandparents were this age, they had a desire to learn. Those fortunate enough to be in good schools under good teachers remember school days as the happiest of times. Those not so lucky still went to school (usually on foot, not in a Mercedes or a school bus) and put up with it because that was the expected pattern. No energy was spent hating school because it wasn't a gala performance!

Of course, I do know children today who find going to school a pleasure instead of a bore. Comparing the two groups, I find that the ones who like to learn seem happier and accept routine calmly. I suppose they should be called realists. The boy in group A who cuts math dreams of being an astronaut, just flying into space free as a bird, but he has no ambition to master mathematics as a beginning. The girl who dreams of being a great actress sees herself standing on stage while flowers rain around her, but she wants to cut English, which is pretty basic to the theater.

One kind of happiness comes from conquering obstacles. I myself reached a peak when I made a B in algebra. Being crowned a queen would not have been so delightful.

The new "freedom and fun" motive affects the older generation, too. The institution of marriage is no more stable than a canoe going over Niagara Falls. Marriage counselors, therapy groups, psychiatrists, psychologists, the churches—all are doing their best to prop up a shaky structure. They work in their various ways to preserve the family, which has been the foundation of civilization since mankind climbed down from the trees and discovered that cooked meat was better than raw chunks. In time it was also discovered that a male and female did better in a pair, caring for their own offspring. As a unit they were safer, ate better and developed emotions unknown before. But this has changed. Now we are amazed because Canada geese mate for life!

The other side of this coin is that for centuries a woman, once married, lost her identity as well as all her possessions.

Even the children belonged to the husband. She was simply a thing owned by the male. No one would wish society to turn back to those dark ages.

Neither would anyone wish to force an obviously mismatched couple to stay together. A basically unhappy marriage is a house built on stilts over a swamp and cannot benefit anyone, not even the family dog or cat. But now many couples divorce because the honeymoon cannot last forever. When it isn't fun, let's split, seems to be the theme song. The family breaks up, and the partners go off looking for the old Bluebird of Happiness in some new place.

Society today needs restructuring, it seems to me. Some old-fashioned words such as "responsibility," "conscience," "caring" might be taken from the attic, polished off and put to use. We need this in every area from government to individual life.

Acceptance of reality is important. No pursuit of happiness alone is apt to bring it. It is as elusive as a sea fog.

"She has everything," we say.

It seldom defines happiness. Having "everything" can be not enough.

When a most glamorous, beautiful, world-famous star marries for the seventh time, I can feel only that her search for happiness has been a sad pilgrimage, no matter how many diamonds she has acquired.

"She certainly knows the marriage vows by heart," I tell Amber. "Too bad they never stick."

Amber has found her Christmas wreath and that, she indicates, is happiness for her. Woven of soft wool, it is about an inch around and fits a person's mouth for carrying.

"Happiness for me," I say, "is watching you right now strutting so proudly around the living room."

Perhaps happiness can never be classified. It can be a moment of joy or a few hours of quietude, a hard-won success or the sight of a red fox running at sunset. Basically it must be an attitude deep within that gives us perception.

I do not believe we find it by trying to be "free," to abandon responsibilities, toss burdens in the deepest sea, ignore the rest of our fellow beings while we seek some mythical euphoria. The happiest woman I ever knew led a difficult, often tragic life but she lived it with grace, compassion, gentleness and humor. She was not liberated, far from it; she had no dazzling career and no memorial was erected to her. But her memory is cherished by everyone who ever met her, even briefly. She would have said, "Of course I am happy!"

"Well, Amber," I said, "I wish my mother could have seen you!"

12

THE DISASTROUS JANUARY STORM moved on
Cape Cod like a squadron of jet planes. Even the weathermen
had not predicted how fast or how bad it would be. Amber and
I were watching television that evening, and she was surprised
when the screen was suddenly filled with zigzags.

"Well, I guess we'll call that nice man again in the morning," I said. She gave a miaow of displeasure as I unfolded my
lap and turned the set off. It was 8:30.

Suddenly the wind moaned against the picture windows.

"This means a blizzard," I told her, an unnecessary remark.

I did not worry, but I did turn the furnace up and turned
on the electric blanket. I checked the window locks. At 9:10

the house blacked out. Amber followed me as I crept to the hall closet, using the last match in the book. She was no help because her small self blended into the darkness.

Two flashlights had died just sitting on the shelf, but I finally found two good ones. Also, the Christmas candles were still around. Already the house was chilly, as if an icy hand had closed around it.

While I sat down to think what to do, Amber moved from one heat duet to another, checking every area where hot air should have been coming out. Her face grew more and more puzzled. She tried them again.

"The furnace is out," I said.

I would surmount this crisis somehow, but I have never felt so ashamed of myself for being utterly unprepared. Some friends had dropped in the night before, and the big fireplace had gobbled up every log and dead branch, plus a basket of old shingles. The garage was neck deep with wood but, because of the high wind and whipping snow, it was as inaccessible as Mount Washington on a stormy night. A tour of the house by flashlight revealed that every old newspaper was also stacked in that garage.

I dug out the fine battery lamp, which gives enough light to read by but only when the batteries are alive. The small oil lamp on the top shelf was in good shape except that there was no oil! The wool blankets sat on the top closet shelf under a pile of extra pillows. I finally dragged one down.

There is nothing colder than an old, lifeless electric blanket, I explained to Amber. She was underfoot every instant. It was getting colder by the minute, and I tried to put the extra blanket on the bed. By the light of one Christmas candle it was hard to keep hauling her out from the folds of the blanket.

Our next venture involved hunting for the ancient Sterno stove, and that search ended when I remembered it had been thrown out two seasons ago, along with a mummified can of heat.

Back on the couch, I wrapped Amber in my best cashmere

sweater and swaddled us both in what they call a throw, made of Scottish wool.

Meanwhile, the worst storm on record in this area did its best to crash the picture windows, rip the shingles from the roof, wrench the doors open.

Amber, buried in my lap and sweater, behaved with complete composure, and I wished I could borrow some. She only began to shiver around one in the morning, just as my feet and hands were growing numb. This was the time to rise above our troubles. I began by taking refuge in Shakespeare, my habit at difficult moments.

" 'All these woes shall serve as sweet discourses in our time to come,' " I assured her.

She poked a pink-tipped nose at me. One visible eye was onyx. I wanted to make conversation.

"I wish I had cat eyes," I said. "I would like to see in the dark. And then in sharp sunlight I wouldn't be hunting for dark glasses.

"Your ancestors came from Egypt," I told her. "That was before you were born. They came to Egypt on fishing boats from Abyssinia and were called fishing cats. That's why you like to wade around in the shower stall or the bathroom basin if there is any water in it, and why you love drinking from faucets."

I burrowed one hand under all the wool and gave her a good rubbing, which resulted in her middle purr. She was warm but not cozy enough for the top purr.

"If I could smuggle you into a museum, I would show you Egyptian bas-reliefs of your ancestors," I said. "They look just like you. Beautiful and elegant. And those cats were very special because the Egyptians were losing all their grain to rats and of course the cats began to kill the rats. So your ancestors were extremely valuable. Kings and queens kept them, and you won't believe it, but if anyone abused or killed a cat, his or her eyebrows were shaved off as a mark of shame."

At that point I noticed that the wind had diminished. I felt better about the picture windows, so I blew out the candle and snapped on the flashlight. Wrapped in our woolens, we crawled into bed. which felt like a polar ice sheet. Huddled under a pile oı blankets, I promised Amber that our body heat would help, but neither of us was exactly feverish just then.

My dissertation was ended because I did not think I could explain about her forebears being mummified and buried in the tombs with their owners. For one thing, it must have involved the cats' being killed when the owners died.

Amber went to sleep at once, but I lay awake worrying about everybody who might be out in that storm. I wished I could check on the neighbors and be sure their houses were snug.

The long night's journey into day was over eventually. Amber had a cold jar of her baby food, and I settled for a can of Coca Cola from the pantry for breakfast, the oddest one I ever had.

The sun came out and the world was polished in crystal. And the Barkers, my next-door neighbors, came plowing through the snow with wood, a thermos of boiling water, instant coffee and soup packets. "Now just keep drinking hot drinks," Kay advised, while Pret got a blaze going on the cold hearth.

The open fire brought back the heat of life. Amber got as close to it as she dared and began to scrub herself. I gulped coffee. At 11:10 the house itself came alive, furnace humming, refrigerator thumping, electric clocks buzzing. Our ordeal was ended. I turned on the radio and heard the news about the whole Northeast.

My final comment is that in the midst of a crisis an individual is likely to be preoccupied with his own trouble, his own immediate world. But I have found that when I need to worry about Amber's freezing to death or the house's blowing down, I seem to extend myself to every human being in the

131

same part of the planet—especially that night to the crews who worked until morning risking their lives to get service restored, roads cleared of live wires, trees dragged from highways, light poles erected again. God bless them, I thought, and God bless neighbors. We are, after all, a caring people.

Amber, of course, had an advantage over me, as do cats and dogs in most situations. They do not keep imagining worse horrors to come. They live in the present. Amber accepted the cold and the dark and the moaning wind shaking the house without ever indicating a complaint. She sought the best security she had, which was my lap, and when I had to get up to check a candle, I carried her like a muff.

The only exception I ever knew to this advantage over humans was one golden cocker named Especially Me, otherwise known as Teddy. Thunderstorms or hurricanes frightened him out of his mind, and he used to crawl under the bed and spend the whole time shaking. No matter how many in the family got down on their stomachs and coaxed, he was unavailable. My bed is one of those old rope beds, bigger than most four-posters and embellished with a deep skirt. He chose the exact middle underneath, just out of reach. After we had tried once to sweep him out with the dust mop but didn't succeed, we gave up.

All living beings experience fear, the experts say, but Teddy's was more than an immediate fear. It was worry, a constant anxiety that lasted until the storm ended. When he finally came out, paw by paw, relieved and shaky, he was ravenous and had to have an extra meal.

Animals apparently do not fear death. Most humans walk with it daily, especially mothers with small children. Such anxiety is, of course, reasonable in our era of crowded school buses, bombs tucked into mailboxes, plane accidents and so on. Even so, it seems to me that we waste a great deal of energy worrying ahead, piling up fears. Animals are superior, no doubt about it.

Amber certainly does not expect that I will die every time I go out and shut the door. She does leap to the kitchen windowsill and press a desperate triangle of face against the glass, but when I start the car I know what she does, for sometimes I forget my bag, and by the time I tiptoe back she is already tucked on her pillow, storing up energy for an ecstatic greeting when I am home again where I belong. The moment I call her name, she explodes into wakefulness, wiping the last yawn from her mouth.

But not only is Amber free from all worries about whatever troubles may be waiting around the next bend, she is also very sensible about accepting the few rules and regulations of our daily lives together.

Her feelings have always been that our few firm rules are perfectly acceptable—for instance, if I call her, she wants to come anyway. If I say "Stay," she stays because she prefers to have the security of her leash before going out that door into the great mystery of outdoors. Even "No" is all right because I do not go around saying No until it is a bore. And she loves praise as a TV star loves applause. The extreme praise that comes when she stops rearranging a bouquet is well worth it to her.

We are very much alike in this respect, for I too relish praise and wilt under criticism. Being criticized by friends for my own good, alas, does not reform me but just makes me miserable.

When Amber wakes me up jumping on me with morning paws, then sits gazing at me with wide candid eyes for long, long minutes, I am not nervous. She is not reminding me that my hair is a tangle or that my pajamas belong in the dump. Her comforting purr and a feather-light touch on my cheek, plus that intent gaze, do convey that she wishes I would get up, but not that I have no business staying in bed.

If I am going out on a special occasion, she watches every move I make, hopping with interest from bureau to closet shelf to washbowl, but not because I have put on the wrong blouse with my pantsuit or my makeup is the worst color for my fair skin. She especially likes my lavender perfume—but then she loves all flower scents.

And when I finally go out the front door, her last look is plain adoration overlaid with wistfulness. It is no wonder my definition of security is an Abyssinian cat.

It is fortunate that Amber finds security in me, for on the few occasions some stranger has snapped at her for inspecting a tray of cheeses too closely, she collapses like an automobile tire with a nail embedded in it. Then she vanishes until I excavate her from the bureau drawer. I once fixed her a special tray of cheeses so she could sniff every kind and decide on her own favorite. We never mentioned the unpleasant incident again.

13

DURING THE FIRST BREAK in a week of blowy, rainy March weather, we made a routine visit to Dr. Kim. We were the last patients of the morning. After the commotion in the jammed waiting room, even Amber behaved very well, except when Kim applied the stethoscope to hear her heart. He said the sound nearly blew his ears out. This is an inside rumbling I can't even hear.

"You couldn't be healthier," said Kim. "Now let's see, how old are you, Amberino?" He glanced at me, then back to her. "Sorry, that's a question we won't bother about."

"I can look it up on her pedigree," I said as I folded assorted legs and tail into her carrying case. "I think she may be nine."

"Let's settle for eight and a half." Kim put away the stethoscope. "Anyway, she's fine. Everything's perfect."

I was thankful that Kim does not go along with those who are dedicated to remembering how old their pets are, then figuring out that this adds up to age ninety-five in humans. I suppose one could try to estimate our human age as compared to an elephant's and come up with something just as startling. This is not my own idea of an interesting mental game.

My only age comparison is made when someone complains that a new puppy is not yet housebroken.

"How old is he?"

"Six weeks Tuesday."

"He's hardly ready for high school in that case. He is still in the diaper age."

The subject of aging in mankind seems to me to edge into obsessions. I know too many people whose first question about meeting a stranger is, "How old is she? How old is he?"

This never occurs to me. I try to get an impression of the personality, happy or sad, intelligent or dull, conservative or liberal, warm or cold, outgoing or introspective. When others in the group try to decide whether the new neighbor is fifty-five or has just turned sixty or is midway between thirty and forty, I blank out. I go on wondering what kind of individual this is, with a hope that I may eventually find out what shaped him or her. This takes all my time, for everyone is a mystery at best.

The bad result of this is that I seldom remember the name of someone new. My friends who concentrate on age always seem able to pinpoint the name after they have settled on the probable age. Later on, it goes like this:

"What did you think of Elizabeth Graham?"

"Who?"

"The one who was at the cocktail party yesterday—just bought the old McGregor house."

"Oh. Well, I think there is sadness in her eyes, but she won't go around talking about her troubles. She has a quiet mouth, but her face has done a lot of smiling, judging by those happy lines. I think she would always be at ease—she never even flinched when the cocktail was spilled on that pink wool dress."

"How old do you think she is?"

"I haven't the faintest idea."

I am no help in this age-tag deal.

"Amber," I said, on the way home from Kim's, "you know who started this age business? It was Bismarck. It must have been in the nineteenth century. He was the first one to decide that at sixty-five retirement was mandatory. I wonder whether he had an ulterior motive. Maybe he wanted to shove someone onto the shelf more easily. In any case, sixty-five was it!"

Since Bismarck's day, of course, the life span of human beings has changed remarkably. My doctor tells me that in the early days of our own country the average woman lived to be thirty-four or so. If women got past their thirties, it seems, they had a good chance of living into their nineties. The death rate in babies was staggering. Parents expected to lose a few children along the way, but there was usually a new baby coming along.

In the days when my parents were growing up, it was common for young ladies to be "frail." Many were taken to eternal rest before they had a chance to get tired. Of course, a particular hazard in those days was what they called consumption, tuberculosis. The Uncle Leonidas who came back unscratched from the Civil War went to his reward shortly thereafter, they said, because he had caught consumption in the South. I think he was in his mid-twenties.

Possibly the fact that the mortality rate was so high resulted in appreciation of those hardy souls who survived. No matter whether they were noble characters or not, they were respected because they had lasted so long. Just to live was admirable, as indeed it was, considering the vast ignorance in the field of medicine. Simply being bled for almost any illness, or having leeches applied between purges, must have shortened many a life. My doctor suggests that the stock itself must have been more rugged in earlier generations, or populations would never have increased as they did.

Reverence for the aged meant that Grandpa and Grandma achieved a kind of royalty, and the wisdom a long life taught them was a rock and refuge to the younger generation. Also, since they were generally an integral part of the family, they were right at hand to give special caring to the very young children while the parents coped with the mechanics of living. So many memoirs are rich with recollections of fishing, berry-picking and building tree houses with Grandpa, or learning fairy tales, furnishing dollhouses and baking cookies with Grandma.

In my own childhood grandparents were still touched with mystique. For years I visualized God as exactly like the portrait of Grandfather Bagg, complete with snowy, flowing beard and a mass of curly white hair with glints of red still visible. The deep sea-blue eyes looked out with such dignity above the patrician nose and imperative mouth. When I misbehaved, I tiptoed anxiously past that portrait, but I needed a figure to revere as a small boat in a stormy sea needs a lighthouse.

Grandma Bagg was not awesome, but when she died the whole enormous house seemed filled with emptiness, although I cannot count the number of inhabitants there at the time. She brought music, color, laughter to everyone, but especially to us grandchildren.

On the other side, Grandfather Raybold was gone before I knew anything about him except that he married Mama and Papa in the little white church on the green. Grandma Raybold naturally lived with Uncle Walter and his family. When Mama and I visited there, it was a special treat to climb the great staircase and go into Grandma's room, the big corner one on the second floor. It overlooked the garden and the woods beyond, although this was a town house, not a farmhouse like the other one.

The room smelled of lavender, and I remember that it always seemed full of sunlight, although I know it must have rained in Pittsfield, Massachusetts, reasonably often. Except for the four-poster, it looked like a parlor, or what used to be called a "morning room." I suspect the furniture had come with her from the manse—the elegant little chest, the lady's desk, the rosewood sofa, the low Victorian rocking chair upholstered in flowered velvety material, soft to the touch of a small hand.

The big woven carpet was soft to walk on, too. The curtains were white, ruffled, tied neatly back. I do not remember the bedspread—was it hobnailed or hand-woven in a pattern? But the down comforter or puff triangled at the foot of the bed was a soft pastel.

To me the most impressive item was something I had not seen before. The bathroom was down the hall, but Grandma had a commode by the washstand. The top was padded and the whole piece encased in flowered chintz. In fact, it looked exactly like the box seats in modern apartments except that they are usually painted orange or black or avocado. The china pitcher, bowl and soap dish on the washstand must have had the moss rose pattern on them, for years later at an antique shop I saw a set, extravagantly expensive, and Grandma's room shone in my memory.

I liked to sit on the commode, which gave a nice view of the family portraits arranged on the dresser and hung in a row on the walls, all in oval gold frames. One showed Grandma and Grandpa on their wedding day, he stiffly elegant in pastoral black, she diminutive and beautiful in antique satin and lacy veil.

When I came to visit, Grandma herself sat in the rocker. Although it was a small one (a so-called lady's chair), she was smaller.

139

She wore a dove-grey frock with trim bodice, rippling full skirt, fine white lace at neck and cuffs. Her slippers were either grey or black. I can't recall her ever wearing the high-laced shoes of her period. She usually wore something on her silvery hair, a kind of lace bonnet or cap (I think this was morning wear) or a black velvet ribbon to keep the fine strands in place (Mama and I both inherited that fine hair). Hairnets were made of stiff, wiry material—horsehair, I think. Hers, of course, was grey.

Her cheeks were still rosy-pink, her blue eyes lake-blue behind the steel spectacles. The locket chain was gold, and tiny blue and pink posies decorated the enamel oval. Pink, pale blue or lilac fringed feather-light shawls were always at hand, for she chilled easily.

I imagine she must have weighed ninety pounds at most. She had been ill after she lost Grandpa and still had a fragile appearance, like a delicate windflower.

Life downstairs went on, chiefly without her except that she came down to dinner and on Sunday afternoons for tea or when Uncle Walter read the Bible. But she was never under-foot, "poking her nose," as Mama said, "into other people's business." Upstairs in her room, she read or stitched or wrote letters in a firm slanting hand (when we were traveling around all over the country, Mama's greatest worry was that she would miss one of those letters; they nourished her through many difficult years when Father's mining engineering career kept us nomadic).

I was too young to realize that such closeness between mother and daughter was unusual. This relationship was not only filled with love but with a kind of sharing as well. I tell Amber that she would have loved Grandma Raybold, too.

Uncle Walter was "in business," having abandoned the traditional ministry. During the week the prosperous paper mill kept him away all day, but my two cousins and I watched for his return so eagerly. He was not awesome like Grandfather Bagg.

He was a big man, handsome, dark-eyed, with gentle humor written all over his face. Another brother had died very young; a daughter married a farmer and "went west" to live in a sod house in Iowa. Uncle Walter became head of the family after Grandfather died.

When he married and built the big house, Grandma was, of course, packed up to move in with the family. I wished I could have seen her own house where Mama grew up, but I never did.

Uncle Walter married a handsome, ebullient woman sparkling with life but temperamental (at least I thought so). She had excellent taste in decorating the home and with the help of the customary Irish girl served elegant meals at the mahogany table, with snowy linen, crystal, polished silver.

My cousins Dorothy and Mildred were lively, alert, full of fun. As an only child never in one place long enough to make friends, I was always sobbing when we took the train to catch up with Papa in some new place. So staying with them was sheer heaven. I was an added nuisance to my aunt, I now know —one more leggy creature dashing around. And the worst was that Uncle Walter had one of the new player-piano attachments for the grand piano and I could put in a roll of "The Whistler and His Dog" and play the same roll for hours. I think my aunt had more headaches and spoke to her husband about it, for he finally suggested gently to me that I play "The Whistler and His Dog" only once—or at most twice—a day.

In any case, downstairs was a moderate bedlam, with streams of company in and out to add to it. Naturally there were quarrels and upsets too. On Grandpa Bagg's huge farm children had the freedom of fields, brooks, pond, barns and icehouses (where you could sneak in for slivers of ice), but at Uncle Walter's much of living went on inside.

Every so often I would simply "give out," as Mama said. Then I ran upstairs to Grandma's room and knocked on her door. It was serene as a still-water pond inside. The lavender fragrance welcomed me, the pastel colors delighted my eyes and the small figure in the rosewood rocking chair always laid down her mending at once.

"Come in, dear," she said. "Have you been out to see the roses?" Her smile was an extra welcome.

Grandma was a listener, which was as rare in those days as now. I could pour out anything cluttering my head and never get interrupted. I was not spoken to about my flyaway hair, messy dress, stocking runs, dusty shoes. The confusion I brought ebbed into peacefulness. If I complained about some injustice she might utter a wise comment, but she never scolded me.

She did not criticize me, although she once spoke to Mama privately. "Grace, can't you do something about that dreadful Midwestern accent Gladys has picked up?" The Massachusetts speech was the only proper one.

Sometimes I had a "sweet" from a china bowl or a thin sugar cookie. In that immaculate room I was careful about crumbs.

I always left this little old woman feeling restored. I also felt cherished as a person, not as just another child.

But I did not know how old she was and never even gave it a thought. We were never there on her birthday, when I imagine the cake was dense with candles. For this was before the obsession with age began.

As I grew older, I knew that obituaries announced the age of the deceased, because I would hear, "Poor Agatha Clark has passed away. The *Post Crescent* has such a nice piece about her. What a pity—such an untimely death!"

Papa would peer at the paper. "Says here she was eighty-six. Must have been something seriously wrong with her."

"I'll make up some chicken and ham and a salad you can take over," Mama said. "You go out, Rufus, and cut the best of the white lilacs."

"You'll have to hurry up." Papa was always in a hurry.

"You go round the garden and pick some vegetables, too. I'll ring the bell when I'm done."

"Where's Gladys?" This always ended his conversation.

"She'll be home in plenty of time to go with you to poor Agatha's." And Mama went off to find a pretty basket.

"No, Amber," I say, "when I was growing up, our attitudes toward old age were very different."

Amber gets up, stretches, then curls up again with one eye open. If I want to keep talking, all right.

14

AFTER OUR FIRST DISCUSSION about growing older, I thought that Amber and I had settled the subject once and for all—at least as far as we ourselves were concerned. But it came to mind again yesterday when I went to a cocktail party given by two unmarried young women who shared the work and expense of entertaining friends of both. Afterward the whole group moved on for supper at an Italian restaurant. On the way home I sat comfortably in the front seat of the car watching moon patterns through leafy trees until someone in the back seat spoke to me.

"I was so impressed at how devoted to you they both are."

"What's wrong with me?"

"Oh, no, I didn't mean that. It's just they are so young! How old are they—thirty?"

"I've never investigated their ages and they have never asked mine," I said. It hadn't occurred to me that the age gap might affect friendships.

The next night my favorite young couple dropped in after a club dance, still glowing from the evening. Then, as he passed us drinks, Bob had a sobering thought.

"Honey, you know this may be our last dance at the club."

"Why?"

"Remember, we can't belong any more when we are thirty-five."

"Can't we get away with an extra year on account of our birthdays being in April?"

"Maybe. We'll work on it."

"Perhaps a few of your best friends will make it to thirty-five next year, too—certainly the Websters will. Then you can organize the exact same kind of boat club with the membership beginning at thirty-five."

I have reflected a good deal on the whole attitude our society has taken toward aging, but I can never make it seem rational. I keep getting right back to Bismarck and wishing he had never been born. Mankind is not, I think, static. All the modern medical discoveries, the knowledge of nutrition, our life-style itself have lengthened the span of human existence immeasurably and also made the species healthier, more resilient.

Besides that, aging is not automatic in its progress. I have known forty-year-olds who were, to all intents and purposes, over sixty. And I have intimately known some in the eighties who have never lost the youthful sparkle and zest for life but have seasoned it with wisdom, deep stores of knowledge and an understanding and compassion such as the middle years often lack.

The mania for being young supports a large part of our

economy, I know. Billions of dollars are spent on cosmetics, wrinkle erasers, face-lifts, hair dyes, false eyelashes and wigs, as well as countless contraptions to jockey bust lines, flatten stomachs. Exercise machines thump and mold legs and arms, correct slight stoops. An endless flood of new diets promises that husbands will eternally chase wives around the house because they will still resemble the sylphs they were as brides. Some of the sensible diets do keep overweight at bay, but others result in dangerous side effects.

The daily fare on television and radio sells the idea that successful marriage depends on the husband's never having a ring around the collar, even if he has been sweating all afternoon repairing the roof in mid-August or murdering Japanese beetles in the roses or commuting home from the office via the subway. To retain his wife's love, he must garb himself spotlessly, rub guaranteed preparations into his scalp, color the thinning hair or wear a modern version of the toupee.

The wife must spend 90 percent of her own time keeping glamorous, waving a lily-white hand at him, with no sign of red, roughened skin to indicate an honest day's work. Care of her face is a full-time job—skin moisturized, soothed, creamed, topped with several layers of makeup base, covered with second coats of Sunglo, filmed with matching dusting powder. Her figure must be slim, lissome, willowy, seductive at all times, even after getting a bevy of children off to school at a hellish hour. What husband coming home at night wants to find that the woman he married has "let herself go"—has tumbled hair, work-worn hands and, God forbid, drops of sweat crystals on her unmade-up face?

Glamour magazines and television can only warn that he will turn on his heel, go off to a motel and pick up some sexy blonde who smells of that eight-dollar-an-ounce seductive perfume.

The message universally hammered in is that without the superficial preservation of youth, all is lost! If this be true, I am a maverick. I agree that external beauty is all very well, and I know that with constant struggle a man or woman can prolong the appearance of youth to a certain extent.

But I worry about the values today. When I meet a middle-aged man or woman who spends so much energy trying to be twenty, I begin to wonder whether all that time (and time is a short commodity at best) is well spent. I indulge in fantasy. Suppose that the same amount of time and also money were used some other way—an extra hour reading a provocative book instead of lying flat with soaked pads over the eyes, or absorbing some good music instead of grinding away at that exerciser. Or investigating nature instead of taking a bubble bath. Or exploring the minds and hearts of the children, if there are any, instead of spending two extra hours at the beauty parlor getting the scalp nourished, the hair streaked fashionably, the split ends cured by a guaranteed new protein treatment.

I see in my mind's eye the beautiful wife (looks not a day over twenty-three) and glamorous husband (not a day older) going out to dinner for an anniversary.

"You look super," he says.

"So do you."

Then they cannot think of anything more to say! They try discussing the security blanket of America, the probable weather, and then they spend a lot of time choosing the dinner and the right wine. Passersby enjoy seeing two such beautiful people who seem to be so happily married. But their own main interest, staying young, is as worn out as an old dishrag.

In the year since their last anniversary the surfaces may have held up pretty well. But what has happened to their inner selves? What discoveries about life, what new understandings, what new horizons have they shared to make life together richer? A few new mechanical aids to help keep that look of youth provide little stimulation for conversation. It is what has gone on deep inside that matters—the core of the personality.

A thoughtful observer begins to note that a beautiful, glamorous face is rather blank, almost like the bisque dolls of early days. The slim figure is as familiar as a model in a fashion show. As time passes, as it has a way of doing, devotees of youth acquire a weary look from the battle that can never be won. They remind me of marathon runners who, no matter how fleet they are, break the tape at the finish line with only a temporary victory.

Stage and screen stars and the great opera singers usually do their best to follow the modern cult. Several I have been seeing for a long time have had so many facial uplifts that I hardly recognize them after the latest remodeling. Much of the charm and enchantment they built up in their careers seems to vanish; they are strangers we do not know. But those who believe it is the essence of their art that matters seem to gain in the mystique of stardom. They are, to me, the truly great. And to me they grow more beautiful as long experience erases the shiny gloss of youth. One can see Jimmy Stewart, for instance, in a very old movie, just beginning to be a great actor, looking so young and so handsome. Now he may shamble onto a television platform, take time to be comfortable in a chair. His snowy hair frames a well-lined face. He blinks those brilliant eyes at the violent lights, and the laugh wrinkles deepen as he begins to speak hesitantly, a little slower than in the early days.

And any audience rises to give him an ovation when he comes on. He is himself, natural, without pretense. Perhaps I only imagine that part of the tribute is a subconscious relief that this actor has not been running in fear all these years from the nightmare of growing older.

As a maverick, I admit that while I love to look at handsome young men and beautiful young women, the men and women most beautiful to me are those who may not be superficially breathtaking. Not at all. They might never win prizes in the glamour contests. They may even be homely, according to today's standards. But some inner, indefinable quality of personality brings a shining to the very atmosphere around them. These are the ones I wish I could paint.

One of them is a dear friend who would be horrified at the idea of even posing for a snapshot. I'll call her Evelyn. She is strongly built, with ample curves. Her fine brown hair (with silvery lights) lies flat except for wisps that fall onto her cheeks as she runs (I have never seen her walk—she skims along). Her eyes are set wide under a calm high forehead. They are the color of a woodland pond on a spring morning, and when she gazes at you that clear, lucent look is deep enough to drown in. Her face is broad, with an unobtrusive nose and wide, gently curved mouth.

She wears unspectacular clothes, including comfortable dresses or simple skirts and blouses and shoes easy to run in. On bitter days I sometimes meet her hurrying along with an armload of groceries, a woolen or knitted shawl blowing behind her, hair dropping like a veil over a rosy face. She stops briefly to say hello in a singing, soft voice.

The wife of an extremely busy medical man, the mother of six children, she never looks cross or harried or low-spirited. She finds time to do more good in the community than can be added up, but never mentions her activities. I found out about the day a week she volunteers in the elementary school library only because I went there to visit with the children. Somehow she had made stuffed wild animals, all kinds, which the children could take home in turn. They are not whip-ups but beautiful treasures such as one sees in Fifth Avenue windows in New York City, valued at thirty-five, forty or more dollars. To see a small, thin, young fourth-grader cradle the lordly giraffe she can *take home* gives a new dimension to life.

I met Evelyn one day when she skimmed into her husband's office with an armload of mail, hurrying but not harried —on the way, perhaps, to a meeting of the historical society or a conservation group or whatever.

So while the doctor was checking my blood pressure, I told him how I wished I could paint so that I could do a portrait of her.

He leaned against the counter thoughtfully. "Yes," he finally said, "my wife has a very expressive face."

Which said it better!

I have never asked how old she is. I only know that, whatever her life span is, she will always be beautiful.

There is something to be done about growing older by every individual who reaches the "retirement age." In our later years we cannot all be Albert Einsteins or Artur Rubinsteins or Arthur Fiedlers, none of whom paused to count when they reached sixty-five or seventy. But how we grow in years does depend on ourselves.

When I came to this conclusion, there was one more mountain to climb in my work on my current book. And Amber began working on the typewriter keys with two flying paws. So we went outdoors and chased a few unidentified flying objects, stuffed the bird feeder, apologized to the mockingbirds because the birdbath was full of sunflower seeds. There is no way to teach chickadees about neatness. What with all these varied activities, we were busy until after supper, when I lit the fire, turned on the sofa lamp, discovered of course that the bulb had burned out during the day, couldn't get the shade off but screwed a new bulb in from underneath.

"Been a long time since the last brushing," Amber told me, planting herself foursquare on my book.

"I have been pondering the problem of aging," I said. "This happens to be a subject you are not interested in."

She purred the high-level purr and half-closed her eyes as she always does when the brushing feels extra good.

"It all started when Kim and I talked incidentally about your being eight and a half and then discarded the subject as totally irrelevant—which it is."

She swiveled her head around, wide-eyed, curious.

"Only human beings have such problems with growing older," I explained. "I wonder why? When did we begin?"

I examined her carefully, feeling the firmly molded bones, the lustrous coat, the erect ears. A few whiskers on the left side had broken off, giving a lopsided effect—too much rubbing against the window screen when a bevy of plump quail came for the cracked corn?

When we began life together, she was tiny and her eyes seemed bigger than all the rest of her. She soared like a bird through the house, in the air more than out of it. She had left her mother before being housebroken and used any spot she lighted on for a bathroom. Too often it was under the four-poster or the lowest couch in the house. During her childhood we worked at this problem, using our reward system of training as we did with the puppies.

She also drove us crazy in her eating habits. They consisted of not liking anything she should eat. This coincided with a small boy in the household who decided he would eat only spaghetti, so it was a time of turbulence.

Her favorite occupations were shredding upholstered furniture or new draperies and unraveling wool from imported sweaters. As a change, pushing pens and pencils from all the desks and tossing them until they went under the couch somewhere alternated with the same pursuit of erasers and paper clips or the munching of rubber bands whenever visible.

Since she operated at such a high level, she made more work than a whole litter of lively cocker puppies would. She could also claw more successfully. They only chewed!

Her insatiable curiosity led her into open drawers, cupboards with one open crack in one door, kitchen sinks, stereos with the lid up, china closets, guests' coat pockets. Once she almost went off in a laundry bag, and another time she was fished out of the dishwasher just in the nick.

She was a kitten, she was enchanting and life was never, never dull. The family spent a lot of time calling one another,

"Come and see Amber! Come look!" She might be a small figurine in the middle of a top shelf where the Belleek tea set lived, or a triangle of face poked from the middle of the filmy lilac sweater she was nibbling. Or she might be playing games with a bunch of car keys fished from a shopping bag, or simply folded up on a visitor's new coat in the exquisite manner only a kitten achieves. At that time she brought a drift of laughter to a house silenced by sorrow.

The years have brought changes. The wiry body is more solid, the whiskers silvery instead of tawny, and the downy white under that determined chin has spread. The wild racing spells, suggesting a jungle pursuit, are limited to occasional flurries of activity. She plays more selectively with one or two toys instead of tossing them all wildly. She dozes more, paws under chin, tail carefully arranged to frame all five pounds of her.

Perhaps the apricot eyelashes are not as thick. And sometimes if she pounces on a pile of manuscript the pages slide and she suffers the indignity of falling down, scattering sheets all over the floor. The greatest humiliation a cat can have, I have observed, is to fall.

She follows the aging pattern of life by having occasional bouts with colitis and recurring attacks of asthma. She sheds more often and has more trouble getting rid of fur balls. She is, by nature, a tropical cat and now dislikes the cold more and chooses nap places right in front of heat ducts. And when she claws a window screen, she may get stuck and need help in getting unhooked.

But she, as a personality, is even more endearing than when she dazzled us with her aerial games as a kitten. The living we have shared is a rich and growing bond. Every scrap of happiness is tucked away in memory. The sorrows I have had to face have found her always comforting me. Like the cockers and Irish, she has ESP and knows instantly when my personal skies have no stars lighting them. She accepts her few limitations with grace, and her purr rate is even more constant.

Some animals I know get crotchety when they are very old, usually because of aches and handicaps. But the happiest person I know is my friend Olive's miniature schnauzer, who is "going on fourteen." Trinka is blind and deaf. She has, at times, attacks of colitis, especially if she has eaten too much sand. And yet she is the gayest, jauntiest, most charming person in any group. She prances, skips, pounces. She is proof of the theory that the blind have an extra sensitivity, for she receives vibrations from furniture, walls and doors. She threads her way nimbly through a house. Only rarely, if she is running fast and someone has just moved a chair into a strange place, does she bump her small nose into it.

She is a focal point in a circle of intimate friends—Helen, Vicky, Linda (who has her own ebullient dog). When we all sit around the open fire trying to solve world problems or dipping into nostalgia over past crises which are now hilarious, Trinka gets the attention of a reigning princess (which bothers Amber). When Trinka indicates that she would like to go out, two or three people drop their drinks and jump to attention. If she wants a snack, the Middle East is dropped while she is waited on. Her blue water dish is beside her red security blanket, and when she wakes from a doze someone runs to the kitchen to bring *fresh* water.

In between, Helen scoops her up and carries her around or Vicky finds a small tidbit to be snapped up.

When all this gets too much for Amber, she makes a quick landing on my lap and paws the brush on the couch.

The basic gift most animals have, it seems to me, is acceptance of circumstances and "making do," as Mama would say. They keep the essence of their personality.

"Now, Amber," I say, "you are growing old gracefully. I hope I can do as well."

I retrieve my best pen from under a cushion, substituting a pencil as a toy.

"Human beings journeying toward old age should learn from you," I tell her. "Part of their trouble is their own making."

I made a list to help clarify my thinking.

Some people concentrate on whatever ailments they have; in fact, this can become a career.

Some ascribe any failures to being senile. If they were absentminded at twenty and now forget an engagement, they declare, "Well, I am senile—no good to anybody."

One man I know has habitually mislaid auto keys. But now this causes deep depression. "I'm just an old useless relic." He adds, "Might as well be plowed under, I guess."

Another dear friend, who is both elegant and handsome, is preoccupied with pointing out that her hair is thinner, she can no longer touch her toes with her hands and some joints are swollen. But if I ask her opinion on any profound subject, her judgment, perception, wisdom and wit suddenly arise, lovely as a bird's flight.

"It's all a question of mind over what's the matter," I tell Amber.

I believe that if a member of my species hammers long enough on what aging is doing to his mind and body, he or she will be believed in the end. But who will benefit?

This habit also invades the young and middle-aged. Once a person begins to concentrate on the negative, it increases.

"What a perfect dinner!" I say.

"I think the hollandaise wasn't quite right. And the squash rolls were a bit soggy. The Coq au Vin lacked something. . . ."

"I thought everything was the best ever."

A tour of the newly decorated bedroom comes off no better.

"The drapes are marvelous!"

"The one on the left is an eighth of an inch too short. And I know the valance is too short, too. As for the new rug, it is a shade too long; it goes *under* the legs of the four-poster. And that spring watercolor is hung too high, isn't it?"

By now Amber is sound asleep, left arm stretched out full length on my knee. This spells complete relaxation, because she is so vulnerable in this position. A wild cat is not apt to let one arm lie so flat, since it takes longer to organize for a leap in case an enemy nears. Two half-closed eyes gaze at me, the dark irises elliptical.

So I have time to ponder a bit longer, but not aloud.

Clocks may be turned back—and what a nuisance when daylight saving begins or ends. But Time herself never turns back (and I always muse on just where the missing or added hour goes). Our physical self must suffer wear and tear, although not according to Herr Bismarck's plan.

Therefore, as the patina of youth fades it is, I believe, the time to build up inner resources. It doesn't matter in what area, but we all need something permanent that will not wither when the office door is closed for the last time or the children have bulleted from the nest into an enlarged world. I don't like the word "hobbies," for they sound to me like idle games, but a constant, growing interest in something outside the routine self can strengthen and enrich. The blessing of beginning this pursuit early in life is that it also grows with the passing years.

I used to know a businessman, very successful, who had just one outlet, which was golf. A leg injury made that activity out of the question, so after retirement he spent a good many years in a rocking chair.

His sole remark, day after day, was, "I'm just passing the time away." It was a sad story. He had many possibilities, but he simply gave up.

It was very difficult for his family, all of whom, children and parents, found one extra hour of time a precious gift. And what made it worse was that he felt deserted, neglected, because the rest of the busy household could not afford to sit in a rocking chair beside him for long hours. He gave them a sense of guilt that grew as the years went on.

Possibly today one of the senior citizens' organizations

could have helped, but these were not in action then. So there he was, a sad figure rocking away the hours.

In contrast to this gentleman, I know a woman who was incapacitated in her eighties and unable to walk, and so she decided to take up rug-hooking. She made beautiful hooked wool rugs, enough to carpet her own house and that of her daughter. She is now at work on one for a granddaughter.

She is happy as a songbird all the while and certainly wants no sympathy because of that wheelchair.

When I read last night of a woman just receiving a graduate degree from college at age sixty, I know she would not like sympathy for the many years she spent raising a big family of children. Conversation with her would be inspiring.

"Amber," I said, "there is really no limit to learning—and learning is the basis of living."

Amber stretched her toes happily. The fluent movement distracted me as always. The delicate precision of her paws and wrists fascinates me. I had to remind her that the anthropologists say the distinguishing feature of man is having an opposing thumb, which no other species has.

"Some say the development of that thumb made man a superior being."

"I do very well without it," Amber remarked, scooping up her brush.

"You cannot thread a needle, Sweet. But then I am not very good at it either."

"I'd rather play with buttons than sew them on anyway."

My long thinking ended, not because I had exhausted my ideas but because the sun was walking the blue sky toward the West with the mysterious decision of nature. The air smelled of dusk—cool and dewy. Bird songs muted, except for the mockingbird who denounced the low level in the birdbath.

"One more thing," I said, as Amber drank from the kitchen faucet while I told the mockingbird to wait a minute. "I remember when I was in college there were difficult times, including a war and my nearly dying of flu in the unheated attic of a dormitory jammed with cots. I kept quoting my then-favorite author, Hugh Walpole. 'It isn't life that matters, it's the courage you bring to it!' That's been a good motto ever since."

Amber did not listen, for she was on the counter pawing hopefully at the refrigerator door.

15

TODAY WAS THE BEGINNING OF SPRING on Cape Cod, and the little house overlooking Mill Pond brimmed with gold light. The outside world was gold too—forsythia a fountain of exuberant bloom, daffodils opening wide cups, three late crocuses the rabbits missed under the split-rail fence.

Amber celebrated by racing through the house, barely touching the floor, pausing to fly to bookshelves, tabletops, window ledges. The pagan in her flowered.

Then she settled on the round table by the picture window. I sipped my coffee and began our morning conversation.

Amber, I love to watch you thinking. It is always fascinating to watch people think, but especially you. Now you stop scrubbing, prick up your ears and decide to check on the birds because that lyric song of the redwings and song sparrows means birds. So off to the window by the kitchen table, which is closer to them. The brilliant light turns your eyes to gold. Then you begin lashing your tail and chittering; you think it would be fun to go out.

You decide that if you claw the screen I might go for the leash, but when I pay no attention you sit motionless while you decide the next step. The next step is obvious. You fortify yourself with some breakfast and proceed with dignity and switching hips to the bathroom (your own). Now I lose you, for you adopt the pose of one of your ancestors in Egypt four thousand years ago as you stare into space. If I speak to you, you do not hear me—your eyes are glazed. Are you back in time? I shall never know!

But once this ritual is done with, you begin to think what you will do next—jump on the bed and fix the pillow, go back to the kitchen or get into my lap and poke at your brush. Decisions are not easy; a few false starts are necessary. Sit in the middle of the floor, make up your mind. I think along with you and opt for the lap. So do you. Purring means lap. Moments of indecision appeal to me, for I have them so often. A prowl gives time to go over things—my mind prowls with you. When you make up your mind, I make up mine.

Thinking, Amber, is a curious process. You, I may say, think with better direction than I do. You take a problem and stay with it. Once you reach a decision you do not waver.

I, alas, waver most of the time, and I must try to do better! I spend too much time thinking about what is most important for me to do next. Perhaps I should clean up the kitchen. On the other hand, the dishes can be done when the next meal is under way. So why not start the car and run down to the village (really a town now) and do the errands? But they can wait until later when all the other people presumably have done their own errands and I can park within screaming distance of where I want to go.

What I should do right now is sit down at the typewriter and try to finish that difficult chapter. But this isn't fair to a houseful of plants dying of thirst or to the harvest table brimming with unanswered mail—tons of it.

I could clean up the fireplace, of course, and lay a good fire in case someone drops in tonight for a drink while we exchange problems. However, I know that the mockingbird will not stop scolding unless I fill the birdbath. The cardinals want their half grapefruits stuck on the split-rail fence posts. The chickadees are making a racket for more sunflower seeds (apparently nothing fit to eat is left).

Olive says all I need to do is make a list the night before and cross items out one by one. But is it better to list first the things I hate, hate, hate to do or those I enjoy? I must think about this. And then I must remember where I put the list, which is another task right there!

One persistent job is telephoning. This takes a terrific amount of time, since the line is always busy or I get the wrong number. The telephone does not like me, and if all else fails and my call goes through it will wind the cord up like a writhing snake. Why not put off calling until I have some leisure? Somehow leisure is what I have least of, morning, noon, night.

While I have been standing in the middle of the living room thinking (so much that I am already tired), you have been planning your own activities, and I must apologize for wasting your time listening to me. I wish I could think as constructively as you do, Amber!

But before you unfold a rose-petal yawn and go off to sit on the high shelf with the milk glass, I want to explain that we limited humans do have a kind of thinking you lack. It is rather abstract and often does not get us anywhere. You, for instance, never concern yourself with *love*. You practice loving me but you never meditate on its meaning.

I am thinking now that this is the most important emotion in life, and its by-product is compassion. No place on this spinning planet lacks some form of love, even among the most remote tribes in their own spot in the jungle or on snowcapped mountains. The love of parents is basic even when it is masked by cruel actions. In our particular piece of the world, the love between man and woman is the foundation of the family which our social structure is built upon. Our civilization depends on personal love—love of parents, children, friends. This widens to include our community and our country (how many die for it). The greatest men and women also love mankind and nature herself.

The love of music, art, literature—how many facets there are! For most of us, the love of home, whether a dingy apartment or a mansion, is very special, although some people prefer wandering to putting down roots. One of those tiresome, inevitable polls would find them a small percentage, I am sure.

Love of God gives sustenance to almost all human creatures, although the meaning of God varies from a deity who is infinite love to one who punishes mankind for its sins. Those who do not believe in an infinite being suffer an emptiness in life, I think, which is as sad as being in an underground cave where no gleam of light penetrates.

The more one loves, the more the capacity to love develops. For loving involves reaching outside of oneself, sharing with others, joining in someone's grief as well as joy. It means keeping an open heart, never a closed one. No amount of meditating can explain the mystery of it, yet it is a free gift for all who receive it.

Hate cripples the power of love much as Japanese beetles devour the heart of opening Peace roses. Any old hate will do it—hate of other races, other countries, other ways of living or next-door neighbors. Bigotry is a strong form of it. Oddly enough, any kind of hate destroys the hater more than the object; it is more corroding than any chemical.

So, Amber, you can snuggle down in your love for me while my love for you widens my horizon so that I love all creatures in the world we inhabit!

The first warm evening came, when the air was still and the moonlight was tender. The worst winter in 177 years ebbed reluctantly, but now men no longer walked across Mill Pond and the water rippled with silver. The sea winds slept. The air smelled of promise.

At eleven o'clock I opened the inner front door to look out across the greening yard. At first I thought I was dreaming, but what I saw was definite, tangible.

"Amber, come quick!"

Amber roused herself and moved light as a shadow to stand beside me.

By the bird feeder a round furry stranger moved about, eating the cracked corn the quail had left. He was a black-and-white etching against the night, bushy tail dragging, wedge of nose scattering corn. The white streak on his back was as broad as his whole back and extended the length of his tail. When I turned the yard light on, his lifted head moved back and forth checking for scent.

"Amber, do you remember Blackberry?"

Amber leaned against the screen, standing on tiptoe, fascinated.

"It isn't Blackberry," I said. "He left us during that skunk epidemic. Try to remember him now."

I am sure she did, for during the six years Blackberry was our special friend she grew accustomed to seeing him eating his meals in the yard or coming to the stoop to claw at the door when he wanted more. She was used to sitting in the lawn chair with me at sunset when Blackberry poked a sharp nose over the edge of the bank.

Now suddenly an exact replica ambled over the grass, sniffing, snuffling. He was not the six-year-old, obviously, but an adolescent. As skunks age, the ermine turns a bit rusty and the body is heavier.

"Amber, he couldn't be a son—maybe a grandson? But how could it happen? The path downhill to the burrow is long since grown over, but he came that way. If only you could communicate with him!"

"What for?" Amber unhooked her claws from the screen and went back to her nest in my tawny sweater, a nice match for her.

As far as she was concerned, this was the same old story.

But I stood there, trying to believe the unbelievable. I have observed many skunks in my day. Sometimes a couple of friends came with Blackberry, and at the farm in Connecticut we had families of skunks who lived underneath the shed by the swamp's border. I also met a few that neighbors fed with scraps, just as they fed all the wildlife around. And my daughter and her family once had a house skunk from a fur farm. Add to that the limp, pitiful bodies along roadsides who have died because of speeding cars. But nobody ever looked like Blackberry because of the amazing spread of the ermine, really covering the whole upper half. Nobody, that is, until this newcomer arrived.

When the small visitor wended his way back down the tangled path Blackberry had made, I put fresh ice in Amber's glass and sat down with a cool drink of my own.

Amber slept on, paws folded under chin.

I could not solve this new mystery. The time sequence did not fit. Any offspring of Blackberry's would be much older than this skunk. Also, that epidemic had presumably wiped out the whole skunk population. Any surviving kit would have turned up long since from the home burrow.

Then, too, the past dreadful winter had decimated wildlife. Surviving birds and animals moved to friendly places for scraps, and tons of cracked corn were lugged to the beaches for starving seabirds. Skunks only semihibernate and in hard winters emerge to find food to carry them over.

But Amber and I had not seen a trace of any skunk. Nevertheless, here he was, materializing on an April night right outside a house that for so long had been home base for that other one.

I began to make a list. Blackberry's rubber dog dishes were in the dump long since. Originally we had fed him on the aluminum plates that frozen food comes in, but he always tried to carry them down the bank to his burrow. Some sturdy human had to crawl down through the brush and poison ivy and retrieve them before we had a dump just below the front terrace. The stock of cat food was gone via the raccoons.

I listed bowls, cat food, canned tuna, kibbles, milk. Blackberry loved milk above all edibles. Perhaps once again Amber and I could look out the kitchen window as we ate our own supper and see a happy bundle of fur eating his.

"I shall call him Snowdrift," I told Amber when she woke up.

A fine surprise for the beginning of spring.

Both Amber and I feel the excitement of the new season. When the first daffodils open gold or white chalices, Amber investigates them. Where there was a drift of snow, here are these blossoms to smell, to touch with tentative paw, to rub against. Our whole world is no longer white but scattered with gold. The grass is green and soft to the paws.

I notice the lemon color of the willows and the purple cornucopias of the skunk cabbage down the marsh. The wild roses put out tiny pale leaves. Crocus carpets the border. The air no longer smells of snow. The redwings are back, the males coming first. Robins find the crumbly mounds of dark earth where earthworms work. Quail stuff themselves with the ground corn we put out.

But perhaps the final sign is the oak that gently begins to let russet leaves fall. This begins at the top of the tree, as if the oak is doubtful about the whole process. All winter I admire the tenacity of oaks, but the first serrated pale leaves of spring are a special joy.

As always, the cycle of mating, nesting, raising the young reaffirms nature's plan for the survival of life on the planet. It never loses its wonder.

Amber and I bring in the first daffodils.

"Remember, we do not nibble these," I say.

I am reminded of a friend whose cat makes it impossible to keep bouquets. Any vase of flowers, from violets or crocuses to huge peonies, inspires him to carefully paw out blossoms, take them in his mouth and carry them over to drop in his mistress's lap. Helen Delbridge has a houseful of cats but says no other cat has ever done this. She also says nobody could ever teach a cat to do this (as if they would want to!). This cat taught himself.

Fortunately for me, Amber usually confines her interest to smelling flowers (she particularly loves roses) but thinks only baby's breath and sea lavender are good for eating, which of course they are not. If any strange flower comes into the house, I watch carefully.

It is sad to know how many houseplants are not edible for dogs, cats or children. Some are poisonous, which may be their protection. Wild animals presumably have built-in safeguards. Rabbits and skunks devour the bulbs of tulips, for instance, but leave daffodils alone. Birds eat poison ivy berries and scatter enough to make the ivy spread. Yet whoever heard of a bird coming down with that dreadful rash?

In areas such as Connecticut and Massachusetts, poison ivy flourishes like the green bay tree, a species I have never seen. But bird lovers hate to hire a special crew of men to spray all the poison ivy and deprive the birds of all those juicy ripe berries. We tried spraying once but gave it up and settled for keeping a prescription from our doctor in the medicine chest for times when the children who pick wild sweet blackberries discover poison ivy cozily tucked around every bush.

So far as I know our animals are immune, and I suspect coons and skunks also are. As a dedicated ecologist, I think poison ivy must have some function beyond providing berries, but I can't decide what it might be.

Man is forever upsetting the balance of nature—for instance, the terrible spring floods come chiefly from tree cutting along the upper reaches of streams. We know that when the Pilgrims came to Cape Cod it was heavily forested, but once the great trees were cut down the Cape changed so that even today it is mostly scrub pines and locusts. A few deciduous trees may be found, but the vast great forests are only legendary. This is why in autumn Cape people go to New Hampshire and Vermont to "see the color."

Amber and I settle for the shades of cinnamon of the beach grass, the steady green of junipers, white and red pines and the tawny thickets. The ponds, inlets and eternal ocean give deep sapphire to the view and the marsh grass seems to give out a rosy glow. The sky echoes the blue of the sea—the sea reflects it when the sun shines.

In April, when we go back inland to the Connecticut farm, hundreds of daffodils bloom on the slope above the pond, so the whole world glows.

By May the whole valley sings with color. We must walk on violets when we go out, wild white ones in the yard, deep blue above the pond, variegated Confederate violets spilling over garden borders.

And the lilacs lift white and purple blossoms over dark green polished heart-shaped leaves. At the farm they reach the attic windows. Throughout the countryside they still mark where homesteads once stood. They are not bushes or shrubs but almost as tall as trees.

The ancient farmhouse smells of lilacs, the loveliest of all fragrances.

When I tell Amber that lilacs were planted by the earliest

settlers and that they give me a sense of belonging to the past, she is too busy chasing butterflies to listen. Her own world bursts with excitement. The air is full of flight, the ground with squirrels, rabbits, chipmunks, raccoons. She cannot chase the muskrats down at the pond or get at the minnows, but at least her winter dreaming by the fire is over.

There is, alas, one experience in our life she cannot share. In May my unicorn comes again, bringing my special magic. He comes on a moonlit night, stepping delicately from the woods down the hill to the pond. He is the color of moonlight himself. His silvery horn lances the shadows in the old apple orchard. I must stand quietly on the opposite bank of the pond. He pauses a moment to look across the dark water and gives me a silent greeting. Then he bends his graceful head and drinks the sweet cool water. In the morning I can trace his footsteps by the crushed violets where his silver hooves have trod.

I could not carry Amber in my arms to see him because a unicorn is visible to only one person. Everyone needs a personal magic, but it is a lone possession.

The unicorn has been a legendary figure as far back as when Noah built the ark, for it is said that this was the only creature not in the ark. The other animals went in two by two, but the unicorn came alone and a little late, and so the ark sailed off without him.

In 400 B.C. the unicorn was described by a Greek, and later physicians in Greece stated that if a man drank from a cup made from a unicorn's horn he was immune to poisoning as well as to many illnesses. This belief definitely suggests that there were unicorns in ancient Greece—or at least that people believed in them!

The Middle Ages added interpretations. The beautiful milk-white creature was the symbol of purity, the symbol of Christ, and could never be approached except by a virgin. Around 1500 the Hunt of the Unicorn acquired immortality in the incredible tapestries the Cloisters Museum in New York City displays so superbly. These great wall hangings were years in the making, every tiny stitch flawless. Birds, beasts, flowers, the hunters, woods, streams are dominated in every panel by the mysterious unicorn. When finally trapped, a circular fence impounds him, but his pose is royal, head up, horn lifted. There is a serenity in the scene despite bright blood flowing down the silvery breast. One expert believes that the blood is actually pomegranate juice, which is another symbol—I think of purity.

My own love for the unicorn began in early childhood, about the same time I met fairies and elves in a secret nook under the blossoming syringa bush. The little people gradually left me as I grew up, but somehow the unicorn never did. Nobody knew about him. The pressures of reality kept me silent, even to my best friend.

But in Shakespeare class at Wellesley College we studied *The Tempest,* and when I came to the line "Now I will believe that there are unicorns," I felt sure that the "immortal bard" was a true companion.

Years later I visited The Cloisters, which in all the metropolis of steel, cement, noise and smog is islanded in upper Manhattan, high above the Hudson River. Going in is like entering a monastery, and the stillness of past time falls gently on the glowing tapestries. I felt I had reached the end of a long journey.

I knew the spell must be universal when a friend took his four-year-old son to see them. "Oh, look, Daddy, there is a rabbit!" said the boy, pointing a happy finger at one small form nested in the flowery mead. Someday he will take his own son, because he will not forget that rabbit.

The dogs in the tapestries fascinate me. They are smooth-coated, medium sized or very small, resembling greyhounds but with blunter muzzles and curling tails that seem to wag right out of the fabric. They wear collars, which I would not have expected in the 1500s. The other animals are equally beautiful.

An embattled stag is familiar, but a beast like a lion is strange in this setting.

One of my favorite characters is a small, slim white cat dozing in the flowered background above a beautiful maiden garbed like a princess. This would not interest Amber.

A botanist could identify the countless flowers, bushes and trees, but all I can do is admire the intricate shapes and glowing colors. These tapestries re-create a world forever lost. We can only be thankful to the artists who labored to depict it. I cannot imagine the years it took or how many people must have lost their eyesight bending over the huge panels. No machine ever stitched a thread. In gloomy, unheated stone chambers, fingers surely grew numb.

Most early art, I believe, was religious, except for royal portraits, and was hung in palaces or churches. Tapestries had a practical asset since they helped keep icy winds from blowing in. The unicorn tapestries also gave bright color to shadowy interiors. And on bitter days summertime bloomed in the flowers.

Just why my unicorn decided to come once a year to a Connecticut valley is a mystery. Perhaps the ecstasy of flowering in May reminded him of that lost world. Perhaps he came because I needed him. I never question him, although I would like to know where he goes when snowdrifts lean against the windowsills and branches crash in the yard at midnight and the snowy owl cries from a sugar maple.

He must return to a never-never land and sleep in violets.

Some years ago I heard from a charming lady whose husband is very realistic. "I don't believe in fairy tales. But if Gladys Taber sees a unicorn, there must be one," he told her.

I am happy to leave it like that.

16

AMBER AND I CAME IN YESTERDAY with the last of my favorite lilacs, which are called French lilacs in our area. Whether they were from France originally I do not know. I call them the black-purple ones, for actually the purple is so dark it has a tinge of black. It is not as common as the other varieties. The season is almost over, but we had enough for one more bouquet.

Late-afternoon light slanted in the western windows. Shadows already fell under the harvest table. It was still warm enough for Amber to ask for fresh ice water while I had a cool drink. The stillness of day's end had a dreamlike quality.

As she looked at me, the irises in her eyes shone delicate

green, the pupils narrow lanced onyx as they do only at this time of day. She stretched her left arm across my lap and yawned. But then her ears alerted. She fixed her gaze on the wing chair and her tail unreefed itself.

"Who's there?" I asked.

A long reflective gaze was my answer. When she turned her head toward me, her look was inscrutable.

Presently her attention was drawn to the doorway. Her whiskers quivered.

"Amber, who is standing there?" I whispered.

The room was filled with presences I could not see. But it seemed that she could. My human eyes were limited.

"Tell them they are welcome," I said.

We sat quietly until day ebbed. When she finally jumped down, she walked around the corner of the sofa that still belonged to the Irish, whom she had never seen in real life.

"Thank you for letting me know," I said.

I knew the room was empty when she ran to the kitchen and planted firm paws on her tray. I had forgotten the time, but Amber is more reliable than any clock.

Spring is for remembrance, I thought, as I minced her asparagus tips, but only for the happy ones.

Moonlight silvered the world as we finished supper, and the daffodil stars blossomed.

"What a wonderful world!" I said.

Amber stopped scrubbing her paws to sing her loudest purr song.

She is sensitive to so many things that ordinary human companions miss. One afternoon last week I was sitting outside in the captain's chair on the terrace, looking out from the top of the bluff to the pale gold sands, Mill Pond and the farther slopes on the other side. The quiet inlet is cupped by the wooded bluffs that are ancient sand dunes. That day the color of the sea reminded me of the blue of chicory flowers. And the blue transported me instantly to my teenage days in Wisconsin. I was riding along a country road that simply went from farm to farm. Papa was driving, as always. Mama sat quietly as he spun past an oxcart. Timmie, the Irish, sat in the back with me.

Mama wanted to stop and pick a bouquet of chicory blue, but Papa never wanted to stop until he got where he was going. If we had a flat tire, which often happened, Mama and I secretly rejoiced because we could pick wild flowers while Papa jacked up the car.

For a moment I was there again, which meant I was off in a strange world where Amber had never been. She suddenly stopped nibbling a chosen grass blade, leaped to my lap, gave me a long look and began to paw me back from yesterday.

I find this a curious but very special quality of Amber's. How does she sense that sometimes I move into the nowhere? I am now looking at a jeweled arm of the sea. The early June sun is comfortable; it lacks the molten vigor of July and August. The sky is full of space and sea-gull flight. Our resident mockingbird interlaces the air with melodies. My lap is warm for sitting. Her fur looks polished.

"Come back," Amber says with earnest paws.

So I return to actuality, which is here and now. But how did she feel my absence when I had not moved at all? How could she realize that I was breathing the farm-rich air of dairy country in Wisconsin and walking on a dusty inland road half a country away from sand and sea and gulls crying over?

When I go away from the house in real life, not in imagination, her reaction is very different. Perhaps it is because I explain where I am going, how long I shall be gone, and the probable snacks I plan to bring back. It is a normal accepted procedure, even if deplorable. But when I make my occasional departure into a world she never knew, she somehow senses it and feels anxious. In fact, she has almost cured me of travels in time.

When I try to share the actual happenings in our life

together, she listens patiently because she is in the picture.

"Amber, remember you were six weeks old when you plopped from that carrying case into my arms? You gave a squeaky mouse-cry and then practiced a tremble of purr. I did not do any of the things that are supposed to be important when a kitten comes from a long first journey out of a cage. I was not calm, relaxed, quiet. I did not leave you to wander around in this strange new world. I broke all the rules. I sobbed. I held you up to my neck and kissed you and cupped my hands close around this small new kitten, really not big enough to be weighed on the vegetable scale.

"But you seemed to understand me immediately and to believe we belonged together. From the days when you were an apron-pocket kitten to your current five-pound handful, our companionship has never failed to enrich our lives."

Amber twitches her delicate triangular ears. By now the sea is swallowing the blazing colors of sunset, and the inevitable cool salty breeze of dusk drifts in.

She yawns, stretches, flicks her tail, suggests that it has been a long time since she has had anything to eat. There is a pink fillet of flounder and she would like it broiled in butter for about two minutes.

So she leads me into the house to the kitchen and sits on the counter to supervise the cooking.

"Amber," I say, "when we go out tomorrow, I promise I won't sit in a chair dreaming. We'll go for a walk in the pansy bed. The yellow ones are just beginning to come out and you'll see how they turn their faces to the sun."

Amber turns her face to me. As I dish out her supper, she begins a soft purr of appreciation.

"Your purr is lyrical," I tell her, "and my humming is off-key. But even so, the same song is in our hearts."

Now it is time to change the calendar, as if tearing off the sheet marked November really means tomorrow is winter. Nature's rhythm is more rational. There are slow sunny days, last leaves drifting to a quiet earth, Mr. and Mrs. Cardinal still dipping in the bird feeder. Then comes the first snow—like a postcard from winter.

Amber greets the white starry flakes that idle against the picture windows by leaping against the glass, paws outstretched, tail very busy. Her chase is successful as far as she is concerned because the early snow melts in the warmth of the windows. When she comes to check on me, she is smiling and carries her tail like a banner.

When the furnace goes on (oh, sweet music from the cellar), she tours the hot-air vents, settling before the kitchen one as a rule. Her tropical heritage comes out, for she likes her fur to be so hot that I worry lest it fall out. At night when the fire burns in the fireplace she snugs down as usual in the low chair by the hearth.

On the other hand she waits for me to open a window. We always keep one window in every room that may be opened to get some oxygen into the winter house. I apologize to my neighbor, who pulls down the storm sash as soon as the temperature goes down to fifty degrees at night. Both Amber and I get drowsy without occasional fresh air, although it could be our imagination since the two of us could hardly use up a whole houseful of oxygen. But the moment I open one window three inches Amber leaves the hot-air vent and leaps to sit on the sill with pink nose-tip pressed against the screen. She may shiver with the sharp bit of air, but she loves to fill her lungs with it before returning to the heat—at which point I close the window and try to conserve energy.

My Siamese and Manx loved outdoors in winter, especially the foot tracks of the wildfolk patterning the snow, but Amber only once slipped out at the farm in January when company came. She landed in a snowdrift and her efforts to get all four paws in the air were rather like *Swan Lake* ballet. I shall never forget my panic as I floundered out. Perspective is a strange proposition. Inside the farmhouse Amber was a normal kitten, but outside in a vast expanse of snow she looked no bigger than a gold thimble suddenly dropped from a basket. Had she gone farther away I never would have seen her.

When we both recovered she gave a few final miaows to suggest it was my fault but she would forgive me as soon as her cold paws were warmed against my cheek a bit longer.

My conversation was brief. "Everything is relative, Sweet Peach. Human beings often get diminished by being catapulted into the wrong setting. Sometimes it is their own fault, but sometimes it is caused by circumstance. At least you did not decide to 'make it' anywhere. You knew a snowdrift was not your métier. You did not attempt to copy the barn cats, who are as casual about snow as Eskimos. Now let's forget this frightening incident."

I often wonder whether Amber has a memory of past winters or merely an instinctive knowledge as birds, squirrels, skunks—all wildlife—do. In any case, she is content unless the electric goes off and we huddle up and listen to the north wind screaming. She cannot gather and store nuts, berries, etc., but she does eat more—just in case, I wonder? She also changes her schedule as to when she must wake me up—much later, she concedes. On dark days (winter has so many) she spends more time in the exact middle of my bed pillow at night when the furnace is turned down, but the electric blanket warms the bedding.

Christmas is wonderful, she thinks, because there is so much to do. Cartons to climb into, packages to help unpack, mail to sort, greens to paw into better arrangements, the tree to inspect (now she is not going to climb it or knock down glass balls—well, maybe one or two). The kitchen is a special treat: nibbles of turkey or roast beef available plus a spoonful of gravy, a bit of Yorkshire pudding or giblets (not advisable for most cats or dogs).

Then January and February take over New England, and if you live at the end of the road, it is easy to be shut in a good deal. I do not like it. I miss not getting out and friends not coming unless they have beach buggies. It can be a very lonely time even though there is plenty of it for working. But when I feel sorry for myself, a small person appears, yawning a pink yawn. Sitting on the typewriter, she polishes a few whiskers. "Just thought I'd find you here," she intimates. "I am getting lonely out there. I need a lap."

Soft and warm she stretches on that lap, one arm out, purr loud. Who could be forsaken with a lapful of beauty, mystery and love?

Her eyes are onyx this time of day. She gazes at me steadily.

"I find you practically perfect," Amber tells me, "except you do have some odd ideas now and then!"